P9-DVS-567

East Is a Big Bird

East Is a Big Bird

Navigation and Logic on Puluwat Atoll

Thomas Gladwin

Harvard University Press

Cambridge, Massachusetts

London, England

To my "coauthors"

> Charles Bechtol
> Hipour
> Dick Neisser
> Seymour Sarason

Contents

Maps and Diagrams

DRAWN BY SAMUEL H. BRYANT

Preface

Most of this book is about a beautiful tropical island and its proud, seafaring people. Yet the book's beginnings and central purpose derive from the experiences of poor people in the United States.

Several steps are required to link the ghettos and shacks of America with a jewel-like island in the Pacific. These steps of reasoning are set forth in some detail in the last chapter. Here at the outset it is necessary only to alert the reader to the plan of the book by outlining briefly the argument upon which it rests.

Poor people in the United States, regardless of their color or origin, tend to do badly in school. They are also inclined to achieve low scores on intelligence tests. These two phenomena are widely agreed to be closely related both by cause and in the sharp curtailment of opportunity which results from them. Educators have, however, been handicapped in their efforts to remedy these intellectual deficits by a lack of clear understanding of how the quality of thinking differs between people who are poor and those not-so-poor. Tests can of course pinpoint quantitative differences, but the results of testing educationally nonachieving poor people are far more ambiguous when it comes to isolating the specific *qualities* in thinking which are distinctive and handicapping to them. Indeed, as we shall see, there is even reason to suspect the validity of the one distinction upon which there is now considerable agreement, that between "middle-class" abstract and "lower-class" concrete thinking.

The failure thus far to identify clearly the distinctive characteristics of the thinking styles which develop under conditions of poverty has led to an impasse of tragic proportions. Schools keep penalizing children for the poverty into which they have unwillingly been born, while one remedial scheme after another disappoints its sponsors by imparting only trifling or temporary benefits. A new approach is needed. This book is the chronicle of one effort to open such a new avenue of inquiry.

Yet why seek an answer to the problem outside the United States, and in a place where poverty does not exist, or at least is irrelevant? Furthermore, why an island in the Pacific, and why particularly Puluwat (Poo-loo-watt)? In preliminary answer to the first question, there is a time-honored and often fruitful tradition in anthropology of looking to another culture for perspective on processes which are at work in our own. This strategy is especially appropriate to the problem at hand because, without making any assumptions whatever about cultural deprivation—its presence or absence, or even its relevance—one can simply state with ample supporting evidence that non-European people who have not had extensive Western schooling, whenever they are tested, tend to perform on intelligence tests in much the same way as do poor people in the United States. This in itself does not prove anything about non-Europeans or about poor people, but it suggests that maybe, just maybe, some of the same factors are at work in both settings in shaping a style of thinking which is poorly adapted to the demands of intelligence tests, even those which are nonverbal and designed to be "culture-fair."

It therefore seemed at least possible that by looking at the process of thinking in a non-European low-test-score cultural setting I might obtain some new insights into the problems which tests and schools present to poor people in our society. At once the question arose of how to "look at the process of thinking." It seemed the answer might lie in finding, recording in detail, and then analyzing a coherent body of native knowledge, not just traditional or descriptive knowledge but knowledge so arranged and utilized that it serves to answer important questions. Starting thus afresh with problems new to our own cultural setting, problems in other words for which I could not know in advance the "right" answers, I hoped to enhance my perspective by discerning which cognitive processes are used and which are not needed in working with such a completely non-European system of practical knowledge.

With the task so defined, Puluwat, place I had known before, became a natural choice. Here there exists in use, perhaps to a fuller degree than anywhere else in the Pacific or maybe the world, a system of interisland navigation which is complex, rational, efficient and almost entirely non-European in origin. It is taught as a logically coherent system and can therefore be recorded and analyzed as such. It is used by living people whose thinking in other domains and on other tasks is also available for study, comparison, and perspective. Because of my earlier work on nearby Truk I had particular reason to believe the Puluwatans too would do poorly on any foreign test of intellectual performance. Finally, the necessity for recording in detail the entire navigation complex (and also the theory of canoe design which is closely related) would make available a systematic description of a complex of skills which has incited much curiosity among scholars and sailors alike, but about which only fragmentary information has until now been available.

The plan followed in this book is first to describe Puluwat, its seafaring culture, its canoes, its navigators, and its system of navigation. Only in the final chapter, with the data before us, are cognitive issues examined in detail, and only there will we be seeking perspectives to illuminate the issues of intellectual deficit among disadvantaged people in the United States. Until then we may immerse ourselves in the beautiful and often dramatic world of Puluwat.

Puluwat is a tiny island, or more properly a cluster of islands, in the western Pacific Ocean. More specifically, it is part of the Caroline Islands of Micronesia. It lies one hundred and fifty miles west of Truk, the center for United States administration of the Truk District of the Trust Territory of the Pacific Islands.

Although my project was many years in development I spent only two and a half months early in 1967 in actual fieldwork on Puluwat. The several factors which made it possible to complete the job in this short span of time require some discussion because they must be taken into account in judging the validity of the entire study. They fall into two categories, the accidents of my own background and the substantial help of a number of professional colleagues.

I arrived on Puluwat with several personal advantages. A number of years before, I had visited the island many times in an administrative capacity. I therefore had friends and an apparently good reputation with the Puluwatans and also with Father Fahey, the Jesuit missionary who was in addition an always generous host. Both the Puluwatans and I were fluent in a common second language, Trukese, closely related to Puluwat. Prior to my becoming a professional anthropologist I had been employed for some years as an engineer, a source of insights both technical and theoretical which were of use in the research. I have had some personal experience in sailing. Finally, in the past I traveled repeatedly between most of the islands which are regularly visited by Puluwat navigators so I was familiar with their seaways.

In reviewing the help furnished by professional colleagues both in preparing for the field study on Puluwat and afterward in analyzing the results, I am attesting not only to their creative share in the work but also to a personal debt of gratitude larger than is usual in such cases. This study extended into more domains than I could possibly master. I had therefore to rely upon the wisdom and patience of others, some of whom helped on a scale such that they became almost coauthors. It is indeed an insufficient gesture of appreciation to dedicate this book to them.

Seymour Sarason's contribution as a psychologist really began twenty years before the present research. I was then preparing to go to Truk for my first fieldwork, a study of Trukese personality, and he instructed me in projective testing.

We later wrote this up in collaboration (Gladwin and Sarason, 1953) and went on to collaborate on another project even more relevant to the aims of this book, a review of research in mental subnormality including "subcultural retardation"—which is the way we used to refer to what happens to you intellectually when you are poor (Masland, Sarason, and Gladwin, 1958). These two collaborations developed in such fashion that they came to encompass most of the interests and premises which underlie the present book. Inevitably, therefore, Seymour Sarason has been a source of continuing stimulus and insight throughout this project.

Another psychologist, Ulric Neisser, not only introduced me some years ago to cognitive psychology but also was instrumental in helping me clarify a programmatic paper from which the idea of this research emerged (Gladwin, 1964). More immediately we worked intensively together, both before and after I went to Puluwat, developing the strategies, interpretations, and ideas upon which the theoretical aspects of the study principally rest. Irving Sigel initiated me into the world of Jean Piaget, and thereafter Jacqueline J. Goodnow proposed and then instructed me in a Piaget combinatorial task which proved unusually salient to the issues under investigation here.

In the realm of the sea I was educated by Charles O. Bechtol, an orthopedic surgeon of considerable accomplishment who has a formidable record in ocean racing and as a hobby-within-a-hobby is an authority on the design, handling, and navigation of native sailing canoes. Virtually all the inquiries and interpretations upon which the chapters on canoes and navigation are based were developed with him. In this area I also benefited greatly from discussions and a review of my manuscript by Howard I. Chapelle, naval architect and historian. In addition, my analysis of wave forms and other natural phenomena is largely guided by an extraordinarily complete and lucid short course of instruction generously given me by Julius Marcus of the United States Naval Oceanographic Office.

On Puluwat somewhat longer than I were two additional colleagues, each conducting independent but related research. Not only did this provide the usual opportunities for interchange of findings and insights which simultaneous research makes possible but also through the prospect of publication of their work I am gratefully saved many reporting chores with which I would otherwise have to be concerned. Saul H. Riesenberg studied and will be publishing an analysis of the social organization which underlies Puluwat's seafaring culture both traditional and modern. Samuel H. Elbert prepared a dictionary and syntax of the Puluwat language which among other things relieves me of the need to reproduce native terms and phonetics. Accordingly, I use only English equivalents for Puluwat terms and spell the names of Puluwatans (all of them real) in simplified form with popular phonetic equivalents. (Stress is equal on all syllables.) On Puluwat I was also substantially aided by two Peace Corps volunteers assigned there. Phillip D. Bogetto not only accompanied me on canoe performance runs but also shared a variety of his own observations of the seafaring life of Puluwat; Peter Silverman, who learned as a hobby to sail his own small canoe and reviewed my notes on canoe handling, saved me from blunders of interpretation too grievous to describe. He also took the photograph used on page 129. John K. Fahey, S. J., whose role as generous host to the three of us has already been noted, served also as a mentor whose helpful advice and suggestions were too numerous even to recall. In addition, all five of these have offered helpful comments on the manuscript.

The brevity of my stay and the richness of my data must be attributed above all to the exceptional knowledge and explanatory skill of my instructor in navigation, Hipour (Hee-power), who is described with affection in Chapter 4. I am one of those fortunate anthropologists whose native instructor (we call them "informants" and do them an injustice) almost wrote the book for him. Not only that, but the formal instruction for which I had allowed two to three months was completed in little more than one. My research assistant, Teruo (Tare-oo-oh), also saved me weeks of work by collecting many categories of data on all the canoes of Puluwat. In addition he assisted me with the psychological procedures, went along to keep me out of trouble at sea, and helped me in innumerable other ways.

Reaching and living on a remote little island can present formidable problems. For us, all was made easy. I can principally thank Tosiwo Nakayama, Assistant District Administrator and also a close personal friend of twenty years, who kept our many needs constantly in mind, and Henry T. Chatroop and the staff of the Truk Trading Company who outfitted us on Truk and then sent additional supplies faithfully on every kind of craft, official and otherwise, which traveled from Truk to Puluwat during our stay. Always in the background was Alan M. MacQuarrie, Truk District Administrator, who was unfailing in his support and courtesy. I must also mention one more time in this context the role of Father Fahey, for he not only made ready our quarters in the lower floor of his own residence but also provided us with invaluable advance guidance on things we should prepare and bring along.

When all of this work began to get on paper I relied from the first draft to the final revisions upon the endless patience and typing skill of Mrs. Mary Ann DiGiovanni. She was able somehow to fit my typing tasks into her already full days as wife and mother, and in the process even managed to add to her household a new baby, who arrived somewhere between Chapters 3 and 4!

Finally I express my appreciation to the National Institute of Mental Health which employed and supported me during the period of my fieldwork on Puluwat. Those of the staff who arranged the fulfillment of this final commitment by NIMH to me are aware of the roles they played and of my gratitude to them.

T. G.

Oxon Hill, Maryland
August 1968

East Is a Big Bird

Hipour the navigator

1 A Sail in the Sun

Puluwat is an island of green, edged in white and set in a tropic sea. Already distant, a canoe is sailing away. Its sail accents the scene, a white cockade bobbing over the waves, impudent and alone on the vast ocean.

Then the canoe and its crew are gone. In the days or weeks thereafter no one on Puluwat can know where they are. Finally someone, perhaps high in a tree picking breadfruit, sees a tiny white triangle on the horizon and emits a whoop. The cry is carried from voice to voice and within a minute everyone on Puluwat knows a canoe is coming. More men climb trees and soon eyes practiced in the scrutiny of sea and sails distinguish a familiar mark or shape. The canoe is identified. The studied indifference of those left behind gives way to excitement. If the journey has been long and the day is pleasant the lagoon will fill with canoes paddled out to greet the travelers as they enter the pass in the reef. Each will receive some little gift from another island. The voyage is over. All of Puluwat shares in the reaffirmation of a proud heritage.

From the canoe the perspective is quite different. Anyone

who has sailed a small boat in the open sea need not be told that the image of a little sail bobbing over the water would scarcely come to the minds of those on board. The sail dominates them, by its size but more by its tense struggle to contain the wind it has deflected to its own use. Vibrating, it strains at its lashings. Alternately the sail shades the crew and blinds them with its whiteness. The spars sway and shudder as the boat lifts and plunges through the steep waves of the open Pacific. The canoe itself, a narrow v-shaped hull usually about 26 feet long, with platforms extending out both sides, lurches with a violence which requires constant holding on. If the crew is lucky and the wind holds steady, this pitching and twisting will go on without rest day and night for the day or two or three it takes to reach their destination. But the wind may drop and leave the crew drifting or dawdling along under an equatorial sun. Or it may rise to a storm with gusts wracking the canoe and driving chilling rain into the skin and eyes of the crew. Through all of this the navigator, in sole command, keeps track of course and drift and position, guided only by stars and waves and other signs of the sea, and in recent years by a large but unlighted compass. Even at night he stays awake and vigilant, trusting only himself. They say you can tell the experienced navigators by their bloodshot eyes.

There is a heroic quality to this kind of sailing. Happily, everyone on Puluwat and the other islands of their seafaring world agrees as to its heroism. Even more happily, virtually every man, every child, and any woman who cares to can experience again and again the life of a hero. It is thus a hospitable sort of heroism despite its frequent hardships. Sailing canoes are complex and temperamental craft, but manageable enough that anyone brought up on them can qualify as crew. One is therefore not faced with a fear of failure. True, only a few can achieve the skills of the navigator, but you do not have to be a navigator to be a hero.

Voyaging is hospitable too because, unless there is some occasion for worry or bad weather is making everyone miserable, the prevailing mood at sea is one of good fellowship. Jokes find an audience eager for amusement, tales can be embellished endlessly without fear of losing listeners, and on most trips there is food to eat any time one becomes even a little hungry.

Canoes leaving on a journey—the far one with sail already raised—while old
and young watch from the canoe house

On all these islands in the Central Carolines happiness is having lots of food, and provisioning a departing canoe becomes a major undertaking—for all the relatives of the crew when a canoe leaves home, often for the entire island when a canoe ends a visit elsewhere. Life at sea is a good life, a life of contentment and self-realization.

There are discomforts of course, and also risks. Without them there would be no zest, and no occasion for heroes. But the discomforts are transitory and, when you are used to them, quite tolerable. The risks are real, but not nearly as great as one would expect contemplating the vast stretches of ocean, the tiny slivers of wood and cord which are a canoe, and the little dots of land which are the islands to which Puluwatans sail. The reason the risks are not greater lies in the realm of technology. It lies in canoes which may look complicated and sometimes crude, but which are extraordinarily tough and versatile in the responses they can make to all manner of conditions and crises. It lies in a system of navigation which in the hands and eyes of a gifted and vigilant navigator covers just about every contingency. But above all it lies in the skill and resourcefulness of a people born to the sea and proud of its mastery. This book is principally concerned with the enabling technologies of sailing and navigation, and with the psychological processes which govern their application. Yet these cannot be understood apart from the way of life in which they are embedded. We must begin, then, with a brief sketch of Puluwat and its seafaring people.

Puluwat is one of a long chain of low coral islands which lie between volcanic Truk on the east and Palau and Yap on the west. Taken all together, these islands comprise the Western and Central Carolines; they cover more than a thousand miles of the Pacific Ocean north of New Guinea. The low islands, from Puluwat and its neighbors westward to Sonsorol, southwest of Palau, share a similar culture and languages. They are closely related also to Truk, but differ sharply from Yap and Palau.

According to local tradition, the low islands were settled from the east, from Truk. The Trukese in turn look eastward to Ponape and Kusaie, from whence the first woman arrived pregnant, sailing on a coconut frond. Linguistic evidence seems in this case to support tradition, pointing to an original settlement a few thousand years ago on Kusaie or the nearby Marshalls and spreading outward from there.

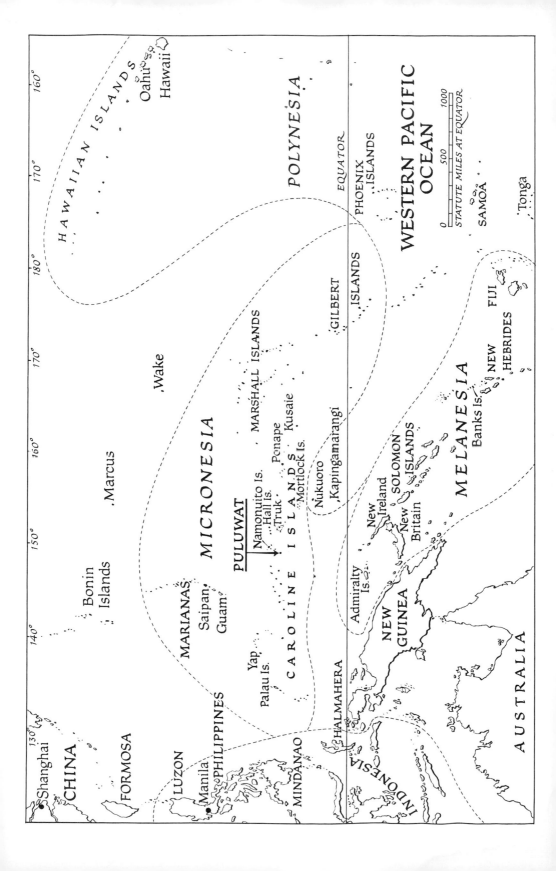

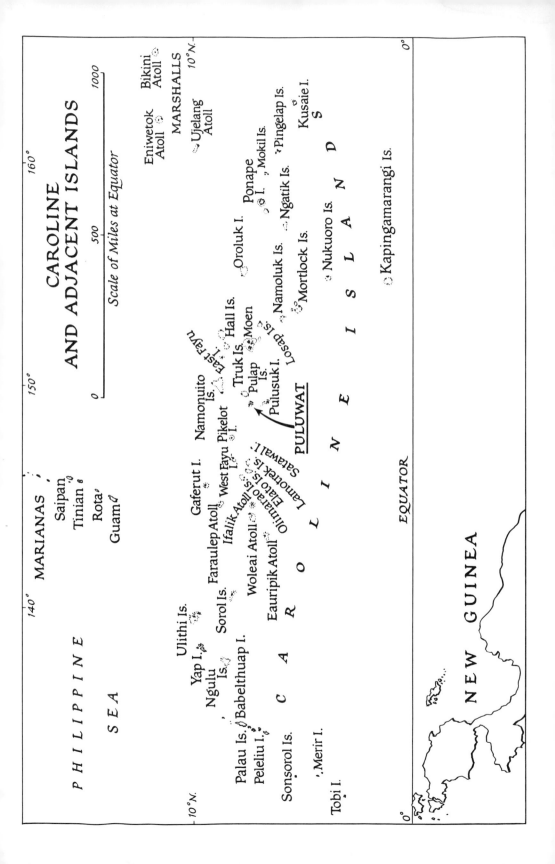

CAROLINE
AND ADJACENT ISLANDS

Scale of Miles at Equator

0   500   1000

MARIANAS

Saipan
Tinian
Rota
Guam

Eniwetok
Atoll

Bikini
Atoll

MARSHALLS

Ujelang
Atoll

Oroluk I.

Ponape
I.   Mokil Is.

Pingelap Is.

Ngatik Is.

Kusaie I.

S

PHILIPPINE

SEA

Namonuito
Is.

Hall Is.

Moen

Truk Is.

Pulap
Is.

Puluwat

Puluusuk I.

Losap Is.

Namoluk Is.

Mortlock Is.

Nukuoro Is.

I   S   L   A   N   D

Gaferut I.

West Fayu   Pikelot
I.   I.

Faraulep Atoll

Ifalik Atoll

Sorol Is.

Woleai Atoll

Olimarao Is.
Elato Is.
Lamotrek Is.
Satawal I.

Eauripik Atoll

C   A   R   O   L   I   N   E

Ulithi Is.

Yap I.

Ngulu
Is.   Babelthuap I.

Palau Is.

Peleliu I.

Sonsorol Is.

Merir I.

Tobi I.

EQUATOR

NEW   GUINEA

Kapingamarangi Is.

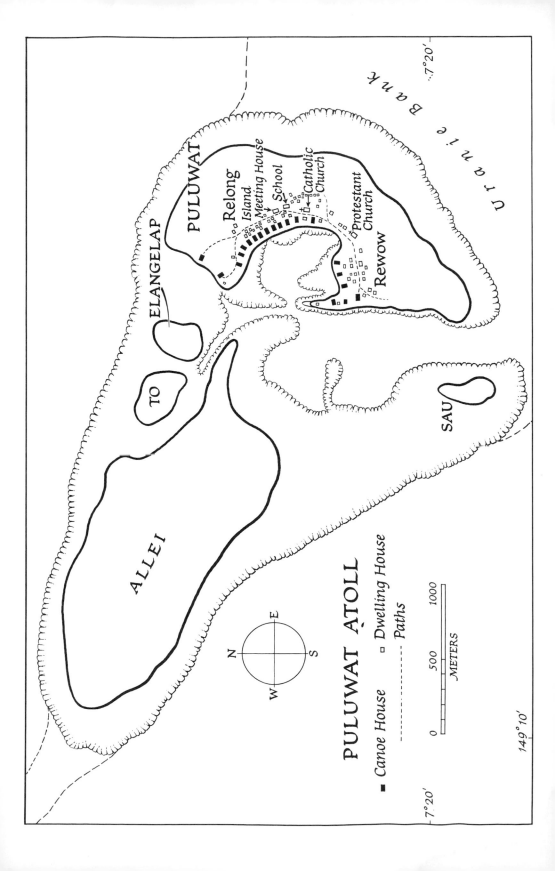

PULUWAT ATOLL

■ Canoe House   □ Dwelling House
------- Paths

0   500   1000
METERS

ELANGELAP

PULUWAT

Relong
Island
Meeting House
School
Catholic
Church
Protestant
Church

Rewow

TO

ALLEI

SAU

Uranie Bank

7°20'

7°20'

149°10'

N
E
S
W

In recent centuries the Carolines have been controlled successively by Spain, Germany, Japan, and the United States. Through most of this time, however, Puluwat was little influenced. Explorers, traders, missionaries, and administrators remained on the island only occasionally and temporarily. During World War II the Puluwatans were evacuated by the Japanese to nearby Pulusuk for military reasons, but thereafter they returned to take up a life little different than before. Only the Americans who came after the war have tried to bring about radical change, principally through education, Christian missions, and indoctrination of leaders. These have had some impact, yet thus far one is more struck by how little has changed than by how much.

The five compactly clustered little islands which together comprise the Puluwat Atoll are arranged in most unusual fashion. Whereas most coral islands in these tropic seas lie along a reef which rings a large lagoon, or else stand alone as islands with no lagoon at all, the Puluwat Atoll is a tight grouping of two relatively large islands, Puluwat proper and Allei (Al-lay), and three small ones. Between them lies a relatively small area of lagoon. In its longest direction the whole atoll is only a little over two miles, but of its surface area over two-thirds is land, almost every inch of it potentially useful and productive. With big taro swamps on both of the large islands, with the rest of the land almost too heavily forested, and with a good balance of useful trees and plants, principally breadfruit, coconut, and pandanus, Puluwat can support many more than its current population of less than four hundred people, all of whom presently live exclusively on the main island of Puluwat.

The lagoon is not only small but is divided in two. An outer lagoon faces the southwest, which is usually the lee side of the atoll, and is protected only by a reef through which boats pass to the open sea. A smaller inner lagoon is almost encircled by Puluwat itself and further protected by Allei and Elangelap, one of the small islands. It thus adds to the resources of Puluwat a perfectly sheltered harbor for boats, so well protected that canoes can be moored, instead of carried up on the shore, under almost any conditions short of a major storm. Most of the people live near their boats, in houses clustered around the arc of this inner lagoon.

Two canoe houses

The balance of land and water not only brings with it many practical benefits; it imparts also to this tiny atoll a beauty exceptional even for a coral island. Look across the little lagoon from anywhere along its crescent shore. The luminous green of a tropical forest shimmers under the sun, above it the china blue sky is splashed with lustrous flat-bottomed clouds, and below lies the mirror of the water. The edge of the land is a sandy shore, seemingly pinned down by hundreds of coconut palms stuck in at all sorts of crazy angles. Through the trees a dozen or more massive canoe houses shoulder their way almost to the water's edge. Often a small canoe with one or two people aboard paddles across from one side of the arc of land to the other. It is easier to use a canoe than to walk, especially if there is something to be carried, and there are always plenty of canoes drawn up along the shore. In the morning and at the end of the day people also paddle over and back from Allei to work in the gardens or taro swamps. Occasionally a sailing canoe sets

Two paddling canoes, drawn up on the beach, a sailing canoe moored offshore

out on a journey or to fish on the adjacent reefs, or perhaps one sails in from a far island. At once the perspective changes. The lagoon becomes an amphitheater and the canoe under its white sail the star of the show, holding all attention as it tacks back and forth to its place along the shore or toward the freedom of the open sea.

Beauty suffuses more than the lagoon. The island of Puluwat is broad enough to protect its inner side from the full fury of tropical storms. The breadfruit trees have therefore been able to grow to great size and, by shading the ground below, limit the growth of brush and lesser trees. Thus, the principal living area of Puluwat lies among the spacious green pavilions characteristic of a mature rain forest. The path through the central village area winds past the buttressed trunks of one huge tree after another. Between the trees are nestled small family houses, some built of unpainted lumber or crude concrete, but most still hunched low on the ground with a thatch roof and dirt floor. In each live half a dozen or more people closely related by blood or marriage. The few clearings which have been made— for the school and meetinghouse, and for the Protestant and Catholic churches—are flooded in unexpected sunlight which lends a special drama.

The island meetinghouse (center) and school (right)

The Catholic church

A woman carries her child along the main island path

Along the paths people are moving, singly or in pairs or threes. Most are women and children, for the men are likely to be in the canoe houses working on their boats, or perhaps at sea fishing while the women tend the houses and children and gardens. Crossing back and forth on the paths and running between the houses and down to the shore there are astonishing numbers of children. Laughing children of three and four jump into the water and swim out again around and around in an endless circle. Older children move in small groups of boys or of girls, occasionally both together, playing whatever game has caught their fancy on that day. Sometimes this is walking with coconut shells cupped under the feet to "clop, clop" on the ground, or pitching a plastic can lid which twists and veers in the air so that a batter armed with a stick or coconut rib almost never hits it. Adolescent girls stand or sit in small clusters, gossiping, only occasionally joined by a boy or two. Usually the older boys like to loaf with the men in the canoe houses or range around the island looking for entertainment or diversion.

Young and old, all are handsome, their light brown skins contrasting with the brightly colored loincloths of the men and the long lavalavas tucked around the waists of the women. Almost always now these are made of cotton purchased from the trading companies on Truk; until recently they were of hibiscus fiber woven on a backstrap-loom. Except for an occasional skin disorder and sporadic outbreaks of respiratory infections, the latter coming particularly after the visit of a ship from Truk, everyone seems very healthy. Even old people in their sixties or more carry themselves well.

To one familiar with the closely related people of Truk, one hundred and fifty miles to the east, one of the most striking qualities of life on Puluwat is its warmth and spontaneity. This is nowhere better expressed than in the affection and attention which every child can command, not only of his parents but of all adults, related or not. In contrast to the inconsistency and frequent callousness of Trukese parents (Gladwin and Sarason, 1953) Puluwat children are met with warmth. If they have a question or cry or are hungry they are attended to. No matter how much they swarm around when work is going on they are never banished unless they are physically in the way. When they are still very small, only

Children watching a canoe come in from a trip

Children idling by a canoe house

four or five, children are frequently taken along on long canoe trips so they will learn to love the sea. Everyone pampers and plays with them and they have a joyous time, ending when they return full of the importance of their adventures. Having such little children on board can only be a nuisance, yet no one seems to object as long as they enjoy the experience.

Presumably because of this consistently positive response by adults, Puluwat children seem confident, poised, and quite without fear even of strangers. Whereas Trukese children flee in sobbing terror from a white man although they may have seen him dozens of times, even the tiniest of Puluwat children soon learned to follow us with curiosity even when no adult was anywhere in sight for reassurance. Children barely old enough to talk, when met on the path would ask in Puluwat, laboring over each syllable, "Where are you going?" This is the friendly way for one adult to greet another on the path and it never would occur to a Puluwat child to do otherwise, even with an American. Like tiny children everywhere, of course, once the question was asked the little Puluwatans were likely to be overcome by their own cleverness and run off giggling in excited embarassment without awaiting a reply.

The Puluwatan who starts his life unafraid of strangers will

An old woman, cooking

never learn to fear them. In days gone by when wars were fought between islands, wars of clubs and spears and later of guns, the Puluwatans were the scourge and terror of the Central Carolines. At various times Puluwat controlled several of the large islands in the Truk lagoon. The mere threat of a coming Puluwat armada was said to have been enough to frighten the entire population of the island of Ulul to the north of Puluwat into boarding a passing Spanish ship which was leaving for the Marianas, and they never returned. In one of these conquests Puluwat wiped out the chiefly clan of Pulusuk, forty miles south. A Puluwat dynasty was installed and Puluwat claims titular ownership of most of Pulusuk to this day.

There is a modern tale about this. One day only a few years ago a Puluwat man, living on Pulusuk with a wife he had married there, tried to exercise his hereditary rights to the fruits of the trees on "his" part of the island. When he picked coconuts from these trees, which Pulusuk families had been using for years, they became angry and, brushing aside his claims to ancient rights of conquest, threatened him with harm if he did not stop. Word soon got back to Puluwat. At once every able-bodied man and every seaworthy sailing canoe was mobilized. At dawn the next morning a flotilla of perhaps twenty canoes was arrayed off the shore of Pulusuk. Leaving one or two men aboard the canoes, the others swam over the reef and onto the land, each with a knife in his teeth. Silently and unopposed they walked up the beach, through the one village on the island, and into the interior. Still without a word they climbed tree after tree and picked one or two nuts from each. Then they returned to the village. The people of Pulusuk, stunned, invited them into the canoe houses and brought the coconuts they had picked and more food than they could eat or carry. The Puluwatans ate and, with an exchange of greetings, solemnly boarded their canoes and sailed home. There have been no arguments since, although this is perhaps in part because Father Fahey, the Catholic missionary on Puluwat, insisted that the Puluwatans apologize to the people of Pulusuk in order to prevent any further trouble.

His insistence upon an apology was honored because most Puluwatans are Christians. Protestants are concentrated in the village of Rewow at the western end of the arc of Puluwat and Catholics in Relong in the other, northern half. Despite earlier missionary efforts, Christianity became an effective force on Puluwat only after World War II. It would be hard to insist that before this time there was any real native religion, but there were many taboos and magical rituals, while divination and sorcery determined the outcome of all manner of events. Almost all of this is now gone, wiped out in little more than ten or fifteen years. Its passing was not only complete but largely uneventful. That all of these magical practices could so easily be abandoned demonstrates a people both pragmatic and unafraid, even of the unknown. But the story of how it happened reflects also the enormous influence exercised by a great navigator in a culture of which navigators are the apotheosis.

In keeping with current mission practice, the missionaries who introduced and taught Christianity on Puluwat tried to limit outright condemnation of local practices only to those which were clearly in conflict with Christian doctrine. Consequently they did not try to outlaw divination, most taboos or many forms of magic. They did, however, insist that none of

Winin, master navigator, on a trip to Truk in 1947. In those days old men still wore the distended earlobes cultivated at puberty, though without the ornaments for which they were intended

these supernatural beliefs and practices were actually effective, and that the outcome of events would be in no way changed if all were disregarded. However, at first they were relinquished only partially and reluctantly. Not surprisingly in a people constantly challenging the dangers of the open sea, many of those conserved were rituals and taboos related to boats and sailing. After a few years, however, one of the truly great navigators of Puluwat, Winin (Wee-neen), who was a Catholic but could equally well have been a Protestant, decided that the priest might be right in what he was saying and the only way to find out was to experiment. Disregarding taboos on sexual activity and on prohibited foods, omitting a variety of formerly essential rituals and precautions, and not even bothering to divine for a propitious day, Winin set out with a small crew on a long voyage. He had a fine trip and returned to report no bad effects from his wholesale disregard of practices which everyone agreed were a nuisance. Almost at once the taboos and rituals surrounding boats and sailing and fishing were dropped.

However, many of these were related to larger complexes of supernatural beliefs affecting life ashore as well. Thus, for example, as in perhaps most non-Western seafaring cultures, women, sexual contacts with women, and above all any contact with menstruating women, were anathema to the forces of the ocean. At sea women were confined to a cramped little covered space on the lee platform of the canoe (a practice which still partially persists, largely for reasons of modesty and convenience), but also were avoided before trips, when building a canoe, or when doing almost any work related to the sea. In particular they were banished to a separate little house whenever they were menstruating. There they had their own food and were forbidden to touch anything which might later contaminate a navigator or a member of his crew. Not directly a part of this complex, but associated with it through a general concern with femaleness, was the belief that a woman should never sit or stand or even walk at a level equal to or higher than her brother or other male relatives in equivalent relationships. Only a few years ago it was common on Puluwat to see women walking along bent over, with their hands clasped behind them in a further gesture of subjection. When their brothers were seated they had to scuttle along almost on all fours in order to stay low enough.

In rapid succession virtually all of these customs crumbled before the realization that if their effects were not to be feared at sea they were certainly of little concern on land. They were dropped with little or no additional pressure from the Christian missionaries and lay teachers. Perhaps even more remarkable is the fact that this occurred with hardly any disruption, often producing little more than a sense of relief that another burdensome practice was gone. There were, of course, some exceptions. Certain customs persist, at least in modified form, such as the isolation of women on canoes, and, especially in traditional settings, women sometimes stooping before "brothers." Some customs which were hastily abandoned are now missed, including an initiation ceremony for new navigators to which we shall return later. This initiation ceremony did, however, include some chants and prayers which were actively opposed by the Catholic priest, and probably the Protestant leaders also, so that it would have been especially difficult to retain it without major modification.

We should not be surprised that abandoning these supernatural beliefs and magical practices resulted in a few cases in a sense of loss or even of anxiety. Rather we must marvel at a people who can so pragmatically assess elements in their traditional way of life which are not in harmony with some new force, and without rancor or dissonance abandon them—or, as the case may be, reject the new. With seemingly little conflict or travail the Puluwatans pick their way among the alternatives presented to them by the past and the present and live at any point in their history with a singularly harmonious mix of customs and life styles. They disregarded determined German efforts to vest title to land in individuals, keeping it instead in matrilineal clans and smaller kin groupings with female descent. They accepted American insistence on the election of magistrates, but then allowed the magistrate power only over new programs and activities sponsored by the adminstration, reserving traditional matters for the traditional chiefs. They readily accepted cotton cloth as a substitute for hibiscus fiber loincloths and lavalavas. At first they insisted on only bright red, but now have diversified their tastes. Thus the acknowledged greatest living master of both canoe-building and navigation, Ikuliman (I-goo-li-man), whom we shall meet

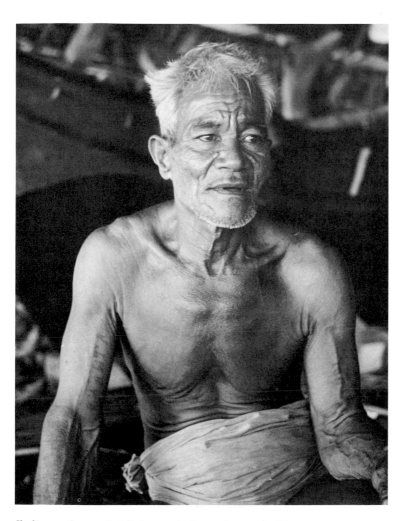

Ikuliman, the greatest living navigator and canoe-builder

often again in these pages, especially favors a loin cloth in pastel lavender. At the same time they have rejected cotton clothes cut in Western style unless they are useful to ward off the sun at sea or to keep out the chill on wet days. Protestant women, and a sprinkling of Catholics, wear dresses into church, and most people have Western clothes to wear when they go to Truk, but they are simply not very comfortable for the Puluwatans and normally they do not wear them. In an engaging adaptation, however, pregnant women often wear skirts with the elastic waist about their necks and the skirt itself draped over their unsightly bulge and sensitive breasts.

Examples of such rational selectivity between things old and things new could be multiplied endlessly. The flexibility of Puluwatans in adapting their culture to the world as it impinges on them is impressive to the outsider. For them it is merely sensible. It spares them the agony of struggles others have experienced, which they probably cannot even imagine, between conservatives and progressives, traditionalists and hucksters, struggles which wrack most of the developing areas of the world. This sophistication in dealing with innovations which come to their island is not exclusively Puluwatan. They share it with all of Truk and the other neighboring islands. The Trukese have made different selections: they took Western clothes as well as cotton cloth, they acceded much broader powers to magistrates, and so forth. These suit the particular circumstances of Truk, but are equally pragmatic and equally adaptive.

It is tempting to speculate upon the source of such useful pragmatism. Viewed from an exclusively Puluwatan perspective it would fit in with the supremely confident way in which they address themselves to their world and its problems. But this overly simple explanation must be rejected because elsewhere in the world people apparently equally proud and confident seem to draw their confidence so directly from their way of life that they are afraid to barter away even one small element of their culture lest it weaken their grip upon the world as a whole. Furthermore, the equally flexible Trukese do not share the fearless self-assurance of the Puluwatans. The Trukese are in fact far more anxious in their conduct of affairs both public and private (Gladwin and Sarason, 1953). Perhaps the explanation lies, as Alkire (1965) concluded on Lamotrek, in the constant travel and resultant flow of ideas and experiences between all these islands.

Such tiny communities can only have grown and developed through sharing unceasingly everything which human ingenuity could contrive on one island or another. For many generations before the advent of European ships the sailing canoe merged dozens of little clusters of humanity into a pool of talent, joint support, and mutual enrichment. Once Europeans came on the scene, establishing centers of trade on a few large islands, the outrigger canoes introduced iron tools and probably tobacco and some other plants to the smaller islands long before any white men reached them. Thus, from time beyond memory there has been a flow of new ideas to be judged, then integrated or rejected as the people of each island reacted to them. Even today the Puluwatans, who trade with the Truk Trading Company, go west to Satawal to find out what the Yap Trading Company is bringing there. The Trukese in their own huge lagoon were apparently never the voyagers that men from the small coral islands have been. The richer volcanic soils and the more generous resources of everything from people to water which characterize larger islands made Truk, like other high islands in the Pacific, a magnet for people from all the surrounding atolls and little islands. Thus the Trukese were more exposed than even the voyaging low islanders themselves to the flow of new ideas and influences, and often provided the gateway into which innovations flowed from the outside world, thence to be diffused by canoeloads of visitors from Puluwat and its neighbors.

Although the people of Puluwat and Truk both enjoy the comforting capability of choosing rationally between new and old alternatives, there are other areas in which their psychological response to the needs they feel in their lives differ markedly. One of these is food. On Truk the giving and withholding of food is tantamount to giving or withholding support and affection. Children are disciplined with threats of refusing food, and they see their parents and other adults continually worried lest there not be enough. Yet, although hunger is a source of recurrent anxiety, this anxiety has practically no foundation in reality: on Truk, as on Puluwat, food is almost always in ample supply and rarely is anyone hungry for any length of time. It seems to be one of those things around which an essentially rather anxious people have focused their concerns out of all proportion to any real basis for worry. Yet on Puluwat, in so many ways culturally and psychologically similar to Truk, there is no evidence of a comparable food anxiety. Puluwatans treat food in a matter-of-fact way as part of the daily routine. They greatly enjoy eating, especially freshly cooked breadfruit or fish, and above all sea turtle, but it remains in comfortable proportion to the rest of their needs and pleasures, testimony once again to a realism which only the self-assured can afford.

The staple foods on Puluwat, as throughout most of the Caroline Islands, are breadfruit and taro. Of these breadfruit is most favored. Taro is so secondary in their tastes that it was only in relatively recent years and under administrative pressure that sufficient effort was invested in dredging out and planting the taro swamps to assure an adequate supply during the periods when the breadfruit trees are not bearing. The months completely without breadfruit are November through February, sometimes longer in poor years. In March a few trees of an early variety begin to bear; by May the majority of the breadfruit trees come into bearing and there is often more than the people can eat. Some of this surplus is buried in pits where it ferments to a relatively stable condition and is edible during the lean months. This preserved breadfruit also lasts a long time when taken on a canoe voyage. In the past when there was little taro even the preserved breadfruit would run out during the lean months and everyone was hungry. This provided the excuse and occasion for drinking a toddy prepared by fermenting the sap of coconut trees; during these months recurrent tipsiness dulled the pangs of hunger and allegedly kept people from being grumpy over the lack of food. It was probably quite rare that the shortage of food became really acute—witness the lack of work on the taro swamps—but mere scarcity was enough to provide the men an admirable excuse for their favored pastime of drinking.

Nowadays the excuse is gone, and there are recurrent efforts to discourage the making of coconut palm toddy because it interferes with the growth of coconuts and hence with the production of copra, which is made from dried coconut meat and is the principal cash crop. This has probably helped conserve the supply of coconuts, but it has not brought the end of drinking. Quite the opposite. To prepare palm toddy it is necessary to tap a coconut tree and then wait for the sap to ferment naturally. Now one can get out some sugar and some yeast (imported for baking bread), or buy them if one of the local entrepreneurs has them in stock in the little shack he calls a store, mix them in water, and wait a very short time. The result is a vile brew which nonetheless has a formidable impact. There is actually quite a bit of drinking among men on Puluwat, especially when the rather stern Catholic missionary is away—which is quite often because his is a far-flung "parish." The principal reason for this drinking is the same the world around: most people enjoy the effects of alcohol, and many people enjoy getting drunk, despite the distressing side effects of occasional fights and of inevitable hangovers. In addition, drinking is an almost exclusively male activity and as such can be seen as an enhancement to masculinity. This seems to be a factor of consequence for some men more than others, but only one grown man is said never to drink at all.

Returning to the more mundane matter of food, breadfruit and taro are both rather large and starchy. Breadfruit grows on magnificent tall trees from which it must be picked, a job performed by men who climb up carrying long slender poles forked at the end. As their wives stand below to warn the passers-by the heavy fruits, twisted off their stems, come crashing to the ground. When they are too ripe they explode on impact and spread wide a ghastly yellow mess. Taro is a more humble plant, a gray or somewhat purple tuber which grows in swamps, although there is also on Puluwat a little of a distantly related variety which grows on dry land.

Both breadfruit and taro, and such occasional foods as imported rice, are usually prepared by households, extended family units covering three or often four generations. Cooking is best done by steaming in an earth oven, often in a separate little cookhouse, followed by pounding and packaging in breadfruit leaves. Fresh breadfruit is also tasty when roasted in the coals of a fire and then scraped free of its charred exterior. Most commonly, however, it is simply boiled. Generally this is women's work, but men and women sometimes work together

A family pounding food for a voyage

in the hard task of pounding breadfruit or taro with coral rock
pestles on hardwood planks. This is especially likely when
everyone in the household turns to the task of provisioning a
canoe about to set off on a trip. Much food is also prepared on
Saturdays.

Food is readied on Saturday because one of the Western
customs which Puluwatans (and Trukese) have embraced with
unreserved enthusiasm is the observance of Sunday as a day of
rest. After church people take walks around the island, sleep,
gossip, flirt, sing in groups, drink (usually to get drunk), tell
stories, whittle, and in general express each his own individual
nature. The only thing these activities have in common is that
they are pleasant and are not considered work. In order, however, that people have something to eat on Sunday—which is
also the time for feasts to celebrate holidays and special occasions—food must be prepared on Saturday. The custom has
evolved now to the point that virtually everyone works hard on
food production all day Saturday and enough is thereby
amassed to last for several days.

On Saturdays men may help their womenfolk pick bread-

A fishtrap on the shore

fruit in the morning, but thereafter most of them go fishing. There are many different ways of catching fish on Puluwat. Occasionally schools of fish get trapped in the lagoon and can be surrounded by canoes carrying a long net, half of which belongs to the village of Relong and the other half to Rewow. In the daytime fish are speared in crannies in the reef by goggled swimmers. At night in the dark of the moon fish are also speared underwater using a light; in the past, and sometimes now, this was a torch of dried coconut fronds held by a partner in a canoe. At present it is more commonly a Japanese waterproof flashlight held by the fisherman himself under the water, a spooky sight if you are not prepared for it. There are also fishtraps, beautifully contrived of slender sticks lashed together into an elongated basket with a conical one-way entrance. In the past huge fishtraps were planted on the Uranie Bank, a broad deep reef which extends twenty miles to the east of Puluwat; each canoe house had its own area of the reef reserved for their traps. Now the traps are smaller, three or four feet in length, and are used only inside the lagoon. With the advent of good steel hooks fish can more readily be caught outside on the ocean reefs by dropping baited lines over the side of a canoe. This latter means may in fact be the most efficient and most reliable way of catching fish known to the Puluwatans, but perhaps because it is rather dull and undemanding it is not their favored technique. Nevertheless, a lot of fishing is done with baited handlines. Even paddling canoes are taken out from the shelter of the lagoon and anchored a little distance outside the pass, while small sailing canoes are taken farther from the island. The larger sailing canoes are also used for fishing with baited lines, sometimes by prior intention, but more commonly when it is found that the fish are not biting on trolling lines. A set of smaller handlines and hooks are customarily carried aboard for this eventuality. Granted, handlines offer a rather routine way of fishing, but on a large canoe wth a full crew of five or six men it can be a mighty productive routine.

For this kind of fishing sailing canoes are usually not anchored. Instead they are allowed to drift, with the sail slatting in the wind, as long as the fish are biting in a particular location. As soon as the biting stops lines are pulled in, the sheet is taken in to fill the sail, and the canoe moves on to try another spot. Not more than five or ten minutes at most are wasted on a new location before moving on again if the fish do not strike. Hooks, lines, and lead sinkers are imported by the trading companies; all fishline is now of nylon. The meat of freshly caught fish is used as bait for the hooks. It may be necessary to bring along something else—many things are used—for starting bait. If canoes have set out to troll and given up for lack of catches, usually one or two canoes will at least have had a little luck. The handful of fish they may have caught are then offered to other crews to use for bait if they have nothing.

The drifting canoe typically rides with the outrigger upwind; since the waves usually follow the wind at least approximately, the hull is likely to be parallel to the troughs and rolls up and down over each wave following its outrigger float. Although the sail is usually left hoisted when fishing, even when the sail is lowered there is enough wind resistance in the hull, the bodies of the crew, and the mast and rigging to keep this part of the canoe downwind, an important factor as we shall see in keeping track of where you are going when drifting in a storm. This orientation of the drifting canoe has the result that when the fishermen sit around the edge of the outrigger platform their lines drift away from the boat and stream off relatively separately one from the next; surprisingly little fouling of lines occurs. Although numerous, reef fish are only of modest size. They are of many different varieties. Each time a fish is hooked the line is pulled in, the fisherman removes the fish, throws it toward the middle of the boat, and at once rebaits the hook and throws it back in. One man does nothing but wait to grab the twisting, slapping fish off the platform, bang their heads with an iron bar if there is one, or else anything hard and heavy, and throw them into a basket secured below the outrigger booms in the middle of the hull. If the supply of bait is low this man scrapes off the scales and makes some cuts near the tail of the fish, tears off the meat with his teeth and tosses the pieces onto the outrigger platform behind one or another of the active fishermen. Two or three pieces of bait always wait behind each man. They take turns at the tiresome job of killing and stowing fish, but it usually seems to fall to the junior members of the crew. Meanwhile the captain or one of the senior men stays seated near the sail, ready to grab the sheet in response to a gust of wind or other sudden happening. So the routine goes, not enough happening to make it exciting but too much to permit the pleasures of relaxed storytelling.

If this kind of fishing is dull, trolling is the opposite. Trolling from a sailing canoe with the fish schooling and a fresh breeze blowing is all raw action. Usually more than one canoe is out and on a Saturday as many as half a dozen may be working a mile or two of reef where there are fish. The canoes vary from full-sized interisland sailing craft to little one-man outriggers which are really no more than paddling canoes rigged with a sail. On the bigger boats four long heavy nylon lines are trailed behind, each firmly secured, two on the outrigger platform and two on the opposite side on the lee platform. Within the limits of the number of men available someone tends each line by keeping it deflected with an arm or leg or toe so that if it tightens with a biting fish the change will be felt. Care must be taken, however, lest a heavy strike cut the flesh or even sever a toe. At the end of each line is a heavy steel hook, usually with a feather lure, but sometimes a lure made of coconut leaf strips or even some bait. This, then, is the equipment of each canoe.

Smaller canoes have fewer men aboard and fewer lines out.

The canoes work back and forth over the reef, lines streaming aft and everyone alert. If the wind is good they are making six knots or better. Fish are most likely to feed and therefore to run at the edge of a long reef or around a smaller single reef where the current is rising into the shallower water, bringing smaller fish and other food up from greater depths. The meeting between the force of ocean currents and the great reefs creates steep waves and a wild sea. The wind whips the white tops off the waves and throws them into biting spray, while the hull and outrigger float fling themselves through the surging water and throw up more stinging wetness into the wind.

Even under the best of conditions, however, random trolling over the reefs results in few strikes. Generally the fish run in schools, large numbers of fish of many kinds pursuing in their turn schools of smaller fish. The small fish jump at the top of the water, its surface alive with thousands of tiny flashes. From above the seabirds, mostly terns, some white, some black, wheel and dive and dive again, trapping the little fish in their frenzy between enemies above and below. It is the birds which signal to the fisherman that the fish are running in a school. All the canoes turn and plunge toward the birds which are pirouetting over the surface of the sea, the boats beating up against the wind and waves if they must, but hoping that when a big school of fish comes along it will be downwind from them and they can run foaming down upon it. If they do, it will be with the sail as full as the captain dares and with every bit of the boat tearing and straining at the resisting water. This is work as rough on boats as it is on men. The schools of fish shift and disperse as suddenly as they appear and every moment counts.

The canoes converge over a school of fish. They plunge past one another, each carrying its cargo of furiously active men. One man after another cries "a strike!" and hauls on his line with long sweeping strokes of his arms, almost oblivious to the struggles of the fish on the other end—unless it is one of those huge fish everyone hopes for. If the fish is really big the rest of the crew join in the battle, forgetting the lesser catches they have hooked or may later catch on their untended lines. Time enough to see what is left when they have brought the big one aboard. Usually no one bothers to kill the fish. They pull them to the middle of the canoe, get out the hook as best they can, wasting time stunning the fish only if they have to, and with a kick or heave fling the fish into the bottom of the boat. Later when the frenzy is over they will kill those which have not yet died and stow them in the big basket slung below the outrigger booms in the middle of the hull. Meanwhile they get the nylon line back in the water as fast as possible and hope there is no snag in the coils which fell in a pile on the platform as the fish came in. With luck there will be a second strike, especially if the school is moving along with the canoe. Or perhaps the crew can leave their lines, quickly reverse the sail, and tack back over the school of fish. Soon the strikes end and the excitement quiets down, with the hope that it will not be for long. If so, there will be another flock of birds, another wild rush, more strikes, more tumult, and more big fish crashing around inside the deep hull of the boat. On a great day canoes return loaded heavily, riding deep in the water with their burden of fish.

But even on a seemingly good day time and again the schools of fish can melt away and the birds fly off to renew their individual searching just as the canoes arrive. Sometimes, too, the fish seem not to be feeding, or the current is running the wrong way. The weather can become so bad that even the boldest of crews will take no more punishment for themselves and their canoes and run for home, chilled to a pasty white by the lashing of cold squalls of rain drawn down from freezing heights on torrents of cold air. Yet no canoe runs for home before everyone aboard has peered through the spray and overcast to be sure that no other canoe has been caught in a squall and capsized or perhaps torn its sail. With a lifetime of practice every Puluwatan, like seafarers the world over, can pick out the tiniest object on the surface of the sea and sense its shape and condition. This is the time when everyone worries about the little one-man canoes which should never be out in such weather. There are always those who feel they can fish best this way, or perhaps can find no one with whom they can team up on that day, so out they go. It falls to the largest boat in the flotilla to brave the wind and seas to escort the little canoe in, cursing its foolhardy occupant but never thinking of leaving him to a deserved fate.

Thus it is that trolling is at best an uncertain way to catch fish, one which can result in a bigger catch than any other, and a catch of big delicious deep sea fish at that, but can also result in no catch at all. Most commonly it yields two or three good-sized fish—tuna, wrasse, or the like—and a few little ones, just enough for the families of the crew. In return the canoe has taken a beating, rougher treatment and more risks than would be acceptable on a long ocean voyage when the canoe must above all be kept intact. Canoes which fish a lot soon have loose lashings; they leak and their rigging is chafed and needs replacement sooner. It is a high price to pay for a few fish. It takes a year or more to build a sailing canoe, and a couple of weeks just to overhaul the lashings and rigging. But fishing is part of what the canoes are built for, and as all the canoes strain toward a school of fish, at once you know which sails the best and which captain is most skilled and daring. This is the good way, the proud way to catch fish.

Doubtless there are many people in the world who go about the business of providing for food, shelter, and their other needs in the most rational way their resources will permit. Probably when survival depends upon wresting from a hostile environment every scrap of sustenance it will yield, productive efficiency becomes the standard by which all choices must be made. Such conditions, however, do not obtain on Puluwat. The sea is full of fish and the land is burdened with all manner of growing things. There are many pathways to plenty, and productive energies need not be guided only by rational economics. If men feel better trolling at high speed over the reefs, what does it matter that this is more costly and perhaps even less productive than sitting on a lurching canoe catching little fish with a line hanging inert in the water? What good is it that a man lives if he is not true to his nature?

2 The Way of the Voyager

Standing on the shore of Puluwat and looking out upon the ocean there is little to see but water and sky. The scene is alive with wind and waves, with birds flashing in the sunlight and clouds marching slowly past, but otherwise it is empty. Puluwat seems a patch of land thrust up from the bed of the sea, alone in an endless expanse of sparkling water. Yet if the view is to the east, or to the west, we know that just a few fathoms down there is a great reef teeming with fish, swimming to breast the current which flows steadily, first this way and then that, over and through miles of coral and sand before its water runs over the edge of the reef and back down again to the cold depths of the ocean. This much perhaps we can picture and make real in our minds. Yet beyond this there is more, and it too is real. It is this farther reality which stamps a unique meaning on the life of every man, woman, and child on Puluwat.

What lies beyond is a world of little islands, some inhabited and some not, but each with its own special shape and nature, and each in its own assigned place upon the vast surface of the sea. As one thinks of these islands, one over there, another there to the north, a third over here closer, Truk rising high from the sea off in the east, and many more among and beyond these, with reefs stretched between, the sea itself is transformed. No longer is it simply a great body of water which, encountering Puluwat, shoves around it and reforms on the other side to flow on to an empty eternity. Instead the ocean becomes a thoroughfare over which one can think of oneself moving, other islands left behind to right and left, toward a particular island of destination which as one comes up upon it will be waiting, as it always waits, right where it is supposed to be. When a Puluwatan speaks of the ocean the words he uses refer not to an amorphous expanse of water but rather to the assemblage of seaways which lie between the various islands. Together these seaways constitute the ocean he knows and understands. Seen in this way Puluwat ceases to be a solitary spot of dry land; it takes its place in a familiar constellation of islands linked together by pathways on the ocean.

The Puluwatan pictures himself and his island in his part of the ocean much as we might locate ourselves upon a road map. On a road map places, mostly communities, appear as locations with names, linked by lines of travel. Those we know from having visited them spring to mind, the buildings, the people, the spirit of the place. Those we know only at second hand have an image much less clear, and some are nothing but names. But each has its place, and there is a way to get to each one. Each too has its part to play in the totality which is a state or region or country. So it is with the island world of the Puluwatan. He knows of many islands and can visualize where they are and how to get to them. Some he has visited; he knows people and places on them which set them apart. Others he has heard about because people from them have visited Puluwat, and Puluwatans have traveled the seaway there on their canoes. Still other more distant islands are spoken of only by their names and legends. The navigators know the star courses to them but have never traveled these courses—but if they did they know the islands would be there.

Historically it was essential that Puluwat be a part of this larger island world. It would never have developed as it has if it stood alone. Alkire (1965) develops this thesis in his monograph on Lamotrek, and his conclusions apply equally to Puluwat. Dozens of islands stretched over a thousand miles of ocean from Yap on the west to Truk and the islands beyond on the east have been linked by their seafaring men and their sailing canoes into a network of social, economic, and often political ties without which they probably could not have survived, much less evolved the complex and secure way of life they now enjoy. The opportunity to exchange people, goods, and information permits these tiny communities to survive disasters, notably typhoons, to draw from a pool of ideas and innovations larger than just their own, to integrate when useful into larger political groupings, and to extend the range of choice in marriage beyond the limited number of unrelated partners available on one's own island.

These are all highly practical, indeed essential, considerations. Yet beyond its practical value the seafaring life, the constant voyaging of sailing canoes back and forth between islands, has acquired a psychological worth of its own. It adds a measure of meaning and value to every other act, on land as well as at sea. Nothing could attest to this more eloquently than a paradox: as the seafaring culture on Puluwat renews itself with undiminished vitality—building new canoes, training young navigators, experimenting with novel techniques—the practical necessity for it has all but disappeared. Virtually all of the exchanges of people and things and ideas outlined above could be achieved reasonably well through travel on the small passenger-carrying ships which have been making regular administrative and trading trips through these islands for the past twenty years. True, the schedules of the ships are uncertain and their capacity limited, and some islands to the west, especially Satawal, being in a different administrative district, enjoy no direct service from Puluwat. However, if the Puluwatans were pressed there are other islands within their own district which could serve the same functional need, which in the case of Satawal is primarily to expand the range of available marriage opportunities. As for the other inconveniences of erratic schedules and crowded quarters, in objective terms they are trifling compared to the effort involved in building, maintaining, and operating a fleet of sailing canoes, to say nothing of the discomfort of riding for several days without shelter on one of them.

The truth of the matter is that the Puluwatans are not objective about their canoes and their voyaging, even less objective perhaps than we in the United States are about our automobiles. Especially for those of us who live in cities the minor inconvenience of public transportation objectively should weigh far less in the balance than the cost and trouble of keeping a car, yet most of us not only keep our cars but at intervals buy new ones. We say the automobile has become part of our way of life and we do not want to give it up. If this be so, on Puluwat the sailing canoe is not merely a part of their way of life, it is the very heart of it. To suggest that the Puluwatans should beach their canoes and retire their navigators would be to foretell disaster. To imagine Puluwat without the élan of its seafaring life one must think of a dispirited people. While the exhilaration of trolling over the reefs can remind men they are men, the canoes that Puluwat builds and the voyages to distant islands which they undertake suffuse the entire island, not just its men, with a sense of purpose and fulfillment. In the last analysis everything on Puluwat is justified by the contribution it makes to the capability of boats and people to travel well and safely at sea.

In keeping with this, even though the canoes are operated exclusively by men, and most traveling on them is done by men, everyone shares at least vicariously in their life and accomplishments. Women make few long trips, and when they do travel it is in the cramped isolation of a little hut lashed on the lee platform of the canoe, but every woman knows about all the canoes on the island and all their voyages. They have strong opinions about the relative ability of each navigator, and even about the seaworthiness of the different canoes. Concerned with the well-being of their men, women's judgments are most likely to rest exclusively upon such practical considerations as safety and reliability, whereas men think also of the seniority of navigators and their grasp of the esoteric knowledge which is still a part of the art even after the disappearance of magic. Yet all will join in agreement that Puluwat canoes are faster and stouter than any others, and its navigators the wisest and most skilled.

There is no sign that this enthusiasm is waning. If anything it is growing stronger. The rest of the world may see virtue in mechanization, and in power and efficiency, but on Puluwat almost every young man seems still to aspire to become a navigator. Only a handful make it, but those who fall by the wayside are willing to settle for the lesser glory of being a crew member on a Puluwat canoe. Thus far very few young people appear inclined to leave Puluwat to seek their futures in the district center on Truk or elsewhere. Rather, the young men are learning to build, to sail, and hopefully even to navigate canoes, and young women are readying themselves to be wives of seafaring men. This eagerness went far enough to create problems for me in obtaining valid information about canoes and sailing. If a question is asked about sailing no man wants to admit that he does not know the answer, that he is ignorant of a matter relating to life at sea. Thus I learned that, while anyone can be relied upon to give a ready answer, only the most qualified can be relied upon for a *right* answer. It is not that the others are lying; they are simply giving the best answer they can think of rather than admit they have no answer at all.

With such abounding enthusiasm for the sea it is evident that taking a trip to another island becomes in large measure an end in itself. Indeed, if one disregards the larger functional advantages which result from the maintenance of interisland ties and looks only at the purported reason given for making any given trip, these reasons often seem trivial, certainly not enough alone to warrant the great amount of effort involved. Trips of one hundred and thirty miles are made to Satawal and one hundred and fifty miles to Truk just to get special kinds of tobacco, the former a particular variety imported from the United States by the Yap Trading Company and the latter a native tobacco which can only be grown on volcanic soils. In actuality the trip to Satawal often does include in its purpose a visit by someone on the canoe to relatives on that island or on nearby Lamotrek or Elato. Or they may be taking someone (often a woman or an older child) to or from a more extended visit of several months' duration. Yet an initial inquiry usually elicits only tobacco as the central objective. Similarly, a trip to Truk will include in addition to getting native tobacco some purchases of imported goods. However, virtually all of the latter could be purchased or at least ordered for delivery on the next trip from the ship which serves these islands around Truk. Many trips are made to Pikelot, over a hundred miles away, to catch large green turtles; they are very numerous and easy to catch on Pikelot (as on any uninhabited island) but with a little effort and persistence they can be caught also on Puluwat and the trip would be unnecessary.

Closer to home, some people seem almost to commute back and forth to Ulul, nearly eighty miles away, for all sorts of reasons, and on an average a canoe travels between Puluwat and nearby Pulap (twenty miles distant) and Tamatam (fifteen) every week or two. Finally, because so many people on Puluwat have relatives on Pulusuk, forty miles to the south, there is a lot of traffic between them also, including men such as canoe builders going to work for their relatives on Pulusuk, or bringing back to Puluwat a paddling canoe built by someone on Pulusuk.*

Travel between Puluwat and the nearer islands less than a hundred miles distant, especially Pulap, Tamatam, and Pulusuk, is augmented by canoes based on those islands coming to Puluwat. However, no canoes come from the more distant islands. This is because there are no sailing canoes on Truk, and although there are a number on Satawal and on Lamotrek, in recent years they have made few if any trips as far east as Puluwat. Neighbors of Puluwat, however, especially Tamatam and Pulusuk, regularly also send canoes on long voyages westward to the Satawal group or east to Truk. In recent years canoes from Puluwat have also gone beyond Truk to the Mortlock Islands on the south and to the Halls on the north. To repeat, however, what is so remarkable about these trips, especially the longer ones which require at least four or five men and a big canoe and last several weeks, is not only that the reasons for making them are often (but not always) rather trifling but also that all except those to Satawal and its neighbors (and to Pikelot) could be made readily by ship. Even Satawal can be reached on a roundabout trip via Truk, Guam, and Yap.

* Quite a number of the paddling canoes on Puluwat actually came from Pulusuk; this appears to be part of a larger system of exchange of goods and services between the two islands. Good sized paddling canoes can be carried lashed to the outrigger platform of a sailing canoe.

All of this traveling keeps the big interisland canoes pretty busy. At the time of this study there were fifteen of them, plus a dozen smaller ones for local use, in active service on Puluwat. During the sixteen months from January 1966 through April 1967 the fifteen big canoes made a total of seventy-three trips to other islands, an average of almost five trips per canoe. One canoe made nine separate voyages during this period, and another eleven. Aside from essentially local trips to Pulap, Tamatam, and Pulusuk, these voyages generally required two weeks or more for completion and involved in many cases stops at several islands en route. To cite a few figures, there were twelve trips to Satawal and its neighboring islands averaging a month in duration, twenty-two trips just to Pikelot (the turtle island) and back taking two weeks on the average, five trips to Truk (and usually other islands also) of three weeks' average duration, and fourteen voyages to Ulul (often stopping at Pulap), which varied from one to three weeks but averaged eleven days. All told, the fifteen canoes averaged a total of over two months away from Puluwat out of the sixteen months for which information is available. The two most active boats were away the equivalent of three and a half and almost six months respectively during the same time.

In addition to their interisland voyages most of the large canoes are used also for reef fishing. Data are available on fishing operations only for the four-month period from January through April 1967; memories of the period before this time were unreliable. Although most of the fishing is done by the smaller sailing canoes built primarily for this purpose, the twelve big canoes which were used for fishing during this period went out on the average twice a month. Furthermore, some of the fishing trips by these large boats were to richer reefs farther away, Manila Reef to the south and Gray Feather Bank to the northwest, usually requiring an overnight sail.

There are good seasons for sailing, and bad. The Puluwatan navigator knows these times by the rising and setting of certain stars just before dawn or at dusk through the cycle of each year. He knows the weather and winds associated with each of these star months and can thus forecast the seasonal changes.

The Western world forecasts the same changes by the movement north and south of the doldrum belt, which extends around the world. Air, warmed by tropical waters and sun-baked lands near the equator, rises. In a vast global circulation it divides at higher altitudes and travels toward the poles, where it comes down again to move outward toward the fat middle of our spinning world. The area where the air is rising from the surface of the earth is known as the doldrum belt. On land it brings monsoons and rainy seasons throughout the tropical world. At sea as the air lifts off it often leaves behind a glassy calm in which not a breath of wind stirs for hundreds of miles. Equally, however, the rising warm air meeting colder air aloft may create turbulent squalls or great storms. At yet other times the winds are fair, but blow from different directions than at other times of the year. In some parts of the world, including the western Pacific, the doldrum belt is driven far to the south during the winter months of the northern hemisphere and to the north in the summer. The winter movement results from the thrust of great high pressure systems of weather which drive down (and eastward) toward the equator from colder latitudes. Winds swirl about the high pressure centers in a clockwise direction in the northern hemisphere and the opposite in the southern. These winds not only affect the weather but also determine the character of ocean swells which the Puluwat navigator knows and uses to maintain his course at sea.

During the midwinter months of January through March in the western Pacific a succession of high pressure systems pour out of the Asian heartland deep into the ocean areas. The doldrum belt moves far south and Puluwat, 7 degrees north of the equator, feels the strong northeast trade winds which drive off the fronts of the north Pacific highs as they swing to their southern limits. Treetops sway constantly and huge waves roar day and night on the long northeast flank of the atoll. Canoes go out only to fish the nearby reefs or to make urgent trips to the closest islands. Even the shortest trip is a hectic and harassing battle against driving winds and sea, hard on men and boats alike. It will be remembered this is also the time when there is no breadfruit bearing on the trees or even preserved in the ground. This season is given a special name and set apart in distaste from the rest of the year.

In April the pressure from the north weakens, the doldrum belt begins to move north toward the equator, and in the Carolines the trade winds, although still blowing fairly steadily from the northeast, drop in strength to comfortable levels. Overhaul of the sailing canoes is completed and one after another, or in convoys of two or three, they set off on their various journeys. The destination of most, although not all, of these first trips of the sailing season is Pikelot.

Pikelot occupies a unique and affectionate place in the lives of Puluwat's seagoing men. It is a tiny island, scarcely five hundred yards in its greatest extent, a hundred miles northwest of Puluwat. There is some water deep enough to swim in between the steep beach and the reef, especially on the north and south, but no real lagoon where canoes can be moored. Therefore they must be manhandled through a small slot in the reef and then heaved in all their great bulk by chanting straining men up the beach onto the wide shelf of sand on top out of reach of the pounding waves. In return for this effort, and also for at least one but often three or four days and nights of sailing each way, Pikelot offers only two things, turtles and relaxation.

Supplying Puluwat with turtle meat is the ostensible purpose of all trips to Pikelot in the spring. Actually, every canoe returning from there does arrive burdened down with three to six large, trussed up green turtles on board, each as heavy as a grown man and mostly females, preferred because they carry eggs at this time of year and are fatter. On land, as they are when they crawl up the beach of Pikelot, turtles are easily rendered helpless by stepping on their tails and flipping them with a quick heave over onto their backs. Then they can be tied up and dragged to the canoe, or tethered with a rope on one flipper and made to swim around the island if they are farther away. Kept out of the sun they will stay alive for a week or more, thus assuring their delivery to Puluwat still fresh. A canoeload of turtles is a treat for everyone on the island. Unlike a catch of fish, which belongs principally to the crew which caught it, the meat of turtles is divided up by the traditional senior chief among all of the households and any visitors on the island.

Despite the joys of feasting on turtle meat, and the satisfaction of providing such a feast, one gets the inescapable impression that this is not the only, or often even the primary, reason for going to Pikelot. Among other things turtles are so plentiful there that a stay of twenty-four hours would usually

Hipour's canoe returns with turtles from Pikelot

be ample to catch a full canoeload, yet it is rare for a canoe to remain less than three days and often they stay for a week or more. A trip to Pikelot has much of the character of a stag party in the United States. The voyages are often organized on the spur of the moment, and an expedition to Pikelot even grows occasionally out of a long drinking party. Someone jumps up and says, "I'm going to Pikelot. Who's going with me?" If the man is not too drunk others join, sometimes enough to commandeer a second or even a third canoe. A minimum of equipment and any available food is loaded aboard and they depart, singing and shouting as they work their way across the lagoon and out to the pass, while their wives and other sober souls scowl their disapproval on shore.* This sort of prank would be

* No one from Puluwat has ever gotten in trouble this way. If they are too drunk someone stops them, or else as soon as they are out of sight they lower the sail and sleep it off. However, two canoes from Pulusuk did get lost recently when they left for Pikelot with a drunk navigator. They drifted for days in strong winds and when they were finally picked up by a Japanese fishing boat they had to abandon their canoes. However, with a characteristic lack of charity toward the seamanship of Pulusuk men, the Puluwatans contend that this particular navigator did not need to be drunk in order to get lost.

unthinkable were the destination anywhere else. For Puluwatans drunk or sober, Pikelot is special. Once there one can do little but eat turtle meat (although this is rich and in time brings on diarrhea), talk, sleep, and bathe in the warm water. There are no responsibilities and no nagging women. Uniquely on Pikelot there are not even any bothersome flies, although the birds are so numerous their noise sometimes interferes with talking and the smell of guano pervades the wooded interior of the island where the wind is cut off. It is a good life for the few days it lasts, and at its end the crews who return blackened by the sun are particularly welcome heroes because of their cargoes of fresh turtle. A few weeks after the sailing season has begun any man who for some reason has not yet been on a canoe going to Pikelot feels aggrieved, chagrined that he has been left out.

At this time of year, during April and even more in May, canoes go also to Satawal and often on to Lamotrek and Elato just beyond. Sometimes the full one-hundred-thirty-mile trip is made directly to Satawal from Puluwat. The small size of Satawal—barely a mile long and without a lagoon—and its lack of flanking reefs in any direction make this the most exacting task in the Puluwat navigator's repertoire. For this reason, and because it is a nice gesture to bring turtles to your hosts when visiting another island, most canoes go first to Pikelot. This is an easy navigational exercise despite its distance because of many deep reefs which provide seamarks along the way. Thereafter they go on to Satawal, a run of less than sixty miles.

All this time the doldrum belt is moving northward, bringing occasional storms but more often good sailing weather. The winds become variable. With luck and good management it is possible during these summer months to sail with the wind to another island and then, after waiting a little while for the wind to change, sail home again with the wind once more pushing along from behind. During July and August the doldrum belt has moved so far north that Puluwat lies south of it. Now the trade winds are coming from the south. Although below the equator the trades typically blow from the southeast, when they cross the equator the same winds turn and come from the southwest. This more westerly wind is fine for voyages to the east. With a southwesterly breeze one can go to Pisaras, East Fayu, or the Halls with the wind astern, and thereafter run down to Truk itself with the same wind comfortably on the beam. Then wait a week or two and the wind will often shift around to blow you home again.

Linger too long, however, and the doldrum belt will have passed again to the south. This usually happens toward the end of September. Cooler air from the north comes upon water heated by the summer sun and by doldrum winds and the mix becomes unstable. This is the season of typhoons, identical to the hurricanes which are spawning at the same time and for the same reasons in the Caribbean and adjacent Atlantic waters. These storms come up so fast and with such fury that only the most daring, or perhaps foolhardy, of navigators venture on a long trip during late September or October. After this the weather stabilizes again, the northeast trades (which actually vary between northeast and east) dominate, and canoes which were caught on Truk can return home to Puluwat with a good wind behind them. Gradually the winds grow in strength, with an occasional letup near the end of December, until the steady, discouraging blow of the drab winter months sets in and everyone stays home to await liberation by the gentler weather of spring.

The intention to make a long trip such as one to Truk or Satawal usually develops over a period of several weeks or more. This is not always true, however. If, for example, a canoe is long overdue, worried relatives on Puluwat may decide overnight to set off looking for them and leave within a few hours. Stops are then made at all the islands, however distant, which the missing craft had planned to visit, plus any others along the way, to learn whether the canoe was sighted and when. For most trips, however, the idea of making a journey is mulled over for some time and alternative possibilities are weighed. If the journey is to the west, to Satawal and perhaps beyond, who is to go determines which islands are to be visited, that is, who has relatives on the various islands. This is especially true if women or older children are to be taken along for visits. If the trip is to Truk the emphasis is likely to be more on trading than on visiting, requiring the weaving of pandanus sleeping mats and the twisting of coir (coconut-husk fiber) rope and twine for trading. In contrast, however, trips to the closer islands are almost never anticipated far in advance. They are usually directed toward some immediate purpose and are undertaken as the need arises.

The initiative in the actual planning of a trip resides with the navigator who will be in charge. Although all large sailing canoes are jointly owned, most navigators have a position of sufficient seniority to control the utilization of a sailing canoe and can leave on a trip whenever they see fit. Each large sailing canoe is actually owned by a group of less than a dozen men, most of whom are related in one way or another to each other, although this relationship is as likely to be by marriage or through their fathers as through the traditional female line. It is usual for most, but not necessarily all, of this same group of canoe owners to be members of the canoe house in which the boat is kept. Canoes are built, wear out, and are replaced. Each has its own set of owners, although some of these may also have interests in other canoes. Canoe houses in contrast go on forever. There are nineteen in all, fifteen of which currently house seaworthy sailing canoes. Each stands on its own plot of ground and even if one has to be rebuilt it remains the same house. Its membership, again not confined to matrilineal relatives, changes as men die or move away and new ones join. Thus, the two groups, canoe owners and canoe-house members, overlap but are not identical. Membership in a canoe house does not automatically grant a share of ownership in the sailing canoes housed there. Correspondingly, men from other canoe houses may have acquired a share of ownership in one or another of the canoes in this one even though they do not belong to it.

Within both of these groups of men seniority is recognized. In most cases there is enough overlap in membership that the head of the canoe house and the head owner of a given sailing canoe are the same man, although in five of the fifteen houses with canoes in them simple seniority has elevated to the relatively passive role of head of a canoe house a man who is too old or not sufficiently competent to manage a sailing canoe. Not surprisingly, looking only at the heads of the canoe-owning groups, we find they are almost all navigators, some senior and highly qualified and some less so, but all of sufficient competence to take their canoes out to sea on their own. Add to this the fact that most of them also head up the canoe house where their canoe is kept and it becomes clear why the majority of senior navigators—the ones most likely to be in command on long trips—can decide virtually on their own without consulting the other owners when and where their canoes will travel.

The actual decision on when to leave, whether or not the trip has been under consideration for some time, is usually reached only two or three days, never more than a week, in advance. If the question is pressed, one is told this short lead time is necessary in order to be able to forecast favorable weather during the first leg of the trip. However, the weather forecasting system operates essentially as an almanac dependent upon the rising and setting of stars and the phases of the moon. The Puluwatans know quite enough about these matters to be able to forecast the positions of the heavenly bodies weeks ahead. Insofar as weather is involved in the final decision whether to leave on the appointed day, it is determined by the look of sky and sea at the time.

After observing the development of a number of voyages, some planned on less than twenty-four hours' notice, and talking in more general terms with a number of navigators about the planning of trips, it became evident that there is a simpler explanation for the short time between decision and departure. The reason is just that there is nothing in the immediate preparation for a journey, either of the canoe or its crew, which requires much time. With respect to those left behind no effort or planning is required to assure that life will go on and the necessary tasks will be completed while the travelers are away from home. As in most seafaring cultures, on Puluwat there are a variety of people—kinsmen or other members of the canoe house, for example—whose unquestioned obligation it is to step in and help as required. Occasionally when a great many canoes are away there is a shortage of men and those who remain have to pick a lot of breadfruit and spend much time fishing, but the worst that results is inconvenience. If there is a more pressing concern such as a sick relative or the need to cut copra in time for an imminent visit of the trading ship a man has only to decline to join in that voyage. Otherwise he can gather up the personal items he needs to take along in a matter of minutes, and his share of the food for the trip can be prepared in a few hours.

Preparation for the voyage, once it has been decided upon, begins with rounding up a crew. Four to six men comprise a full complement. Most of them are likely to be members of the navigator-captain's canoe house or co-owners of the boat or both. There is a core group of men who seem to travel regularly

Tawaru on the lee platform "cabin," during a 1947 trip to Truk

on each canoe. However, there is nothing rigid about this. The canoes are sufficiently alike that no technical problems arise from riding on an unfamiliar craft and there are no special loyalties associated with individual canoes. The word soon gets around that so-and-so is making a trip to Truk or Ulul or Satawal. Anyone who is waiting for a chance to go there can be fairly sure of finding a place on the canoe just by asking. The navigator presumably intends to round out his crew with some of his younger relatives whose services he can virtually command, so he easily makes a place for the petitioner by dropping one of these. He must also if possible include in his crew at least one other man with navigational skills in case he is himself incapacitated.

If women or children are coming along it is necessary to install a small domed cover of plaited pandanus leaves over the lee platform. This little cabin is usually carried also on any long voyage since under these circumstances there will probably be a good number of trade goods, gifts, and personal effects which should be kept dry, and the shelter is welcome too for sleeping if the weather turns wet and cold. Women and children require more, however, than food and shelter. There must also be a man in the crew who is at all times responsible for each passenger. For women this is almost invariably their husbands. Particularly in the old days when women, because they were female, posed a supernatural threat to the rest of the voyagers, it was essential that someone be available to assist them with utmost discretion in any of the bodily needs which emphasized their femaleness. One could scarcely ask anyone but a husband time after time to scoop up seawater for a bath so that as the woman poured the water over herself the sound of it striking the sea below would mask the noise of her urination. Even today, although the threat is gone, embarassment is still very possible when one or two women live with a group of men for several days on a very small boat. In these circumstances the only really appropriate intermediary is a woman's husband.

Children require even more attention. Boys and girls are likely to be taken on their first canoe trip to another island when they are only five, or sometimes even four years old, despite the objections of their worried mothers, so that they will early in their lives get to know and to enjoy life at sea. To this end they are allowed the run of the boat, not cooped up in the little cabin except in bad weather. Thus, in addition to seeing that they are fed and their other physical needs cared for, someone must watch little children all the time. They can swim— Puluwat children swim almost as soon as they can toddle to the water—but falling overboard can still be very dangerous, especially at night. Therefore, for any child aboard there must also be two men, both relatives of the child and responsible for him. If there were only one he would spend all his time watching his charge and fail to do his share of the work with the rigging, bailing, fishing, and other seagoing chores. Nor would he be able to take a nap, even when the child slept, lest the latter wake up and fall overboard. These and other considerations frequently require a little juggling of the roster before the list of crew and passengers is firmly established, but it is usually possible to please everyone—and those who might be unhappy because they have been unceremoniously pushed aside are likely to be related as juniors to the navigator who made the decision, with the result that they may not appropriately voice any public complaint.

After the crew is selected the remainder of the preparations go forward almost automatically since everyone knows what is required to equip the canoe, provision the voyage, and meet the personal needs of each person aboard. This does not mean that the preparations are simple, especially the equipment which must be stowed aboard for an ocean trip. Its complexity can perhaps best be conveyed by running through the list of essential items which must be carried.They include:

a number of paddles, enough for all crew members

two bailers, one for each end of the canoe

spare ropes of various sizes for mooring, repairs, and so on

eight to ten pieces of hardwood a couple of inches in diameter and about 3 feet long used for splicing broken spars, for driving into the sand to moor the canoe, and in an emergency for firewood, lashed to the outer end of the outrigger platform

two longer straight poles about the same diameter as the above but 14 feet long used to replace lost spars and to pole the canoe through shallows

a heavier timber of the same length but 6 to 8 inches in diameter used as a lever to right a capsized canoe or to fashion a spare mast, lashed with the two slender poles to the inboard end of the outrigger platform

a number of mats roughly plaited from coconut fronds used to keep food and other goods dry and to shield the canoe from the sun and drying winds when it is moored or ashore

a box containing an adze, chisel, brace and bits, and a plane for repairs

an open iron box (usually from wrecked Japanese equipment from World War II) for cooking fish caught at sea, with sand in it if the trip is to be short and extra weight does not matter, otherwise empty

dried coconut husks to use for fuel for cooking

cleaned, combed coconut fibers to twist into rope splices

strips of coconut midrib from which to make fishhook lures, formerly used also for divination by knots

a conch shell with a hole in its side to be blown as a horn to announce arrival, to keep track of other boats in convoy at night if there is no flashlight, and in the past to scare away storms and rain squalls

one or two flashlights and batteries if available, used es-

pecially to check the compass at night and to shine on the
  sail when in convoy so that each canoe can locate the others
a large compass, preferably protected in a box, belonging to
  the navigator
needle and thread for sail repairs
sticky breadfruit sap to patch leaks
black paint to cover abrasions and keep the hull from water-
  logging
fishlines and fishhooks for both trolling and handlines
a large bottle or glass float-ball filled with emergency drinking water
if available, traditional conical hats for sun and rain made
  from pandanus and tied under the chin, better than any
  imported hats

These things are brought aboard and stowed away, along
with food, trade goods, gifts, and personal effects, and all are
checked by the navigator before he pronounces the canoe ready
to leave. Assembling the items is not, however, as difficult as
the length of the list might suggest. Most of them are conveniently stowed between voyages in the eaves of the canoe house
and need only be lifted down and carried to the canoe. Only
after everything else is aboard and checked is the sail brought
out. The sail comes last because until it is raised it forms a
bulky barrier impeding movement of men on the readying
canoe.

Meanwhile food for the voyage is prepared and assembled.
There is a special word in Puluwat for the food which provisions a canoe going to a far island, but the food itself is no different from that eaten ashore. If the departure is hasty food may
even be collected from that already on hand in the various
households. It is better, however, if the journey is to be long to
cook freshly picked breadfruit or fresh taro and pound it and
package it in big breadfruit leaves the morning the voyage begins. In this way it will be fresh and last as long as possible under the hot sun. For a long trip there should in addition be
some preserved breadfruit. It is not as good to eat, but lasts
much better even after it is taken from the cool ground. If people
become hungry after several days at sea it is usually not because
too little food was put aboard but because the food became

People waiting in the canoe house to say goodbye

sour. Some ripe coconuts are carried as extra rations. Until the inside shell is cracked the rich, oily meat of a ripe coconut will last almost indefinitely. It is also good to eat along with starchy breadfruit or taro if no fish have been caught. Finally there are several bunches of younger green coconuts, drinking nuts to quench the thirst and provide the extra pleasure afterward of scraping out the soft white meat of the young nut.

Canoes may leave at any time of the day, or even at night, but most depart during the morning or at midday. This is especially true of those leaving on long voyages. The morning is not only available for the preparation of fresh food, but everyone has ample opportunity to learn of the departure and join in the farewells. As one after another of the preparations is completed, people begin to assemble at the front of the canoe house and under the nearby coconut trees on the beach. Talking, joking, gossiping, they express their farewells by their presence rather than in words. Several women of one household may finish a batch of food and pile the packages in the shade of the canoe house, then drop down themselves to sit on the coconut fronds which cover the sandy foreshore. Older boys arrive lugging heavy bunches of coconuts, often two of them with the load on a pole between their shoulders. They stay, moving around restlessly or leaning against the sloping trunks of coconut trees. The older men who belong to the canoe house were already there, or perhaps they went off to help with the food and now return. Others who have no particular job to do that day drift up and join the little knots of people. They talk and watch the men who will soon be leaving climbing over the canoe as it rests in shallow water, each busy loading or stowing or checking some item of gear. No one mentions the imminent trip, however; it is bad luck to talk about the unknowable, whether on land or at sea. Also, silence avoids the risk of betraying an anxiety many feel but must not express. The dangers of voyaging are real even though actual loss of canoes at sea is rare. Everywhere, on the beach, in the canoe house, playing in the water, or climbing all over the canoe there are little children, sharing in the undercurrent of excitement which infects everyone.

As the morning wears on the boat is gradually loaded with equipment and supplies. With everything carefully stowed the outline of the canoe does not change markedly, but it settles in the shallow water and is moved out a little way. Finally, all is ready and the sail, wrapped in loose folds over its spars, is carried out. When folded together, the boom and yard to which the sail is secured do not match in their respective curves, giving a clumsy appearance to the long bundle of wood and cloth. This clumsiness will vanish once the sail is raised. Then these same curves create the graceful, piquant sail profile which is the hallmark of canoes in the Central Carolines.

With the sail aboard there is a pause. The crew comes ashore and may share a cigarette or two, passed from hand to hand among themselves and the well-wishers who will remain behind. Often before a longer trip everyone goes to church for a prayer and a blessing. In a touching gesture the navigator, if his old navigation instructor is still alive, may go to ask his mentor's last-minute advice if he cannot physically lend his presence to the departure. Then without any formal farewells the men wade out through the shallow water to the canoe. If women are going along they board first, settling themselves as best they can in the cramped space under the cover of the lee platform. The line or two which hold the boat are untied and someone shoves it away from shore. As one or two men start paddling the others get ready to hoist the sail. Those on shore watch as the canoe moves away and then drift off in twos and threes about their various affairs. By the time it is out of sight no one is left in front of the canoe house to watch except perhaps some old people who have neither an excuse nor the energy to move elsewhere for a while.

Working through the lagoon to the open sea may take some time, though the distance is not great. Often it is necessary to paddle most of the way across the inner lagoon to the sandspit which divides it from the larger outer lagoon area. Even if there is an offshore breeze at the beach and the sail fills at once, under these conditions it is usually necessary to tack back and forth as the canoe moves on an opposite heading through the outer lagoon toward the pass. In addition there are delays as the rigging is checked and tightened and the navigator has the angle of the mast adjusted by his crew to suit the strength of the wind he senses once he has moved away from the lee of the land.

Coming up to the wide pass, bounded on one side by the southern tip of Puluwat and on the other by a tiny islet which is the roosting place of at least a thousand seabirds, the canoe quickens to the motion of the sea. Inside the lagoon it has been gliding along unperturbed by the rippling water. Now after scarcely a moment of transition it is plunging and rearing through waves flung high as they breast a current which most of the time swirls powerfully outward over the reef. Outside the canoe settles down a little, but a narrow 26-foot hull, even though balanced by an outrigger, has no chance to stay still while moving through the labyrinth of massive waves which march and countermarch across the western Pacific.

Once in the open the navigator establishes his strategy for the first leg of his trip. He sets his course, tests the wind, and often calls for further adjustments of mast or sail. Perhaps he tells someone to move aft so his weight will sink that end of the canoe deeper in the water and thus improve its trim when the wind is on the beam. These are technical matters to which we shall return in the next chapter. What is important here is that only after he is at sea does the navigator determine his sailing plan and make his final adjustments. Before they left he doubtless noted the general weather and wind so that he had some idea how rough it would be and whether they would tack or

Preparing the canoe

The cabin being installed, protective mats and the mast carried out

Raising the mast

Always there are children

Carrying out the sail

Raising the sail

Checking the sail

run before the wind, but if the weather were not such as to create undue risks he paid it little further heed. The sailing directions learned during the years of his apprenticeship are sufficiently complete to guide him in executing the voyage under almost all possible conditions. Beyond these general directions individual judgments must be attuned to the conditions actually observed at sea—seen with the eye, felt with the motion of the boat, and heard in the sound of the wind—conditions which cannot be inferred while standing on unyielding land with the wind blowing at full force only in the treetops.

Putting this together with the succession of earlier phases of preparation we see that at no time is an over-all plan developed for a voyage. It evolves in a series of steps, each decision being made as the need for it becomes imminent. The movement from one step to the next is of course taken only when conditions are appropriate. No one would think of making a distant voyage, for example, during the winter months of high winds. Or if a trading trip to Truk is contemplated no thought is given to setting a date before a supply of trade goods has been collected. Once these preconditions are met, however, each successive decision can be reached entirely on its own merits. There is no need in making one decision to conjure up possible contingencies which might qualify subsequent choices farther along in the sequence of events. The entire culture of Puluwat is organized to assure a favorable outcome. The navigator can be confident that when the time comes there will be no difficulties for which there is not a ready solution. He even sets the actual day of departure before settling on his crew, so sure is he that they will be available. Similarly he need not worry about the readiness of the canoe. Canoes are always ready. As the trip develops, each successive commitment is made without concern for the conditions which must be met if it is to be fulfilled. It is thus not surprising to find the canoe and navigator actually launched upon a voyage for which there is as yet no specially devised plan. The navigator has in his memorized sailing directions a whole portfolio of instant plans. The resources needed to complete the trip are all at hand: the knowledge acquired by the navigator in his training and enriched by his experienced judgment, the capability of the canoe and its crew, the known range of conditions which can obtain in familiar seas, and all the helping signs of reefs, birds, stars, and waves which will guide them on their way. So the navigator senses the wind and sea, sets his course, trims his sail, and, lo, the plan is complete. They are on their way.

Soon the canoe is well out at sea, settled on its initial course. The crew can relax. A line or two may be rigged for trolling, but only if there are reefs below teeming with fish or the trip is short. A trolling line creates drag which on a longer trip can slow a canoe enough that it may not make its landing at a distant island before dark. Like all good sailors, Puluwatans have a constant concern with getting the last ounce of performance from any boat they are on. The rigging and trim are continually readjusted, and even the sand is omitted from the iron cooking box to save weight on a long voyage. Every extra pound makes the canoe ride lower and thus slower in the water.

As the journey goes forward anyone is free to make a suggestion about the course the canoe is on, the set of the mast, the look of the weather, or perhaps a detour over a reef to catch some fish. The navigator is in command, with all the authority and responsibility we are accustomed to associate with the role, but this does not set him apart, aloof from the rest of the crew. He joins in the jokes and gossip and talks about his navigation quite freely, especially if he has a son or other student naviga tor aboard who can learn from his example. If there is some cause for anxiety or question, the responsible navigator feels obligated to pay particular attention to the suggestions or doubts of his crew members. They in turn will not speak up unless they have some seniority and competence to back their views. Examples of these interchanges appear frequently in accounts of voyages told by navigators; it appears they are proud of their willingness to attend to these queries rather than resenting those who question their judgment.

An episode of this sort took place on the return leg of a trip to Pulusuk I made with Hipour. It was a moonless night, but the occasional clouds did not seriously obscure the stars. It was therefore easy to determine our course, slightly west of north, and in any event the whole journey is only forty miles, making it unlikely that we could stray far. There are also reefs which further fix one's position during the early part of the trip, so the length of run in really open ocean without any seamarks at all is shorter still. Yet in time the crew began to become anxious. It was nearing midnight, and the wind, which had freshened somewhat, had veered away from northeast a little toward the north, making it more difficult to hold the course with the canoe hard into the wind. The clouds grew larger and increased in number so that more of the sky was obscured; occasional rain-squalls could be made out in the distance. None of these potentially threatening developments were of a magnitude to offer realistic cause for even the slightest alarm; nevertheless, tension rose. Idle conversation slacked and ceased. Some felt we should already have sighted Puluwat some time before. Making a landfall on a dark night is always tense. Everyone was alert, peering ahead into the darkness. The few words which were spoken were subdued and dealt mostly with the wind, the weather, or our course. Suddenly Hipour turned the canoe into the wind and we stopped, sail slatting in the wind. A weighted fishline was put over the side into the black water to take a sounding. It seems that Kurua (Koo-roo-ah), the senior man of Hipour's regular crew and his companion on many voyages, thought the waves had become unduly choppy and believed we might be over Uranie Bank, considerably to the east of our proper course. We could be passing out of sight of Puluwat in the dark. Hence the sounding. No bottom was found, which meant we were not over a reef, and we sailed on. However, the tense quiet continued. Finally someone peering through the gloom said he thought he could make out Puluwat, a dark smudge at the horizon below the gathering clouds. My unpracticed eye could see nothing, but soon another and another man confirmed the sighting. Conversation picked up, there were some jokes, and finally even I could make out Puluwat, a blackness dead ahead right where Hipour had laid his course. (It might be added that just about that time a rainsquall hit, the wind shifted, and we spent the next two hours tantalizingly in sight of Puluwat, chilled to the marrow, trying to claw our way into the pass against the wind and the rush of an outgoing current.)

Usually canoes travel alone. Sometimes they sail in convoys of two or three, but hardly ever more than four. In addition to companionship the other canoes add an element of safety. Mishaps are by no means unknown. Almost everyone sometime in his life is on a canoe which capsizes, especially at night from an unseen and unsuspected squall. With proper team-work, using as levers the timber carried for this purpose along with the mast, it is possible for the crew alone to right the canoe. Even more complex salvage is possible at sea when directed by a man trained in these special arts, but anything of this sort is safer and easier if another canoe is standing by to help.

Traveling in convoy has other advantages. Among the men on the various canoes the most senior navigator is in charge. In this way men of less experience and ability can make trips they might otherwise never undertake alone, gaining in experience and confidence without undue risk. It also means there is plenty of manpower available on arrival to handle the canoes. This is especially important at Pikelot where there is no one on shore to welcome arriving boats, the beach is steep, and the surf surges dangerously right over the reef. Extra hands can also be important on other islands if canoes arrive unexpectedly and the local men are all out fishing or perhaps cutting copra inland.

A convoy can be a nuisance, however. The canoes must keep in sight of one another because once separated they can seldom find each other again. Thus, the first canoe to get everything aboard and depart cannot travel far before stopping to wait for the others to catch up. Thereafter the faster canoes or those which can beat upwind better must wait for the slower. There is often an appreciable difference in performance between the different craft. Further delays result from even a light rain. Any canoe lowers its sail in a heavy rainstorm, lest it be capsized by a squall approaching unseen in the murk, but in convoy the sails must be lowered as soon as there is any possibility of losing sight of one another.

At night if there are flashlights the lead canoe in a convoy shines a light on its sail occasionally, and at once the others acknowledge the signal in the same way. In the past, and to the present if the visibility is poor or there is a shortage of flash-lights or batteries, someone on the lead canoe blew on the conch shell and the others replied to show where they were. This is done also if canoes momentarily move out of sight of one another in rain or mist. If a canoe capsizes or is otherwise in distress at night a little water dipped into the conch creates a burbling sound when it is blown, an SOS for all who hear it.

Whether alone or in convoy the routine at sea, aside from storms, is relatively undemanding. At times everyone is talking, and at others most are asleep, stretched out, curled up, or propped against almost anything which offers support. No matter how crowded the canoe, people seem to find places to sleep without falling overboard. Occasionally, more often if the weather is rough, the canoe needs bailing. Someone sits on the little bench or thwart installed for this purpose down in the hull and throws the water over the lee side with a bailer, a scoop carved—like everything else—from breadfruit wood. All except the navigator take turns at this wearisome task without prodding or complaint. The crew members similarly relieve each other steering with the big steering paddle astern when this is made necessary by a following wind. Everyone is assumed to have the skill necessary to be a steersman, although it is soon obvious that some can hold a course better than others. Manning the sheet which trims the sail, and thereby trims the canoe, is more exacting. Sloppy work on the sheet can affect all aspects of the canoe's performance, as well as its safety. Most of the time the navigator tends it himself. When he wants relief he designates who shall take over. For a young man this can be an exciting responsibility, a rewarding gesture of confidence by the older navigator.

As with sleeping, so with eating. People eat when they feel like it. Usually one man gets out some food and the others join in. If fish have been caught, either they are eaten raw (especially tuna and bonito) or someone kindles a fire in the iron cooking box. It is set well aft on the outrigger platform so that sparks flying from the little glowing heap of coconut husks will stream over the side. The fish are roasted whole on top of the fire and when they are done the fire is doused so that the husks can be used again and also so no more sparks will blow about.

Nowadays it is unusual for a canoe, if it does not run into some sort of trouble, to be at sea for more than four or five days, or a week at most, at one stretch. In the past it was often longer. Primarily this was because the canoes were slower and it took longer to get from one island to another. More distant journeys than are now customary were also made, but most of these were accomplished as they still are in stages, stopping at one island after another. A few, really long, unbroken voyages were made to islands more distant, islands large enough to minimize by their size navigation problems in reaching them. They could be sighted over long distances and made large targets. These were islands such as Guam, Saipan, and Ponape. The men who made these heroic voyages were probably no better navigators than their modern counterparts, possibly even a little less accurate, but they were rugged and determined.* They arrived at their destination half starved, dehydrated, and so burned by the sun they were black and almost poisoned by its effects. The return would not be made for months, and such trips were at most undertaken only rarely. Those which are recent enough to be remembered at least at second hand were made primarily to Saipan to trade with the Spaniards there for iron tools and knives which could not be obtained in any other way.

Once the canoe has arrived, especially at an island where the crew have many friends and relatives, the welcome is warm and life is easy. No one need work. Their hosts feed them and entertain them with drink, good talk, and often at night a companion for their bed. If a man has not brought his wife along he can expect someone on the island who is his "brother," a relationship no less binding if it is artificial, to offer his own wife for the visitor's pleasure. Apparently not only do the visiting men appreciate this custom, but also the women. The wife who is offered in hospitality appreciates the novelty of a new sexual partner, and even the traveler's wife left at home understands and expects this sort of thing—as long as he does not try it once he is back on Puluwat! When such a warm welcome ashore is added to good fellowship and pride in their skill at sea it is small wonder that men in return take lightly the risks and hardships of their long travels.

This hospitality is found on all the islands around Puluwat which share at least in part in their common seafaring tradition. When a canoe goes to Truk, however, the goal is principally to

* In 1969 Dr. David Lewis visited Puluwat in his 39-foot ketch. With all charts, modern navigation equipment, and even wristwatches stowed below, Hipour navigated the ketch to Saipan and back entirely on the basis of traditional knowledge. Dr. Lewis will soon publish an account of this exercise.

trade. As in the past, the Puluwatans still seek the tobacco which grows much better on the volcanic soils of Truk. Often too they obtain pestles chipped out of solid hunks of coral, used to pound breadfruit and taro on hardwood slabs. Sometimes they bring back cuttings of new species of banana or breadfruit they find growing on the high islands. In the past there was a brisk trade in the finer quality lavalavas which Puluwat women liked to wear but which were made of the fibers of a banana plant which grows only on Truk. Even more important was turmeric, a reddish root which will not grow on sandy soil. It was ground to a powder, mixed with coconut oil and annointed all over the body. It was thought to bring health, cure illness, and make a person beautiful. Years ago Trukese men grew it for themselves and prepared it in little packages. Two hundred of these, or perhaps only a hundred, plus fifty banana-fiber lavalavas, could be traded for a large sailing canoe built on Puluwat. During the Japanese period between World Wars I and II the Trukese stopped using turmeric, but they continued to plant it for the Puluwatans. Thus, until the early 1950's canoes would still come in from Puluwat for turmeric, but their crews had to settle down to wait for it to ripen. Then they would prepare it and bring it home, all the while living in ritual continence. Finally the Trukese stopped even planting turmeric, and about the same time the Puluwatans, having shed all their magical beliefs, lost interest in it. Thus, trading for native Trukese products has diminished in importance. Instead more time is spent at the various trading companies on Truk, locally owned but dealing principally in imported goods. There everything is bought, after much debate, for money, although sometimes coir rope or pandanus mats are sold to the company instead of being traded to the Trukese, thus in effect extending barter into the commercial realm.

Puluwatans have relatives, usually artificial, on Truk as they do on other islands, and in some cases the ties are close. More often, however, these are relationships only of mutual convenience. The Trukese "host" is more accurately an agent. He arranges to collect on his island bottles full of dried tobacco or whatever else is requested by his Puluwat "relatives," and arranges a rate of exchange for whatever the Puluwatans have brought. This may include, in addition to rope and pandanus mats, wild birds and turtles captured and brought in alive from East Fayu, an uninhabited island north of Truk. The crew members often sleep on their canoes or in a village meeting-house, the closest equivalent on Truk to a canoe house. All in all a trip to Truk is likely to be a fairly businesslike affair; the crew which has close relatives and settles in for an enjoyable long visit is the exception. Sometimes the crew can relate only to the island magistrate. This is especially true on Moen Island, the administrative and commercial center for the district. Under these circumstances it is not surprising that, even though a canoe may stop at several islands in the lagoon, its total time in Truk will amount only to a week or ten days, two weeks at the most.

While the men of Puluwat, and sometimes their women and children, are voyaging to far islands, what of those left behind? Life goes on, work gets done, and publicly there is no sign that the travelers are even missed. Yet privately their women are not only lonely but also genuinely worried. True, the last time any-one from Puluwat actually died at sea was in 1945. In that year a canoe with four men and a girl aboard vanished in a typhoon. Since then from hundreds of voyages travelers have always come home safely. Nevertheless, the risks are genuine. That no one has been lost is a tribute to the knowledge and seamanship of the Puluwat navigators and their crews. There have been losses in more recent years from other islands. There are many harrowing tales even on Puluwat of crises and near disasters, told with a flourish when the canoes return. When a canoe is overdue all these stories come to mind—and without a precise schedule a canoe soon becomes overdue in the mind of a worry-ing wife. Even more is this true if her husband has taken one of their children along. Even though women agree in principle that it is good for children to learn early the ways of the sea, in practice they often object, sometimes strenuously, when their own are being taken away to face the risks of an ocean voyage. Yet their objections seldom prevail and they must wait in rest-less anxiety as mothers as well as wives for their family to be reunited.

To express and therefore perhaps to relieve their worries, wives sometimes sing chants for the welfare of their missing men. They call for good winds, a stout canoe, and a wise navigator; they mention the departed husband and the places he will be traveling; a navigator's wife also includes some of the esoteric words and names only navigators know. Women do not know the meaning of these words but they are taught to include them. In the past these chants were composed for the initiation ceremony of young navigators and taught to their women. In those days they had magical powers. Nowadays all women can sing songs for their absent men, but they do so more from sentiment than from a belief in their effectiveness in warding off danger. Yet who can be sure . . . and it is nice to think with a song about a man who is away at sea.

Finally the canoe comes home. In the past the men of the crew spent the first few days after their return living together without women in their canoe house. This ended with a small feast and ceremony in which they put behind them the world of the sea and formally returned to the island and to their families. Now, however, when the canoe has been unloaded and secured, or perhaps carried up into its place in the canoe house, the men disperse to their own houses to take up once again the lives of husbands and fathers.

Yet before long they will leave again on another trip, and another and another. Puluwat is a good island. It is a good place to be born, to grow strong, and even to die. Yet to discover its essence one cannot look only to the land. The land is only the backdrop and the place of preparation. Without its sailing canoes and seafaring men Puluwat would have no past and no future. So with every voyage, and only through each voyage, its worth is renewed and its destiny fulfilled.

3 Canoes

There are lots of canoes on Puluwat. In fact there are so many that their combined carrying capacity is considerably greater than the total population of the island. There are slightly under four hundred people of all ages on Puluwat. Adding up for all canoes the stated number of adults who can be carried on each, the total comes to four hundred and ninety. Obviously no occasion ever arises for the entire population to be afloat at one time. Instead the excess capacity assures that water transportation is conveniently available for every purpose. Whenever any number of people want to go anywhere they can readily find the proper size of canoe or canoes to take them, whether on a voyage to Satawal or an errand to the other end of the island. This availability is furthermore real, not nominal, because flexible customs govern borrowing (and from relatives even permanently appropriating) canoes of all types. In order to use a canoe it is at most necessary only to ask the owner or owners and permission will be granted. With fairly close relatives even this is not required.

Replacing the lashings of a paddling canoe

A paddling canoe waiting on the shore

The largest number of canoes are small, uncomplicated, single outrigger craft used to paddle back and forth across the lagoon on an endless variety of missions. At the time of our study 55 such paddling canoes were in service, plus 6 more under construction. They are simple in design. The hull is hollowed out of a single breadfruit log. The outrigger float is of solid wood and is secured on short struts to the ends of two slightly curved booms. Add to this the ornamental end-pieces of the hull, which rise to a V (said to represent the tail of a frigate bird) and two little thwarts or seats at either end and the canoe is complete. A simple conventional design in black paint decorates the outside of the hull, although this is often dim with wear. The hull of a paddling canoe bears an obvious relation in form to the larger sailing canoe, but is usually somewhat wider and more rounded below. As a result these little canoes can carry a surprisingly heavy load without swamping. Although they vary in size from one almost 24 feet long capable of carrying twelve people to a number of one-man canoes of only 9 or 10 feet, they average about 14 feet in length and at this size can carry four people when fully loaded—which they seldom are. All are individually owned, although they are usually kept in or near a canoe house and are considered to be available at will to all its members.

Some paddling canoes are rigged with a sail. They are slightly larger, on the average two or three feet longer, than those without sails. Their rig is similar in its essentials to those of full-sized sailing canoes, to be described later, but their hulls have the simplicity of a paddling canoe. At the base of the outrigger booms there is a board carrying a socket for the mast, the booms are usually somewhat longer, and in a few cases a rudimentary lee platform has been constructed primarily as a place to stow things away from the wet inside of the hull. Otherwise, they are basically paddling canoes and are frequently used with paddles alone, the sail left stored in the eaves of the canoe house. When the sail is rigged it is often in order to go a little way outside the lagoon, or perhaps only to the end of the lagoon, to fish. Some of the larger of these canoes, however, go outside to troll on the big reefs; these are the ones which cause worry to the crews of the big sailing canoes when the weather turns bad.

There are relatively few combined paddling-sailing canoes on Puluwat now. At the time of this study the count stood at 11, with 3 under construction. However, a separate count of all the canoes built during their lifetimes by the living master canoebuilders on the island showed a substantially larger proportion of little canoes with sails. Although the figures obviously cannot be directly compared, these men, eighteen in number, accounted for the building of 52 simple paddling canoes, and 35 more with sails. Put in a different way, only 1 out of 6 paddling canoes now on Puluwat carries a sail, whereas the master builders have rigged with sails 2 out of every 5 such canoes they have built.

At first glance this difference suggests a marked shift in recent years in the ratio between paddling canoes with and without sails. There may have been some fluctuation of this sort, but this is probably not the principal explanation for the discrepancy. A more likely explanation is that on Puluwat there are two other sources of canoes other than the master canoe-builders, and both favor simpler canoes. One is fairly obvious: the building of canoes by people less skilled, men who are capable only of laying out and carving a simple paddling canoe hull. It was not possible to conduct a complete count of all the canoes built by all the men on the island, but the inventory of existing canoes showed that a number of them had been built wholly or in part by less experienced men. It is also probable—and in the case of a couple of old men quite certain—that they did not remember and therefore did not record some of the paddling canoes they built in their younger years. This could affect paddling canoes of both kinds, but it is likely that the less pretentious the canoe the more probably it would be forgotten. Among other things it often happens that the apprentice canoe-builder is given his first practice in carving the all-important lower contours of the hull on a sailing-paddling canoe, easier and less risky than doing the job on a full-sized sailing canoe. Although this sophisticated work is not really needed on a little canoe, it is a training exercise which assures that the builder will probably remember this particular sailing-paddling canoe all his life even if he forgets a few other plain paddling canoes.

A more surprising source of paddling canoes is importation from other islands, especially neighboring Pulusuk. Whereas Puluwat is famous for its sophisticated sailing canoes and has exported them to islands near and far, it actually imports an appreciable number of the simpler paddling canoes, and exports relatively few. It is not clear whether there is some sort of ultimate balance in the exchange of goods and services between islands, but viewing canoes alone there is a definite imbalance, especially with respect to Pulusuk. In our count, of the 66 paddling canoes of all types in use on Puluwat, 11 came from Pulusuk. Furthermore, very few of these were paid for in any way. Instead they were given in response to a need more or less explicitly stated by a Puluwat relative of a Pulusuk man, often not even a real relative but only an artificial "brother." The other principal source of imported paddling canoes is the neighboring atoll of Pulap, including Tamatam; they have contributed 2 each to the present Puluwat flotilla of paddling canoes. However, over the years Pulap and Tamatam, unlike Pulusuk, have acquired a number of sailing canoes from Puluwat, often on the basis of kinship rather than remuneration, so the balance there is more equal.

Having recorded these few notes on paddling canoes we can turn to the quintessence of Puluwat marine architecture: the interisland sailing canoe. Here we will be considering almost exclusively the 15 large canoes whose style of voyaging was outlined in the preceding chapter. In addition there are in use on Puluwat 4 smaller sailing canoes. These are used primarily for fishing on local reefs, but they can occasionally take up to four or five people to one of the nearby islands and back if the weather is fair. Although these smaller canoes are important in the over-all seafaring economy of Puluwat, in design and handling they differ in no significant way from their larger counterparts. They are easier to build, can be constructed from the trunks of less massive trees, and are completed in less time. To build and sail them, however, calls for the same practiced skill as do the interisland canoes.

All 19 of these canoes were built on Puluwat.* Their builders are a select group. As befits practitioners of a continuing craft they range in age from quite old men to others perhaps in their late thirties, the latter beginners in the art. In all there are only thirteen living men who have completed one or more interisland canoes. Another five have built the smaller type of sailing canoe but no large one, bringing the total to eighteen—out of eighty-one men on Puluwat thirty-five or older. Most of the older canoe-builders are also navigators, but not all. Although it cannot be documented, the impression is clear that those few who build sailing canoes but are not qualified as navigators (including one of the most skilled and productive builders on the island) are lower in prestige than master navigators of comparable age.

A number of the present-day master canoe-builders learned their skills through apprenticeship to their fathers. Others were taught by older men who were usually related to them in

* Two more, one large and one small, both built on Pulusuk, are in Puluwat boat houses. However, both have been taken out of service because of age and poor performance. One of these is waiting to be taken to another island and sold.

one way or another. There were a couple of especially able men who each taught several of the present builders. It is thus obvious that there is considerable flexibility in establishing an apprenticeship. A young man who wishes to learn asks one of the active canoe-builders for instruction. If the latter is willing and the pupil apt they work together until the young man is ready to start building canoes on his own. This may take several years. Often the apprenticeship begins with the younger man watching the older at work, asking questions, helping at first only with routine chores and then gradually with tasks which require increasing degrees of skill.

However informal in its inception, the relation between student and teacher becomes formalized when the apprentice undertakes the supervised construction of his first canoe with a hull contoured for sailing. This may not actually be a full-fledged sailing canoe. The rigging and other secondary structures of the canoe are seen as relatively standardized and in any event capable of adjustment or modification after the canoe is in use. The performance of the canoe is instead felt to reflect principally the skill with which the builder fashions the contours of the lower part of the hull, especially near its ends. Thus, if a man has adequate skill with the adze and other tools of the canoe-builder it can be taken for granted that he will do the upper hull and the rest of the canoe sufficiently well. It is his capability in carving the lower hull to its finished lines which must be nurtured and then tested. If there is pressure of time, lack of a tree large enough for a big canoe, or possibly some doubt as to the ability of the apprentice to complete the task, he may be asked just to build a small paddling canoe to prove himself. This canoe, however, must have the finished lines and smoothly faired contours of a sailing canoe if its builder is to be judged qualified. If his work is approved he becomes his own master and may then build larger craft without further instruction or supervision.

Until beliefs in magic and the supernatural disappeared from Puluwat a few years ago apprenticeships were more formal and restricted, and also more taxing. Not only had the student to learn the theory and practical skills of canoe-building, but he also had to learn many magical rituals and spells and in addition observe taboos against sexual activity and the eating of

Moving with a good breeze

certain foods. There is no evidence that these constraints reduced the number of master builders in earlier generations, but the secrecy with which canoes were built and instruction offered did sharply curtail the spread of knowledge of canoe construction within the larger population of nonbuilders. Thus only in recent years have there been available numbers of men with some facility in using tools and knowledge of what is required to build a canoe, yet without the ability or perhaps determination to learn thoroughly the onerous task of building a large sailing canoe. They are often invaluable helpers to the present-day master canoe-builder and can make his task both less tedious and more thorough than before. All the members of a canoe house may join in to help complete a boat which is being built for them. This is a major gain.

The canoe which they build is remarkably well suited to its

A sailing canoe, showing the outrigger (left) and lee platform (right) on opposite sides

tasks. These are several, fishing and interisland travel being most important, and the conditions under which they are fulfilled highly various, yet the canoe meets them all. Described only in words, with all its platforms and appurtenances, the sailing canoe presents a clumsy and homely picture. Yet as the accompanying photographs attest it has a quality of handsomeness, even of grace; James Hornell (1936) in his classic publication on the canoes of Oceania referred to the canoe of the Caroline Islands as a "flying proa," a name with a magical sound true to its spirit. Because both the canoes and their construction have been described extensively elsewhere (Krämer, 1937; Burrows and Spiro, 1957; Alkire, 1965, 1970) only enough description will be presented here to supplement the photographs in making clear their general configuration.

The hull profile, a sharp V, broader at the bottom. Note the special contours of the bottom, and asymmetry of the end of the hull as shown by strips of masking tape applied on transverse plane for photograph.

The tapered hull, lee platform on left, outrigger platform on right

The sailing canoe has four principal components: the hull, the outrigger, the lee platform, and the rigging and sail. The hull is narrow and deep, in cross-section a sharp V slightly flattened to a broader V at the bottom. Viewed from above it tapers smoothly toward either end, although at its very end it is somewhat blunt. The hull is symmetrical from end to end, but some canoes are slightly curved sideways, curving if at all away from the outrigger. The side of the hull is also higher on the outrigger side, conforming to the upward slope of the heavy outrigger booms at this point. The length of the hull, measured from the base of the V-shaped ornament at each end, averages 26 feet on the 15 sailing canoes now in use on Puluwat. (At the waterline, normally loaded, they run about 2½ feet less.) There is furthermore relatively little variation in length among them. One is 24 feet, one 30, and one 29; the remainder fall between 25 and 27 feet in length. (The smaller sailing canoes built principally for fishing average about 5 feet less, with similarly minor variation.) There is proportionately somewhat greater variability in maximum width, which averages a little over three feet (37½ inches) to the outside of the hull at its top, about 33 inches at the waterline. There is also considerable variation in the relation between width and length. In other words, there are broader canoes and narrower ones. Their breadth depends both on the judgment of the builder and on the size of the breadfruit tree out of which the keel piece of the canoe is hewn. Not surprisingly, the breadth of the hull has its effects on performance, a broader canoe being slower but able to carry a heavier load—although actual performance estimates do not bear out this correlation as fully as one might expect.

The building of a sailing canoe begins with the keel piece, the backbone óf the hull. It is a single piece of wood which is shaped and hollowed to form the lower half of the hull in its full length, except for small pieces at either end which resemble the stem in the bow of a Western planked boat. The size and shape of this large keel piece determines the dimensions of the finished hull. As much of the sides of the hull are formed out of the keel piece as the size of the treetrunk from which it is hewn will permit. The rest of the height is then built up of planks, carved from the same tree or another one depending on the wood available, carefully contoured and fitted at the edges to the keel

Hull joint lashings being replaced at overhaul. Pegs are driven into temporary lashings to compress new caulking in joints; the other lashings are countersunk.

piece. Holes are bored every few inches on each side of the joint and the two pieces of wood are lashed together, temporarily at first. When it is time for the final lashings to be installed grooves are cut to countersink the cords into the surface of the hull, the joint is caulked, and then the lashings are applied and puttied in to provide a smooth exterior with a minimum of drag. It is, however, still possible to see where the planks meet; the line of the joint with the smoothed-over lashings crossing it at regular intervals resembles strongly a surgical incision after the sutures have been removed.

The hull contours are laid out, once the keel piece has been roughed out and its overall size determined, by a system of proportional measurements. The basic unit of measurement is the length of the hull taken along the bottom—in other words, the length of the keel. This is then halved (by doubling over a piece of cord used for measurement) to locate the middle of the hull, halved again to provide reference points for the upward curve near the ends of the keel, and halved yet again to furnish still smaller units of measurement. There are similar procedures for obtaining dimensions proportional to the original unit of keel length for almost every feature of the hull. These have been described by a number of observers, most completely by Alkire (1970) for Woleai. The system used on Puluwat differs only in inconsequential details from that on Woleai.

After the hull is completed the remaining components are dimensioned proportionally to its length. Thus the mast and the boom are measured to the full length of the hull, while the yard is as long as the distance from one end of the hull to the first thwart at the other end. Similar procedures define the size of each element of the outrigger and outrigger platform and the lee platform. With knowledge of this detailed but rather simple system, therefore, the canoe-builder is able to lay out a harmoniously proportioned and well tested design for his craft. This system also assures that when all the work is done a person accustomed to working on one canoe can find everything in just about the same place and acting in just about the same familiar way on any other canoe which he boards.

However, on Puluwat as elsewhere in the world, things often turn out not to be as simple as they at first appear. If designing a sailing canoe ended with the basic measurements, anyone handy with an adze could be a master builder. As it is, scarcely one man in five achieves this mastery. There are two prinicipal reasons for this. One is the practiced skill and eye which are required to translate raw measurements into a symmetrical hull, smoothly contoured and neatly fitted together. No jig or other external means of measurement are available. The dimensions must be worked out first on the rough hewn log, adzed away, redrawn, and once again removed by the sharp blade, and so on until the hull has been sculptured to its final form. As each finer shaping is taking place the builder must have constantly in his mind and in his eye the ultimate contour toward which he is working. Just one cut too deep into the wood can destroy the entire undertaking and waste a precious breadfruit tree.

The other skill, even more critical than being able to create a smoothly shaped and balanced form, is the ability to know how the water will flow along the surface of the fast-moving canoe, where it will form waves, where it will meet pressure, and where it will cause pounding. Knowing this, the master builder can shape his timber so that it will create the least resistance. On one side the water should flow smoothly along the hull. On the other the canoe must press and draw the water so the hull will resist the sideways pressure of the wind. The lines of the hull which will meet these demands are far too subtle to be expressed in the doubling and redoubling of a piece of twine, or even in the smaller measurements made by counting hand widths. Similarly, although the measurement system provides a reference point for the beginning of the upward slope of the keel toward the end of the canoe, the actual point where the line of the keel changes is up to the builder. Some have a longer sloped area, some shorter, and some carry a gentle curve the whole length of the keel. How this change in slope is handled is critical in determining how the canoe will steer—it must not be too skittish, nor yet too sluggish—and how fast it will rise to a steep wave, that is, whether it will remain dry or take on water. This is but one aspect of the systematic theory of hull design with which the Puluwatan builder works; others will be reviewed later. The point emphasized here is the subtlety of the contouring of the hull. Every aspect of a canoe's performance is determined in the last anlysis by the contour of the hull. Yet the distinctions are too fine and the various contours too complexly interrelated for them to be taught in any other way than by example, or learned except by skilled observation and experience. Not everyone is equal to this challenge.

With the remaining parts of the canoe, the outrigger, the lee platform, and the rigging, we are dealing with structures whose components are more complex than the hull but whose design is much more clearly determined and standardized. A lot of painstaking work goes into building them, but within limits anyone could do it. Furthermore, if something turns out to be a little wrong, it usually can be adjusted or even replaced without great difficulty, whereas a hull with bad lines condemns the canoe permanently to inferior performance.

These other components share a basically common mode of construction. Each consists of two or three heavy timbers, either local hardwoods or with luck some nicely seasoned driftwood, plus a variety of secondary structures, all lashed together with coir lines. Coir, ranging from fine twine up to heavy rope close to an inch in diameter, is twisted from soaked (retted) and carded coconut husk fibers. Men rarely sit idle in a canoe house. As they pass the time in gossip, instruction, or discussion,

The lee platform (left) and outrigger (right) are basically timbers bound together with coir.

they endlessly lay little bunches of coconut fiber onto the end of some line already finished and roll it between their palm and bare thigh into a hard strand. Like manila line, these strands are in turn twisted together to make larger ropes. It is excellent for both lashing and rigging. It is strong, it is far more resistant to rot than manila, and its surface bristles with stiff little fibers. This last quality makes it a little hard on the hands, but seafaring hands are tough. More important, it makes coir rope adhere to itself. Coir lashings or even simple knots, once drawn up tight, almost never work loose. It is easy to adjust coir rigging because a simple half hitch will hold anything in place, and the navigator can hold the sail in the heaviest wind just by looping the sheet over a timber and pressing the ends of the loop together with his hands. Without this unusual quality of coir rope it is doubtful that Carolinian canoes could be built in the way they are, for they depend for their fastening exclusively upon this highly efficient lashing material. There are no pins

Canoe being moved to the water, showing outrigger assembly

or mortising, and no nails Although hull joints are caulked with coconut fiber and made watertight with a gooey bread-fruit sap "glue" which does harden somewhat, it would never be strong enough alone to hold the joints together if there were no coir lashings.

Incidentally, an innovation being tried at the time of our study consisted in replacing breadfruit glue caulking with a very tough plastic foamed material available in quantity from a new type of fishing float being washed ashore from Japanese boats fishing in adjacent waters. Different ways of using it were being tried on different canoes in their biennial overhaul, and there was as yet no agreement that any one of these would be a lasting improvement on the traditional coconut fiber and "glue." It provided a nice illustration, however, of the constant interest of the Puluwatans in trying new ways and new things, along with an experimental skepticism as to their worth.

The outrigger assembly is built around two heavy timbers or booms which arch up out of the hull and then curve down to

Outrigger float lashings; Tawaru in foreground, Ikefai, another navigator, beyond the float. At the inner end these timbers pass through the top of the hull and are firmly secured to it, forming with the sides of the hull a strong structural "box" in the middle of the canoe. The end of the mast bears down on top of the box and the long timbers of the lee platform are wedged in under a short beam which is lashed to the underside of the outrigger booms (the top of the box) in the middle of the hull. The booms are curved upward to clear the waves which run between the float and the hull; otherwise splashed water would constantly soak the canoe and its crew in rough weather. At the outer end is the float, a bluntly pointed heavy piece of solid breadfruit wood held onto the booms by short forked sticks and a mass of heavy lashings. This is a critical joint because it is almost impossible to repair at sea, especially if the ocean is rough (and when else would it let go?), and the float takes a terrible beating. One likes to think of an outrigger canoe skimming along ideally balanced so that its float is riding evenly just on top of the water. However, a good sailing breeze in the open ocean means a rough sea. In actuality, therefore, the float most of the time is plunging violently. It smashes down and then as abruptly rises, shedding streams of water, until it momentarily clears the surface before dropping back to plunge again, or perhaps to ride along briefly before the next wave engulfs it once more.

The final major element of the outrigger is the platform on top of the booms. It forms a triangle with its apex well out on the booms and its base running along the side of the hull a little more than halfway out from the middle of the canoe toward each end. This platform not only provides a large area for work-ing, riding, and stowing gear but also serves a structural pur-pose. In the latter capacity it holds the outrigger booms firmly at a right angle to the hull and also stiffens the narrow hull against the buffeting of the waves. The distance it extends toward each end is one of the many measurements derived from the length of the hull, but it often needs to be altered a little if the hull flexes too much and loosens its joints or if it is so rigid that it bangs hard into the waves and is thus slowed unduly in rough weather. In the former case the platform is lengthened slightly to provide more support, and in the latter it is shortened.

Both the platform on the outrigger side and the lee platform

Base of the outrigger platform extending along the hull, outrigger booms angling downward to the left through the hull

Nesting the ends of the lee platform timbers

The lee platform in place

are covered with many small parallel straight sticks lashed to a light wooden frame. This creates a rough but flat surface through which water will immediately drain. At the inner edge of both platforms, next to the hull, the sticks are replaced by flat boards. On the outrigger platform, coming in as it does flush with the hull, this board forms a solid deck running half the length of the canoe.

The lee platform, like the outrigger, rests upon two heavy timbers. Instead of being an integral part of the canoe's structure, however, the lee platform timbers are merely wedged in under a short beam lashed across the ends of the outrigger booms, inside the hull. This means that when the canoe is to be carried into the canoe house the entire lee platform can be lifted off by several men and stowed separately, making the canoe far less bulky. It also has the result, however, of making the lee platform a very dangerous place to be if the canoe capsizes. Canoes capsize only in one direction, toward the lee side, usually a result of a sudden gust of wind striking the sail. As the canoe rolls over, the lee platform hits the water and at once floats upward while the rest of the canoe continues rolling, until it lands on top of the lee platform and its occupants—if they have not dived for safety into the water.

Although the heavy beams which support the lee platform rise out of the hull of the canoe at a rather steep angle, the platform itself is almost level on top. This is because it is actually built on some additional lighter members which run all the way from the outer ends of the heavy lower beams back inboard across the hull until they overlap the inner edge of the outrigger platform. The ends of these lighter beams are held up by flat boards which stand on edge and rest on the outrigger deck. In this way the whole assembly is supported a foot or so above the canoe. The board which forms the inner edge of the lee platform, the counterpart of the outrigger deck, is thus a raised bench. This bench is reserved by the navigator for his own use; it is the most convenient place to hold the sheet which controls the sail, it is a handy and safe location for the compass, and from it one can look out in all directions. Two other benches at right angles to the navigator's are formed of boards extending across the hull along the light platform beams. There are even handrails at their edges, used by those who may be standing up to steady themselves, but also comfortable as backrests. Together these three benches comprise a cockpit in the center of the canoe.

Along with the sail and rigging, which can best be described a little later in the context of boat handling, the hull and these two platforms constitute the major components of the Puluwat sailing canoe. Each contributes to performance but, to repeat, it is the design of the hull which is all-important. It is thus in the last analysis their hulls upon which Puluwat canoes must be judged. The judgment seems to have been positive. Testimony to this is the widespread acquisition of Puluwat canoes by islands far and near (including many islands with canoe-builders of their own), although the export of sailing canoes from Puluwat now seems to be declining somewhat.

However, this decline may reflect only a decreased interest elsewhere in the use of sailing canoes from any source. This is especially true of the islands to the east. There are virtually no sailing canoes left on Truk and only a very few in the Mortlock Islands south of Truk. In the Hall Islands to the north the number is decreasing and a lack of navigators confines them to local use. There is, however, still a demand in the Namonuito Atoll, especially on Ulul, its largest island, despite a lack of qualified navigators. This is because unlike the Halls the atoll is large and its deep reefs offer relatively little protection for a small boat, requiring a seaworthy sailing canoe even for local travel using sight navigation. Even here, however, the sailing canoe tradition is dying and reliance is placed increasingly on the administration's little ships which visit the islands, despite their inconvenience. This leaves only the islands immediately north and south of Puluwat—Pulap, Tamatam, and Pulusuk—and Satawal and Lamotrek plus other islands still farther to the west. On all of these, sailing canoes are still actively in use for inter-island travel, and all except the farthest islands have on occasion received canoes through relatives on Puluwat. However, all of them have traditionally built most of their canoes themselves, and still do, so they offer only an intermittent "market" for Puluwat.

Although positive evidence is lacking, the reduction in exports probably means that the average age of canoes on Puluwat is increasing. In the past it would often happen that a canoe

Moored canoe fully covered with protective mats

built for a canoe house on Puluwat would be used for a year or two, though sometimes more, and then traded or given to a relative on another island. Judging from the histories of the canoes built during their lifetimes by men now alive on Puluwat, Truk seemed to receive in trade the newest canoes, perhaps because the Trukese could offer most in return. When the people on Namonuito traded, or in later years bought canoes for cash, they often got somewhat older craft which had been in use for three or four years. However, instead of trading or buying they now more commonly receive canoes as gifts through relatives and these are generally quite new. This is also true of the islands nearer Puluwat, and of Satawal. The people in the Hall Islands, however, for some reason do not fare so well. Time and again there is mention of an old and practically worn out canoe which was nevertheless traded on fairly favorable terms to the Halls. Even now there is in Hipour's canoe house a large sailing canoe, acquired originally from a relative on Pulusuk, which is not only old but also performs so badly it is never used, but

Canoe with temporary covering only on ends and most exposed parts of hull

which is awaiting only the availability of a crew to deliver it for sale to Fananu, one of the Hall Islands.

In any event, the canoes now in use on Puluwat are in many cases quite old. The ages of those still in active service range from two years up to fifteen, but the average is close to nine. This does not, however, mean that the Puluwat fleet is wearing out. In the first place, new canoes continue to be built as replacements. In 1967 two large and three small sailing canoes were in varying stages of construction, and I have since learned several more were started after we left.

More important, all sailing canoes are very carefully maintained. When they are at home on Puluwat unless in constant use canoes are rarely left in the water for more than a week at a time lest they become waterlogged. Whenever a canoe is sitting still, whether on land or in the water, it is at once covered with plaited coconut frond mats to protect it from the drying heat of the sun which can warp or crack the hull planks. Even inside a canoe house in the shade a canoe needs protection from the dry-

Carrying up a canoe; everyone works to minimize scraping on the bottom

ing wind which blows in the open end and sides of the house. Mats are therefore tied around it, particularly at its ends where the wind usually blows most directly. Similarly, the sail is spread on the coconut fronds in front of the canoe house to dry before it is stowed, still tied to its spars, in the eaves. As far as possible the hull is kept from touching even the softest sandy bottom. It is always moored a little offshore. When the canoe is carried up the beach smooth, hard coconut midribs are laid down close together to be sure the keel slides easily over them; on loose sand (as at Pikelot) larger pandanus logs are used lest the hull sink down and be scratched. Furthermore, the men who bring the canoe up, heaving to a cadenced chant, concentrate their numbers under the outrigger platform where they can lift up as well as forward with their shoulders, thus relieving some of the weight on the keel.

In addition to these routine precautions, and minor repairs when they are needed, once a year the entire canoe is checked over. This usually takes place in the spring and covers every joint and lashing. Depending on how much the canoe has been used, every two years or so this operation becomes a major overhaul. Most of the lashings are then replaced, not only those which hold together the outrigger booms and float but also those which knit together the planks of the hull. The caulking between the planks is renewed, and any softened or damaged places are cut out and new planks fitted in. Then the hull is puttied smooth and painted a shiny waterproof black with decorations in red and white. For the red color an imported enamel is sometimes used, but otherwise the Puluwatans feel their own paints are still superior. Meanwhile the spars receive new lashings as necessary, and the rigging and sometimes even the sail are replaced.

As with all boats, the meticulous care devoted to building and maintaining sailing canoes ashore is usually rewarded by lack of trouble at sea. Although materials are carried for the repair of virtually every part of a canoe, these repairs are difficult to make at sea, doubly so because the only time they are likely to be necessary is under rough stormy conditions when some component has been overstrained. The beating which the complex structures of a sailing canoe take in a heavy storm is severe. It is driven by wind, smashed by the running seas, wrenched upward, and dropped steeply down again on the crests and in the troughs of waves which come in from all angles. That it survives at all is remarkable. That it survives so well is a tribute not only to careful construction and maintenance but also to a remarkably sophisticated and rational basic design.

The design of a sailing canoe, again like all other sailing craft, reflects many compromises. It could be made much faster, but only at the cost of ruggedness and seaworthiness upon which survival depends. It could be made to carry more weight, but then it would be slower. It could stand a lot of improvement in its ability to sail into the wind, but it would draw too much water to be able to get through some of the passes in reefs which it must negotiate. The most striking compromise among many is the relatively small size of the sail, which must not exceed the limits of stability and structural strength of the canoe in the open ocean. The smallness of the sail has the effect of preventing these boats from ever coming close to the maximum speed which the dimensions of their hulls would allow. Nevertheless, the Puluwat sailing canoe does not do badly when compared to other working ocean sailing craft, particularly as very few other such boats are as small. The 26 foot average overall length of the canoe is itself modest, but when the very narrow hull is also taken into account it becomes evident their displacement is small indeed. (As mentioned earlier at the waterline the average width is 33 inches and the length 23½ feet.) Under these circumstances the performance which is achieved is remarkable. It is possible only because the crew is able constantly to get the most out of their craft under all the varied conditions which they encounter. They can do this because there is virtually no component in the rigging of a sailing canoe which is not subject to significant adjustment. This means that in contrast to most Western sailing boats, which have both permanent "standing" rigging (for example, stays) and adjustable "running" rigging (such as halyard and sheet), all the lines on a Puluwat canoe are movable running rigging. This greatly increases the flexibility of the craft and permits keeping full sail under conditions much more severe than would otherwise be tolerable.

The basic functional design of a single outrigger canoe is also substantially different from the fore-and-aft rig we familiarly see in Western sailing boats. This difference leads directly to a distinctive set of principles for handling and sailing outrigger canoes. It will be well to review these general principles before going on to a specific description of the Puluwat canoe. The first important characteristic is that single outrigger canoes are almost invariably sailed with the outrigger on the windward side. That is done so that the force of the wind on the sail will tend to lift the outrigger float out of the water, not push it down. This means that the stabilizing effect of the float derives principally from its weight, not from its buoyancy. Otherwise there could be a crisis every time the float drove under the water in a big wave or shift of wind. With the float to windward its increased drag in the water when accidentally submerged tends to swing the boat around more into the wind; this relieves some of the push of the wind on the sail, lets the canoe slow down a little, and gives the float time to lift itself clear of the rush of water pouring over it. If the float were on the other side, every time it went under it would swing the canoe downwind and turn the sail still more broadside to the wind. This would not only add to the canoe's speed but also tend to push down even harder on the float by tipping the canoe toward it.

Advantageous as having the float always on the upwind side may be, it also brings problems. By far the greatest difficulty arises in tacking upwind. Western sailing craft make their way upwind by sailing along in one direction at an angle to the wind, then after a while turning the boat so it points more or less in the opposite direction and sails along at a similar angle to the wind on the other side. It is just this turning around which the outrigger canoe cannot do because it would put the float downwind. In order to tack back and forth, which is the only possible way to sail up against the wind, the outrigger canoe must therefore actually change its direction end for end. This is done by shifting the entire sail and all its associated rigging bodily from one end of the canoe to the other every time the canoe goes from one tack to the other. In other words, the fore-and-aft-rigged Western sailboat makes a change from side to side with each tack, while the sailing canoe changes end for end. The latter has no permanent bow or stern since it goes first in one direction and then the other. This requirement that the sail and rigging be readily removable from one end to the other calls for ingenious engineering as well as dexterous seamanship. Both fortunately are found on Puluwat canoes.

A second inevitable consequence of having an outrigger is the asymmetrical drag created by the float. With the forward force of the sail applied along the line of the hull, the resistance of the outrigger float traveling through the water several feet to one side tends to turn the canoe off course. Since the float is on the windward side, the canoe is inclined to turn into the wind—unless something else is introduced to counter the tendency.* On the Puluwat canoe this countering is principally

* The turning effect of the outrigger float is actually added to two other forces which also tend to swing any sailboat, including the familiar fore-and-aft rig, to windward. First, with the sail swung out over the lee side (especially when a conventional boat is heeled over by a strong wind) the pushing effect of the wind is moved away from the centerline of the boat. With this forward push on the lee side the boat naturally tends to turn the other way, that is, into the wind. Second, the resistance of the water as the bow of the boat pushes through it is greater on the lee side. Resistance at the bow, which creates a so-called bow

accomplished by positioning the sail well forward of the middle of the canoe. (This does not work when the wind is astern; then the steering paddle must be used to provide an opposing force.) A wind on the beam (that is, from the side) thus pushes on the forward end of the canoe. With the sideways push of the wind at the front being resisted by the hull along its entire length a strong force is generated to turn the canoe away from the wind and thus oppose the effect of the dragging outrigger. If the canoe is properly rigged the two forces balance each other and the boat sails straight.

However, this balance between the asymmetrical float and the asymmetrical sail of the canoe is dynamic and inherently unstable. It constantly fluctuates with the wind and tugging of waves on the outrigger float, and is constantly modifiable. The slightest change in the angle of the sail and therefore in the amount of wind it intercepts changes the balance and turns the canoe to one side or the other. A slackening of the sheet which holds the sail results in spilling some wind; at once the drag of the outrigger becomes the greater of the two balancing forces and the canoe turns into the wind. Take in on the sheet and the canoe turns back, the force of the wind overcoming the resistance of the float. Actually this is the way Puluwat sailing canoes are steered except when sailing with the wind behind them. It eliminates the need for a steersman and places complete control of the canoe in the hands of the one man (usually the navigator) who holds the sheet.

Although it is not essential to an understanding of how Puluwat canoes are designed and sailed, one additional comment on the principles governing outrigger sailing canoes is important because it points to a unique advantage of outriggers (as well as double-hulled canoes or catamarans) which makes it worthwhile to put up with the complexities described. We have noted that the weight of the outrigger float is used to stabilize the canoe and keep it upright. On a fore-and-aft rig the interaction between the wind on the sail above and the resistance of the fairly deep hull and keel (or equivalent board) below causes the

---

wave, is a critical factor in all sailing boat performance. It is greater on the lee side because it is there that the sideways pressure of the wind must principally be resisted. Consequently the bow wave on the lee side is stronger and the boat is forced toward the wind. Compensations similar to those described here, but in lesser degree, are therefore also designed into fore-and-aft rigged boats.

boat to lean over, sometimes to a precarious angle, and incidentally spill precious wind out of the sail. Resistance to tilting must come from a fairly broad hull (and on a small boat the balance which can also be provided by having the crew lean out the windward side). A broad hull necessarily pushes aside a lot of water. This pushing takes place at the front of the boat. It generates a wave which becomes the principal element in forming the wake behind. The size of the bow wave is a good indicator of the amount of energy, and therefore potential speed, which is used up in just pushing water out of the way. By not having to rely on its hull for stability, the outrigger canoe can afford a very narrow body which "knifes" its way through the water, creating remarkably little wake or drag.

In an effort to hold the drag-creating width of a conventional hull within bounds it is common to seek additional stability against the tipping effect of the wind by adding extra weight at the bottom of a deep keel. As much as 30 to 50 percent of the total weight of a racing sailboat may be lead. This extra weight pulls the boat down in the water and adds appreciably to its drag. Furthermore, illustrating neatly the contrast between the two kinds of rig, the weighted keel does not really begin to exert a stabilizing effect until the boat has leaned over quite a way, moving the weight far enough from under the hull to give it some leverage. The outrigger float, however, at all times has the advantage of its boom as a long lever arm. A small amount of outrigger weight thus has far greater stabilizing effect. This permits a narrow hull which, even with the float included, adds up to much less frontal wave-building width than a fore-and-aft rigged boat of similar capacity.

The narrow hull by its nature also has steep sides all of whose surface can contribute to the canoe's resistance to the sideways pressure of the wind on the sail. Not only that, but the narrow profile of the hull is shaped rather like a supersonic aircraft wing, and therefore helps "lift" the canoe to windward. This makes it possible to eliminate entirely the drag of a keel or board without too severe a penalty in sideways slippage. Despite its steep sides this hull still rides less deep in the water than does a hull which has a keel below. Consequently, the outrigger canoe can sail through reefs and shallow lagoons which would be impossible for Western boats. A shallow draft also means the center of resistance is nearer the waterline high on the hull, and therefore closer to the center of wind pressure on the sail. The wind thus exerts less leverage on the boat as a whole and the stabilizing work of the outrigger is made still easier. As a final advantage, an outrigger canoe, when it is drifting naturally, assumes a position at right angles to the wind, with the outrigger upwind. In this position it is both stable and able to offer maximum resistance to drifting. On one occasion with a stiff breeze of perhaps 15 knots and the sail still up and slatting a sailing canoe was observed to drift downwind at a speed of less than half a knot; with the sail down it would be considerably less. This eliminates entirely the need for a sea anchor, without which a Western sailboat adrift begins almost at once to flounder dangerously or, if steered, to drift rapidly downwind.

On a Puluwat canoe the design principles described above are translated into actuality by the four major components of the rigging and the several coir lines through which they are restrained and adjusted. These components are the *sail* itself, tied to a *yard* at its upper front edge and a *boom* below, and the *mast* which suspends the whole rig above the hull of the canoe. It is a lateen rig, by which is meant that the sail, rather than being fastened to the mast itself, is lashed to a yard which is in turn suspended from the mast.

The sail nowadays is made of imported white cotton cloth, rather loosely tied at intervals to the yard and boom. Prior to World War II the sails were made of pandanus woven in much the same way as sleeping mats or the woven table mats (often called by the Hawaiian name for pandanus, *lauhala*) found in gift shops. Cloth sails are a vast improvement. Pandanus was heavier, less flexible, less durable, and less effective in holding the wind, and when soaked with water, its weight made it almost unmanageable. This last characteristic meant that the sail was usually lowered whenever a rainsquall threatened so that it could be kept dry, a great waste of time and effort. Now the sail is lowered only when there is danger of gusts strong enough to capsize the canoe.

The sail is roughly triangular in shape. Its upper or forward edge, tied to the yard, is almost vertical when the sail is raised. This can give rise to the misleading impression that the yard is

Canoe under sail, showing near-vertical yard, S-curved boom sloping to rear, and mast sloping forward

the mast, an appearance heightened by the fact that the lower end of the yard actually rests in a socket near the forward end of the hull and is held down in place there by a short tack line. In reality, however, the heavy mast resting in a socket in the middle of the canoe holds up the sail. The sail is raised by a stout halyard. This halyard is tied to the yard, goes at once through a hole at the top of the mast, and then runs down the far side of the mast to be secured with a couple of half-hitches around the lower part of the mast. The mast is raked or tilted forward in its socket to accommodate the forward position of the sail, and held in place by three stays fastened near the top of the mast and extending to the end of the outrigger and to a thwart near each end of the hull. When it is necessary to change the sail from one end of the canoe to the other the mast is swung over and it carries with it, like the arm of a construction crane, the entire rig: yard, sail, and boom together. The upper end of the mast is gracefully curved in such fashion that bends away from the surface of the sail. This is said to "let the wind in." In our terms this means it reduces the turbulent flow of air over the sail, a turbulence which would otherwise noticeably decrease the aerodynamic efficiency of the sail. This is but one of dozens of little design details, well understood by the Puluwatan builders, which serve to bring performance to its maximum potential.

A related design feature is the curve of both yard and boom. Once again the theory of the Puluwat canoe-builder makes very good sense on aerodynamic grounds. The upward-facing curve at the forward end of the boom, coupled with a full cut of the sail here, creates a pocket or bulge which "collects the wind." We would say it accentuates the contour of the back side of the sail and thereby creates a low pressure area. This is the same as the curve on the top of an airplane wing which produces negative pressure and thus lift. The down-turn of the ends of both yard and boom lowers the effective height of the sail surface and also directs the wind off the sail in a more horizontal direction. The former promotes stability and the latter propulsive efficiency.

The boom is tied loosely at its forward end to the lower end of the yard. Otherwise it is simply suspended from the lower edge of the sail and is held in by the sheet which the navigator tends. However, in a heavy or following wind the boom can be pulled up closer to the yard by lines whose function it is both to spill wind and to reef the sail. These and other adjustments, as well as the rigging which makes them possible, will be reviewed in the description which follows of the handling of the canoe under various courses and wind conditions.

The way any sailing craft is handled at a particular time depends upon the weather and the heading of the boat relative to the wind. Weather conditions include the strength and steadiness of the wind, the state of the sea, visibility, precipitation, and temperature. Headings can range from hard on the wind, which means that the boat is sailing as close toward the direction from which the wind is blowing as its design will permit, through a reach, with the wind blowing generally from the side of the boat, to running downwind with the breeze coming from behind. Although no decision regarding the handling of a boat can be made without taking into account both the weather and the heading desired at the time, for purposes of description they are best treated separately.

In common with fore-and-aft rigged boats, the lateen rig of a Puluwat canoe sails best on a reach, that is, with the wind coming from its side. Although no figures are available on maximum performance with a strong wind, it was possible to make speed runs one day under a light but fairly steady wind averaging a little over 6 knots on a hand wind gauge. The canoe used is considered to be relatively fast, although two others on the island are rated faster. Runs of one mile (in a few cases one-half mile) were timed and measured with a taffrail log at 15-degree intervals from directly downwind (180 degrees) to as far into the wind as the boat would sail. With the wind directly on the beam (90 degrees) the canoe made 5.3 knots. Speeds on headings to windward and downwind of this were comparable (at 75 degrees, 5.2 knots, and at 105 degrees, 5.4 knots, the latter the best speed of the day). Since this is not even close to the maximum speed which a narrow hull, 23½ feet at the water-line, can be presumed to allow, it may be assumed that a stronger wind would result in appreciably better performance, but how much better is conjectural. The only other figures available on performance on a reach are derived from two interisland trips for which elapsed time was recorded. In both cases the canoes were rated slower than the one used for measured runs, but the wind was fresher, ranging perhaps between 10 and 15 knots, and fairly steadily on the beam. However, on any long trip there are diversions, delays, and fluctuations in the wind which lower the average speed made good throughout the trip. In any event the average speed on both of these trips, of forty and one hundred miles respectively, was 4.5 knots.

Not only does a Puluwat canoe turn in its best performance when sailing with the wind on the beam, but this is also the heading which requires the least work and attention from the crew, except for the navigator. Because under these conditions the downwind pressure on the sail at the forward end of the canoe tends to balance the asymmetrical pull of the outrigger float which would otherwise turn the canoe into the wind, the balance is sufficiently good that on a properly trimmed sailing canoe it is not necessary even to have the steering paddle in the water. The crew relaxes amidships and the navigator alone, or someone who may replace him temporarily, keeps the canoe on the proper heading solely through adjustments to the sheet.

The sheet is a heavy coir line which is used to regulate the

Hipour on his navigator's bench; Teruo at left. There is a lot of mechanical advantage on the sheet as it passes up and down, but also a lot of friction as it passes twice under the beam below

angle of the sail to the boat, and therefore to the wind. Since it must restrain the full pressure of the wind on the sail it is usually under considerable strain. In order that the sheet be instantly adjustable and yet not unduly tire the hands of the navigator who must hold it, it is doubled back and forth several times to increase the mechanical advantage of the navigator in governing the sail. It is tied first to the boom a little forward of its midpoint, runs down under the short beam which is lashed to the outrigger booms inside the hull (under which the lee platform booms are wedged), up through a regular Western-made pulley block (usually salvaged from a wrecked ship and handed down over the years), down again under the short beam, and then up to the hands of the navigator. This combination of running free through the block above and slipping (and gripping) twice on the beam below provides just the right proportion of freedom and friction to make the sheet manageable.

When the wind is strong the end of the sheet is held by the navigator against the adjacent portion of the same line which is going down from the block to the beam below. The rope is thus gripped against itself and the clinging coir fibers bind the strands together until such time as the navigator releases his grip. This makes the sheet easy to restrain. It is more difficult to pull it in, especially when the wind is pressing hard on the sail, but with one hand pulling down from the block and the other pulling up on the end a lot of force can be applied to the sheet, usually in a series of quick pulls.

Work with the sheet is distinctly different from that on a fore-and-aft rigged boat. Since the symmetrical hull of a Western boat is inclined to stay on course unless something interferes with it, when the force on the sail is released by letting out the sheet the boat simply keeps on going the way it was before, or if the mast is placed forward (as in a sloop or catboat) may fall off the wind a little from the pressure of wind on the mast. On an outrigger canoe, however, letting out the sheet when on a reach reduces the effect of the sail in countering the off-center pull of the outrigger float. Immediately the canoe begins to turn into the wind. A similar result follows upon a drop in the wind, while a stronger blow will turn the canoe the other way. This means that the navigator must be constantly vigilant, continually adjusting the sheet. The sheet must also be relieved briefly if an unusually steep wave tilts the canoe sharply enough to threaten capsizing, or a sudden gust does the same thing. Yet the sheet may be eased only momentarily. Otherwise the pull of the outrigger will swing the canoe too far around and spill the wind from the sail entirely. When this happens it is necessary to wait until the canoe has stopped dead in the water; then it begins to drift down, swinging around the outrigger, the wind pushing the canoe around to a heading on which it can again sail away. Thus we see that the forces on a sailing canoe are in a dynamically unstable balance or, to put it in different terms, that the navigator has a tricky job which calls for skill and constant attention. It is no wonder that a member of the crew asked to spell him on the sheet feels complimented by the delegation of responsibility. The word for sailing on a reach in Puluwat translates as "pulling on the sheet."

In addition to its overall efficiency there is another advantage to sailing on a reach. Because the canoe is held on course by keeping it trimmed to a constant heading relative to the wind, if the wind changes in direction the canoe will also change its direction. Since the ocean swells do not quickly change in their orientation, the feel of the boat as it rides over the wave is at once altered. The crew is sensitive to this and thus is warned immediately of any wind shift, an important asset in navigation as it is practiced in these islands, especially when the visibility is poor.

When the heading is changed farther into the wind so that the canoe is sailing close-hauled the balance of forces and general handling of the boat do not change appreciably. Nevertheless, in this change from a reach to hard on the wind an outrigger canoe goes from its most efficient mode to its least efficient. The reason for this is as follows. On a reach the narrow hull with its minimal wave-making action offers little resistance to forward movement, a real advantage. However, it is offset to some degree by the relatively small resistance offered by the hull alone to the sideways pressure of the wind on the sail, a resistance which, despite the hull's steep sides and airfoil shape, is less than it would be if there were a large keel or board down in the water. When sailing on a reach efficiency is high because this sideways slippage is not critical. The hull is pointed a little upwind to compensate for the drift and all is well. Continuing the airplane-wing analogy, this pointing up on a reach increases the angle of attack as an airplane does when its nose is raised at lower speeds to maintain its lift. If, however, the canoe is sailing hard on the wind, and especially if it is tacking and thus trying to make as much headway upwind as it can, this slippage downwind becomes a real handicap. Furthermore, because the wind must be fairly well on the beam in order that the forward-placed sail may counterbalance the drag of the outrigger, a canoe which tries to point up too sharply into the wind will find itself past the point of balance, swung willy-nilly by its outrigger directly into the wind and stopped dead in the water. Occasionally when it is necessary to maneuver in tight quarters, as in going through a pass in a reef close on the wind, the steering paddle can be used instead to counter the pull of the outrigger. This permits sailing a little closer-hauled, but at the same time creates additional drag on a canoe already not sailing at its best. The use of the steering paddle when close-hauled is therefore not appropriate for normal travel.

The result of this unfavorable combination of factors can be seen in the performance of the canoe referred to above, which was not only ranked fast but also unusually efficient among Puluwat canoes in sailing into the wind. Close-hauled, the best bearing it could hold was 62 degrees off the wind—in contrast to the 45 degrees toward which the designer of an ordinary fore-and-aft rig strives (but does not always attain). Furthermore, its slippage, or leeway, estimated by the angle of both the wake and the log line, amounted to another 15 degrees. Thus the canoe was able to make good a course no better than 77 degrees off the wind. Put in another way, the angle between one tack and the next was only 35 degrees. Not only that but the speed dropped to 3.9 knots. Yet I was assured that compared to most canoes we were doing very well. It is not surprising that interisland trips are rarely undertaken when the wind is such that a lot of tacking will be required.

Nevertheless, Puluwat canoes do tack quite often. Tacking is normally required in order to maneuver a canoe from the inner lagoon out to the pass in the reef. When canoes are fishing, going out and returning the same day as well as working back and forth over the reefs, they usually have to do some tacking. Even trips to other islands, especially the short seventeen-mile run to Tamatam, are sometimes made when it is obvious tacking will be necessary, while every ocean voyage presents the real possibility of a change in wind which will force a lot of tacking upon the crew if they are to reach their destination. In the long run everyone gets plenty of practice despite their efforts to avoid it.

An experienced crew can make tacking look quite simple, but it remains a notable sight. In essence, the entire rigging of the canoe including the sail is moved bodily from one end of the canoe to the other so that a craft which was just now sailing in one direction becomes a mirror-image of itself, sailing in the opposite direction with every line and spar in exactly the same adjustment and relationship as before but facing the other way. All this is completed in scarcely a minute. The canoe is actually dead in the water even less time than that because it starts moving out on the new heading before everything has been fully secured in the new positions.

The process of tacking or changing ends begins with the boat

Changing ends

Releasing the tack line

4

Straining to heave the rig around the mast, which is now vertical

5

The instant the rig passes the mast the captain gives the handlers plenty of slack in the sheet. The man at the mast has been handed the thin lee stay, which he holds with his left hand. (This picture is from a different sequence.)

8

The rig is pulled down both by the end stay and by its own weight

9

Bedding the yard in its new socket, tack line looped ready over the end man's hand, while the other takes in the end stay. Note vortex in the water as canoe drifts sideways, while still moving in its former direction.

2

Ready to take the rig

3

Carrying the rig to the other end; Teruo on the stay easing it out as the other stay is hauled in

6

Heaving the rig toward its new position

7

Meanwhile, at the former front end the end stay is snubbed and paid out, with the rig further steadied by the middle man on the light lee stay

10

Securing the tack line

11

Securing the end stay. The sail begins to fill as the sheet is taken in. In the foreground are a nylon fishing line wound on a board, pandanus sun hats, long poles used to repair broken spars (lashed to the outrigger platform extension), and ripe coconuts.

sailing along routinely. The sail is suspended from a mast which is tilted forward and held in position by three rope stays running downward, one to the outrigger and one to each end of the hull. Its base rests in a socket at the edge of the hull on the outrigger platform, a socket which is at the midpoint of the hull and in which the mast is free to pivot. The yard, held near its upper end to the top of the mast by the halyard, rests at its lower end in a small socket in a board at the very end of the hull. The weight of the entire rig bears down on this socket but the yard is further secured against popping out by a small tack line. The first step, therefore, is for a man to go forward and untie the tack line. With this done he then unties the forward stay from a thwart just behind him, but holds it taut still looped under the thwart. At the same time another man has gone to the other end and released and held the stay back there. Nothing has moved yet. Then the navigator lets go the sheet and the sail swings wide, spilling the wind from it and relieving the strain on the rigging. At the same moment a fourth man—it is very difficult to change ends on a large canoe with less than four men—runs forward. The man who is already forward lifts the yard and boom at their base with one hand and with the other slacks off the stay which he is still holding. He heaves the rig backwards and hands it to the fourth man. This looks like a rather heroic heave, but in actuality most of the power for it is generated by the man at the other end of the canoe who gives a mighty pull on the back stay and thus pulls the mast, with the rigging hanging from it, up and backward away from where it was resting. The man who ran forward (the fourth man) now carries the rig back with him toward the cockpit, clambers around the benches, and gives the yard another great heave to get it past the mast. If there is a fifth man aboard he helps push the rig around the mast; this is the clumsiest part of the entire operation because the sail, swung out at right angles to the canoe in the middle of its reversal of position, tends to swing inboard against the mast. At this moment it is essential that the navigator has run the sheet all the way out to give the sail full freedom to pass the mast. Thereafter he must quickly take in the sheet in order to be ready to swing the sail in line for its new heading.

Once the sail is past the mast the rest is easy. The man carrying the rig continues to guide it along. The men on the two stays cooperate in taking up on one and letting out the other to swing the mast backward. The rig moves in an arc down to its new position. The man who has been on the back stay then guides the yard into its socket, while handing the stay to the man who carried the rig there, and at once secures the yard with the tack line to hold it down. Then the stays are made fast. Meanwhile the navigator has taken in the sheet and the canoe is already moving off on a new course. Note that the third stay, which runs from the mast to the outrigger, was not touched but instead allowed to swing with mast. Consequently the lateral angle of the mast remains unchanged. Further, the fore-and-aft angle of the mast depends on the length of the yard between its suspension point on the mast and its base on the canoe; since this has not changed either the rake of the mast is also unchanged. It is therefore evident that the entire rig is necessarily now in exactly the same relationship to the canoe as it was before, but at the opposite end.

There is a fourth or lee stay, a light line used only when the sail is lowered to keep the mast from falling onto the outrigger, a function normally served by the weight of the sail and the pressure of wind on it. When the sail is up this fourth stay is stowed by tying it lightly to the back stay. In tacking if there is a fifth man aboard he holds this extra stay and helps the man on the regular back stay give the critical initial pull which lifts the rig up from its position at the front end of the canoe. He then carries the light stay to the other end, pausing to help the man who is carrying the sail get it past the mast, and then helps steady the rig down in its new position until all the other lines are secured. Then the lee stay can be lightly tied again to the new back stay.

The existence of this lee stay, which is secured to the lee platform only when the sail is down, brings to mind a question whether when the canoe is under way the wind ever catches the back of the sail and brings the whole rig crashing down by blowing it over onto the outrigger. The answer is that it does not, at least under normal conditions. This is because when the canoe is sailing along, if it turns into the wind for any reason it almost at once stops. Immediately the wind begins to drift it around, pivoting as it were on the outrigger and thus protecting the back side of the sail from catching any wind. Actually

When the canoe is anchored the lee stay runs down (right) from the top of
the mast to the lee platform

the only way the wind can back the sail is if the canoe is paddled or otherwise turned around. This would only happen
when maneuvering in the lagoon. It happened once when I was
aboard. It was a dark night and the canoe was close to the beach
on a lee shore with the wind blowing fitfully through the trees,
first this way then that. It was being paddled as well as sailed.
Momentarily the canoe grounded and swung around. At once
the sail, glowing dimly in the dark, began to swing over. There
were cries of real alarm—it is a heavy rig to have crashing down
uncontrolled—and everyone aboard grabbed anything he could
reach, a line, the sail itself, the boom. The fall was checked, men
jumped over the side to manhandle the boat around, and the
crisis was past. Both the alarm and the uncoordinated confusion
of everyone grabbing in the dark testified to the rarity of this
experience, but at the same time the instant awareness of what
was happening showed that everyone had been through it at
least once before.

In contrast to sailing hard on the wind, turning instead away
from the wind first onto a broad reach and on around until the
wind is directly astern, speed performance falls off only slightly, but the way the craft must be handled changes markedly.
With respect to speed on the performance runs cited above once
the heading reached 120 degrees off the wind the average
speed, although fluctuating a little from one run to the next,
remained slightly less than 5 knots all the way to 180 degrees,
that is, until the canoe was running full before the wind. If the
wind gauge used was accurate in indicating an average wind
speed of 6 knots, the canoe was moving through the water only
a little more than one knot below the wind speed. Such efficiency appears unlikely, yet due to a discrepancy between two
scales on the gauge it was carefully recalibrated by the manu-
facturer upon return from the field and the low reading was
confirmed. However, the gauge was also checked against several others in the open and in this context seemed to be reading
a little low, which would mean that the wind was actually faster
than 6 knots.

In any event, regardless of the accuracy of the gauge it is
probable that the speed of the canoe on these runs was fairly
close to its maximum when running before a wind of any veloc-
ity, in contrast to sailing on a reach, where a stronger wind
could mean considerably faster travel through the water. The

reason for saying this is as follows. Whereas on a reach a sailing canoe can, with only minor adjustments, handle a fairly strong breeze with full sail, this is not true when it is running before the wind. With the wind pushing from behind the high forward position of the sail creates a substantial danger of driving the bow under and swamping the canoe. Therefore, beginning at wind speeds only slightly greater than those experienced during the performance runs, it becomes necessary to spill more and more wind out of the sail as the wind blows harder. It is thus probable that there is a steadily increasing disparity in achievable maximum speeds between reaching and running as wind speed increases. However, no data are available to support this conjecture.

With regard to handling the canoe, the need for changed procedures once it turns downwind immediately becomes obvious if we recall the important role played on a reach by the balance between the turning effect of the wind on the forward-placed sail and the opposite force created by the pull of the outrigger. With the wind coming from behind, the sail lines up more with the hull and is thus less effective in countering the turning effect of the outrigger. Furthermore, as the wind comes around still more astern, the sail swinging out over the lee platform is inclined actually to augment rather than oppose the asymmetrical force of the outrigger, although other adjustments minimize this effect.*

No adjustments in the rigging alone are enough to keep the canoe sailing straight once the wind stops pushing sideways on the sail at the front of the hull. At first, when still on a broad reach, the turning force of the outrigger can be overcome by placing one of the crew members aft. This changes the trim of the canoe, sinking the rear deeper in the water and raising the front a little. Since the wind is still somewhat from the side there remains some sideways push and its leverage is maximized by working only against the deeper-riding back end of the canoe. Sailing a broad reach is thus called "sitting at the rear."

---

*Although secondary in importance, when the canoe turns downwind the pressure of the wind at its side is reduced, and sideways drift diminishes and ultimately disappears. It thus sails straighter in the water. This has the effect, through reduction in the angle of attack, of moving the center of resistance on the hull backwards and thus helping somewhat with the problem of outrigger drag.

Teruo on the steering paddle, which is deflected only by the cross-pull of the lanyard secured to its forward end

However, sitting at the rear will serve only through a narrow range of headings. Once headed a little more downwind the unfavorable combination of forces can only be overcome by the deliberate measure of putting the steering paddle in the water. Although called a paddle this is actually a long flat board. It is put in the water only on the lee side of the hull and is rigged to press against the hull, pushing the rear end of the boat upwind. The reason it is never deployed on the windward side is that its only purpose is to counteract the turning effect of outrigger drag when the sail is no longer equal to this task. Sailing downwind is referred to appropriately as "sailing by steering."

The steersman sits on the little socket-board at the very end of the hull, the board which when the sail is reversed serves as the resting place for the lower end of the yard. He holds the steering paddle against the hull and down into the water by a long handle extending backward from the top of the paddle; the paddle board is snubbed against the protruding end of the same thwart to whose other end the heavy end stay of the mast is secured. The paddle is further held in position by a lanyard which runs from its upper end forward and across the hull to the next thwart ahead, where it is secured at the outrigger side of the hull. The way this lanyard runs diagonally across the hull is important because when it tightens against the pull of the water rushing over the immersed part of the paddle it necessarily pulls the upper end of the paddle inward toward the middle of the canoe and correspondingly forces the lower end outward into the water. This automatic deflection of the paddle makes the rather tiring task of the steersman easier because he need only pivot the paddle, forced outward by the lanyard, up and down by its handle around the fulcrum of the thwart to produce more or less turning force on the rear of the canoe. However, this is often not enough, especially when the wind is strong and the outrigger float is smashing into one wave after another and wrenching the canoe violently around. Then the steersman not only holds the paddle down hard into the water with the handle, but must also push it down and outward with his foot to a sharp angle of deflection. For this reason the steering paddle is called a "step-on paddle."

When strongly deflected the paddle creates a considerable drag. However, this is of relatively small consequence because the speed of the canoe must already be sharply limited by spilling wind from the sail in order to avoid the real danger of driving the front of the narrow hull under. The slope of the steering paddle is such that it not only deflects the canoe sideways but also acts as a vane to pull the rear end of the canoe down, as does the weight of the steersman, and thus both forces help trim the bow of the canoe upward, counteracting the downward push of the sail. Once again we see illustrated the extraordinary fashion in which under each different set of conditions almost every component of the Puluwat sailing canoe helps to maintain the stability and performance of the canoe in separate but coordinated ways.

This is evident too in the wide array of compensatory adjust-

As the canoe is turned a little more downwind, the paddle must be deflected still further out by pressure from Teruo's foot

ments which can be made in the rigging under different weather conditions. These adjustments are the key to an adaptability which makes the canoes able to perform well in the face of virtually every challenge the Pacific Ocean can throw at them short of a full-scale typhoon—and even in a typhoon it is navigation which is most vulnerable and probably has accounted for more historically known canoe losses than has failure of the canoes themselves.

Adjustments to the rigging are made primarily to accommodate to increases in the strength of the wind, either actual or —as with a gusty rainsquall bearing down—anticipated. There are no special means available to cope with the opposite condition, very light airs or calms. The adjustments can be divided into fairly lasting compensatory settings for various rigging components and more transitory changes subject to constant revision, of which the most continually changed is the sheet.

Another change fairly readily made and altered is the spilling

Spiller line in use, reefing the sail and dumping wind from the top. All the principal rigging is visible in this picture. The line running large off the top of the picture is the near end stay. Clockwise around the mast next comes the light lee stay, also running off the top of the picture. Next comes the spiller line tight against the back side of the sail, seen also running taut from the yard down toward the base of the mast. The other spiller line flops loosely across the front of the sail and swings freely downward toward the deck below where it is secured lightly to the base of the mast. Spiraled around the mast is the heavy halyard, while the other end stay runs down toward the far end of the canoe. Off to the left, toward the end of the out-rigger, are the fairly heavy weather stay, its other end attached above the outrigger float, and the lighter parrel line which at its end is secured to the weather stay.

of wind from the sail. This is done by one of two lines tied to the boom near its midpoint and run from there up on either side of the sail to a block near the top of the yard through which they pass through two separate holes, then down again to be secured with a half-hitch to the lower part of the mast. Which of the two spiller lines is used is determined by the location of the sail at one end of the canoe or the other: the line on the back side of the sail, away from the wind, is the one taken up. When not in use both lines are left slack so they will not disturb the smooth contour of the sail. With an increase in wind the line at the back of the sail is tightened. This has two consequences. One is that the boom is drawn up to the yard. This has the effect of a reef, reducing the amount of wind which can enter the sail.* The other consequence is that the sail presses against the tightened line and folds over it; the upper part of the sail now flaps or slopes away from the wind and effectively spills out its force. This spilling not only reduces the working area of the sail but also lowers its center of pressure, especially when the canoe is running before the wind and the sail has swung around sideways into a more vertical position. Because a sailing canoe is particularly liable to having its bow driven under when sailing with the wind astern it is under these conditions in particular that spiller lines are almost routinely employed except in relatively light winds. By simultaneously reducing and lowering the pressure on the sail they provide instant and effective protection against being swamped.†

On a reach the spiller lines are much less advantageous. Not only does lifting the boom in this configuration raise the center of pressure on the sail more than it is lowered by the spilling of wind at the aft edge, increasing the danger of capsizing, but the distortion of the natural contour of the sail impairs its efficiency much more when the wind is sliding across its face on a reach than when the wind is running straight into the sail from astern. In this configuration there is also a real danger of jibing. For these reasons spiller lines are very rarely used on a reach and then only on a broad (downwind) reach; they are a last resort short of the ultimate "adjustment" of lowering the sail entirely and waiting for the wind to abate. Also, it should be noted that under any conditions a spiller line chafes the sail and wears it out faster, although this is much less serious now than in the days of woven pandanus sails. In the past

*However, when the boom is relatively horizontal, as on a reach, it also raises the center of pressure on the sail and makes the canoe more liable to capsizing, a side effect which often requires a different kind of adjustment (described later).

†Although I have never seen it done, I have been told it is also possible to square-rig the sail amidships when running before an exceptionally strong wind. This locates the center of pressure lower and farther aft than in any other configuration.

spiller lines tore sails up badly and were used only with great reluctance.

Actually, on a close reach or with the wind directly on the beam it is most unusual for the force of wind to be so strong that the canoe cannot be stabilized just by weighing down the outrigger with a crew member or two. This is aside from gusts which are taken care of by letting out the sheet. However, if the wind is unusually strong two precautionary steps can be taken. The first is to change the slope of the mast sideways. Normally the mast is sloped slightly away from the outrigger, just enough so that its upper end is directly over the middle of the hull (its base, it will be recalled, is off center at the outrigger edge of the hull). This causes the yard, and therefore the front edge of the sail, to be exactly vertical. The sail is thus presented most directly and efficiently to the wind. If strong winds are expected, however, this slope of the mast is often changed, even before the canoe has left the lagoon for the open sea, although the adjustment can readily be made under almost any conditions. It consists in taking up on the stay which runs from the mast out to the end of the outrigger. This moves the mast to a vertical position, or even past vertical, and slopes the sail toward the wind. When this is done it causes the wind to flow in a more downward direction across the sail, thus lowering the center of pressure. It also has the effect, when the canoe turns downwind and the sail swings to a more transverse position, of moving the center of pressure toward the outrigger side and compensating a little for its off-center drag.

The center of pressure on the sail on a reach can also be lowered more substantially by lowering the position of the yard, and therefore the sail, on the mast. This is a more complicated adjustment involving four separate lines, preferably adjusted simultaneously by four men. Central to the operation is slacking off the halyard the desired amount, often a foot or more. However, if it were not restrained this would leave the yard swinging free at some distance from the mast at the end of the lengthened halyard. To prevent this there is a parrel line available—a line not previously mentioned—which serves this purpose alone. The parrel line is attached to the mast below the halyard but above the stays, passes around the halyard loosely when not in use, and runs down to be secured with a couple of half-

The parrel line in use with the yard lowered below the top of the mast. It is the light line running near the weather stay from the right, past the mast, around the yard and to the mast just below the top. It is not tight enough to hold the yard snug against the mast, but tight enough for stability.

hitches on the larger coir line of the outrigger stay. If it is necessary to let out the halyard and lower the yard on the mast the parrel line is at once pulled up tight. It binds the halyard against the mast and keeps the yard from swinging. However, another problem remains. It will be recalled that the spars comprise a triangle. Its base is the hull itself between the socket for the mast and the socket for the yard. One side is formed by the yard from its lower end up to its attachment to the mast at the halyard. The third side of the triangle is the mast from the yard attachment down to its base. By lowering the yard the mast side of the triangle has in effect been shortened and the shape (that is, the angles) of the triangle must be adjusted accordingly. This means reducing the forward rake of the mast, bringing it to a somewhat more vertical position, which is accomplished by slacking the forward stay and taking up on the aft stay in much the same way as is done when the sail is changed from one end to the other.

With this rather complex adjustment of the height of the sail on a reach we have completed the inventory of different ways in which a sailing canoe can be handled and modified to meet the multitude of conditions it will encounter. Although the descriptions in the preceding pages are cast in Western terms, including repeated analogies to fore-and-aft rigs and airplane wings, the principles involved would be explained by a Puluwatan boatbuilder in a very similar way. Puluwatans not only know what to do with their canoes, they also know why they are doing it. In other words, the design and operation of Puluwat canoes is governed by an explicit theory, a body of knowledge expressed in cause-and-effect terms. This is unusual among non-Western boatbuilders, or indeed among Westerners who build sailboats of conventional design. Even when pressed many boatbuilders fall back on explanations from tradition rather than rational principles.

The theory of canoe design on Puluwat is by no means confined to the sail and rigging, where causal relations are fairly obvious and immediate. Earlier in this chapter a number of relations of balance, rigidity, clearance, and strength were mentioned with respect to the outrigger and lee platform. Each of these statements was drawn directly from explanations made by one or another canoe-builder on Puluwat. However, in Puluwat design theory the most complex and the most critical relations exist within the contours of the hull itself.

The manner in which the major measurements of the hull are laid out have already been described. They depend largely upon halving and halving again the length of the keel, with the use of measuring lines. These dimensions are traditional, with minor variations between two schools of boatbuilders, and they are essentially uniform. The system of dimensioning taken together with the size and shape of the available breadfruit tree from which the keel piece is hewn determines the principal proportions of the hull. It is only after these major proportions are established that theory and deliberate individual variation come into play. It will be possible here to outline only the broader aspects of design which occupy the attention of the master canoe-builder. For me to have learned the more subtle relations would have required constant attention and inquiries throughout the many months which are required for the building of a large sailing canoe. Much of the final design of a hull on Puluwat as elsewhere depends upon the refined judgment of a practiced eye. Ask a man as he decides upon each next step why he made that particular decision and he can probably tell you. Ask him later how a canoe is designed and he will have forgotten that he ever made the decision.

The contours of the lee side of the hull are said to be the primary determinants of the speed of the boat, while those on the outrigger side are responsible for its weatherliness, that is its ability to resist drifting sideways under the pressure of the wind on a reach or especially when close-hauled on a tack. Our general knowledge of the behavior of hulls, including analogies drawn from aircraft wings, tends to confirm this general proposition.

The main areas of the hull which ride under the water are the sides, relatively steep and straight, and under a fairly sharp break inward a broader V-bottom area below. The sides, viewed more closely, are actually convex, both of them bulged a little but always more on the outrigger side. Similarly, when viewed from above one side may often be curved more than the other, and if so the more curved side is toward the outrigger. However, equally often the two sides are symmetrical in plan. The generally more convex contouring of the outrigger side in all directions is said (and here again our Western theory would agree) to be essential to the effective weatherliness or resistance to sideways drift of the canoe.

The lower or V-bottom part of the hull, separated from the sides by a sharp break in contour (a break also seen in the hulls of some contemporary America's Cup defenders), is frequently concave for the full length of the hull, or else it is flat. Unlike the sides it is almost never convex. This concavity is apparently intended to channel the water more smoothly along the hull, although it was impossible to arrive at complete clarity on this point. Again, the concavity is usually less, never more, on the

The hull of Hipour's canoe, showing slightly greater convexity on the outrigger (right) side. Note the slight convex break in contour on the outrigger side just above the horizon line.

Hipour's canoe, showing the end contour fairing out and a new contour fairing in above it and running the length of the hull

The lower hull of Ikuliman's canoe, viewed from the side, showing its unique double contoured concave surfaces running the entire length of the hull

outrigger side, thus carrying through to the very bottom of the canoe the principle of more fullness on the outrigger side and a sparer lee.

All of these contours become more critical near the ends of the hull. At the end of the keel the lines of the fairly blunt end of the hull carry underneath into the bottom area where they are faired out and disappear into the concave or flat bottom contours. On only one canoe, that of Ikuliman, were these lines carried down from the end of the canoe and continued along the full length of the keel. This resulted in a hull bottom with two separately contoured areas running in parallel. Ikuliman was not able to convey to me an explicit theoretical reason for doing this, except that it made the hull more efficient and faster. Since this canoe did in fact beat every other canoe from all the neighboring islands in a series of races he evidently knew what he was doing even if I did not!

The area on the side of the hull immediately above these complex end contours is considered especially critical. If it is too full the canoe will make big waves, push aside too much water, and be slow; if it is too spare the boat will slice too deeply into the waves and take on a lot of water. The balance between the weather and lee sides is also crucial in determining the ability of the canoe to sail into the wind. Here the practiced eye is essential. When a canoe is virtually finished, the hull smoothed, the platforms built, and only final lashing and painting remains, two stump logs are set up on end in the boat house and the canoe is lifted up on them. The outrigger is propped up at exactly the attitude it will assume in the water. Then the canoe-builder sits down in front of his canoe and spends a long time studying just how the front of the hull will slide through the water and rise on the waves. He gets up, shaves off a little wood, perhaps only a paper thinness, and sits down again to look some more, his eyes flowing with the water over the hull. He rises, shaves some more, and sits down once again. Finally he is satisfied, and only then is his act of creation complete.

Surprisingly, the very end of the boat, which meets the water first, is not only rather blunt, but variations in its width and shape are not believed to play a critical role in the performance of the canoe. Sometimes the flat surfaces are the same width on both sides, sometimes one side is wider; the latter is true only of hulls with an asymmetrical plan, and the wide side is then on the more curved or outrigger side of the hull. This bluntness and variability is surprising for two reasons. At a naive level one expects a hull to be sharp in cleaving the water, not blunt, and most small Western boats are built this way. It is surprising too, however, because the bluntness conforms to principles which have been worked out as preferable only in recent years in tow tanks and model basins in the United States and elsewhere. Furthermore, this research has indicated that a wide range in the amount of bluntness frequently makes little difference in performance, precisely as the Puluwatan builders contend. That they are right is attested to also by the very small bow wave which the Puluwat sailing canoe produces despite its bluntness even when it is traveling quite fast.

Whether all the principles through which the canoe-builders guide their work would prove out as fully as the design of the hull ends cannot be established. It did not prove feasible to obtain lines from the hulls, lines which could be translated into models and tested. A tabulation was made of some dimensions and some characteristics of all the interisland sailing canoes, along with ratings of the relative performance of each under different conditions. However, the simple measurements and observations which could be recorded in this way did not show any significant correlation with the performance ratings for the canoes. Even such obvious things as the width of the hull (measured at the top) relative to its length did not seem to predict either speed or load-carrying ability. However, since some men, most notably Ikuliman, can consistently build canoes of outstanding performance, and have reasons for doing what they do each time even if I was not able to understand and record them all, the conclusion is inescapable that there are principles which predictably govern performance and my tabulation was simply too crude to capture them.

In concluding the discussion of sailing canoes one other set of scattered observations should be brought together. These have to do with recent innovations in the design and manufacture of the canoes. They are important not merely because they reflect the ability of Puluwatans to integrate innovations creatively and selectively into their traditional ways. They are important also because they have resulted in very substantial improvements in the performance of sailing canoes. The most important single innovation was the replacement after World War II of woven pandanus sails by cloth. As we have seen cloth is not only more efficient and durable but also is lighter and more manageable, especially when wet, and among other things does not need to be shielded from rain. The sheave block on the sheet is another improvement. It has relieved just enough of the effort of adjusting the sail to give the navigator considerably improved resiliency in his response to minute changes in wind speed and direction, so he does a better job of sailing.

Finally, the surface of the hull has become much smoother. It offers less resistance to the water and the canoe therefore goes faster. This smoothing was accomplished in two stages. The first came when iron tools were traded from the Spanish, beginning in the eighteenth century, often by making grueling trips of over six hundred miles to Saipan. These tools included not only iron blades for the traditional adze but later also planes, tools especially well adapted to smoothing off a finished surface. The second stage came in very recent years, and resulted from dropping the taboos and rituals associated with canoe-building, opening up the basic skills of canoe-building to everyone. Many more men are now available to lend a hand with adze and plane and thus spend more time on the tedious and time-consuming task of smoothing every tiny imperfection in the contour of the hull. However intangible their achievements in other contexts, this is once when the impact of Christian missionaries is concrete and measurable, even though perhaps not planned! The smoother canoes built since the taboos were abandoned actually do in general go faster.

In combination these innovations have made a real difference. Trips which formerly took four or five days are now made in two or three. Tacking, although still not highly efficient, is more readily undertaken and is not just a last resort. Not only have these improvements in performance made canoe travel easier, they have also increased its reliability and safety, because the shorter the trip the less opportunity there is for the navigator to be led astray by changes in the weather, vagaries of current, or unexpected storms. This is an art which never stops growing.

4 The Navigators

The masters of Puluwat are its navigators. True, in some situations there are traditional chiefs who take charge, while on other occasions responsibilities are assumed by the island magistrate or other officials elected under the aegis of the administration. Each of these in his time commands a measure of authority and respect, but to none accrues the prestige and distinction accorded a navigator. Often the formal offices themselves are filled by navigators, just as navigators are frequently also canoe-builders. Even here, however, men seem proudest and most comfortable in their roles as navigators.

On neighboring Truk until the 1920's the highest status was accorded to a class of diviners and magicians known as *itang* (Gladwin, 1960: 44-45). Their power, their knowledge, and an esoteric form of speech known only within their ranks set them apart from other men. On Puluwat there were itang too who could talk in their own tongue to their colleagues on Truk and the other islands. For Puluwatans, however, even the knowledge and powers of itang were less than those of the navigator. The principal advantage of being an itang was merely that when a Puluwat canoe visited another island the Puluwat itang could talk persuasively and privately to his influential counterparts there.

This limited use of itang neatly illustrates why it is almost inevitable that navigators must have the highest status on Puluwat. In their seafaring society the most important happenings are those associated with travel by sea to other islands. Since this travel is, or was until recently, performed exclusively on canoes commanded by navigators it follows that most of the really significant occasions in Puluwat life are controlled by them.

Yet navigators are not overbearing or haughty. They derive from their status an assurance sufficiently complete that it requires no continuing reaffirmation through displays of dominance. Ashore they seek no special deference and feel no need to protect their dignity. Some of the finest navigators enjoy on occasion getting drunk and making fools of themselves, but this is no discredit to them. Nor do they change their modest manner at sea. Theirs is a relaxed and informal command.

Half a dozen men on Puluwat are considered master navigators. This is a status compounded both of seniority and of skill and knowledge. Seniority has a somewhat ambiguous quality now since initiation ceremonies for navigators were abandoned a few years ago. This ambiguity will doubtless become more severe as the older men whose primacy is clearly established die and younger men who were never formally initiated into the ranks of navigators take over. Even now some of the older men who have never formally sponsored a student's initiation feel their own stature is slightly diminished. Already too one young man still in his thirties, Rapwi (Rah-pwee), feels the lack of this ceremony. By studying diligently with his paternal uncle from the age of twelve he has mastered all the skills of navigation. During our stay on Puluwat he even completed the most taxing of all the exercises in the navigator's repertoire, the direct trip from Puluwat to Satawal. Yet he was not included among the list of senior navigators which I requested early in our stay in order to find an instructor for myself. Subsequent inquiries created discomfort and an unhappy agreement that by rights he should have been on the list—yet how could he be when he had never been initiated? That Rapwi has a problem now is attrib-

Rapwi, Puluwat's youngest navigator, setting out with his aging uncle-instructor Angora on his final apprenticeship trial, the direct 130-mile run to tiny Satawal

utable to his precocity. Other young men are pressing close behind, already navigating alone on short trips and gaining experience by sailing in convoy to more distant islands. These include, for example, the island magistrate, in his late thirties and soon in addition to come into his own as a master canoe-builder. Behind them are yet others, still in training, some growing rapidly in knowledge and skill and others not, some eager and some lazy—although perhaps this "laziness" is a way of explaining ineptitude, a sign that they may never qualify to navigate alone.

Navigation is not easy to learn. The senior navigators often discourage young men from trying because they are fairly sure they will not make it. For the same reason many young men never even volunteer to try. Presumably too some do not actually care enough to bother with the long grind. Although on Puluwat this may seem improbable, there is perhaps no culture in which a central activity, no matter how heavily favored and rewarded, is uniformly embraced by everyone eligible to participate. In some cultures it is more difficult than others to avoid joining in. On Puluwat it is easy. Although the role of navigator brings rich rewards of virtuosity and membership in a distinguished elite, the many who for whatever reason are not so accomplished are never publicly criticized. This is true whether they tried and failed to learn or never cared to try.

Despite the several ways in which young men can be deterred from entering training, of those who do undertake it less than half, probably substantially less than half, complete the course and achieve recognition as master navigators. Others, having completed their training, are known as navigators but are also known never to have achieved the skill and precision of judgment necessary to complete long trips. They too make only short trips or travel in convoy even though in point of years many are quite senior. Because of the rich satisfaction and prestige which reward the master navigator, failure even though private must come very hard. Despite our relationship of complete trust, Hipour would not identify for me any men of whose failures he was aware, and he was sure there were many more about whom he had never heard. Failure of anyone in the study of navigation is not a decent subject for discussion.

Navigation is taught both at sea and on land. In a sense every Puluwat man has had some instruction in navigation at sea because every man travels on canoes. Whether or not he is destined to study navigation, he is bound to learn how the canoe feels as it rides over the waves, and how this feel alters with changes in course, in wind, or in weather. He acquires skill in steering, and perhaps in handling the sheet. He becomes familiar with the different kinds of seabirds, and with the habits of those which can guide a canoe to its destination. He comes to know how a canoe handles, how fast it travels under different conditions, how it drifts with the sail down, and the differences between various canoes. Nowadays he may learn a little about the compass, especially if a navigator is thinking of taking him into instruction. He can detect reefs many fathoms down by subtle changes in the color of the water and in the character of waves on the surface, and he learns to see them under all kinds of sky and conditions of the sea. No man can avoid being exposed to all these things and learning them all if he lives the life which is the heritage of birth on Puluwat. Some learn them better than others, and this can have an important bearing on their eligibility for instruction as navigators.

Formal instruction begins on land. It demands that great masses of factual information be committed to memory. This

Angora teaching new apprentices the star compass with pebbles

information is detailed, specific, and potentially of life-or-death importance. It is taught by a senior navigator to one or several students, some young, some older. Often they sit together in the canoe house, perhaps making little diagrams with pebbles on the mats which cover the sandy floor. The pebbles usually represent stars, but they are also used to illustrate islands and how the islands "move" as they pass the canoe on one side or the other.

In the past instruction was very secret. There was much magic and esoteric knowledge which could be known only by the privileged few. Some of it could be used against the navigator in sorcery if others knew it. In addition the navigational skills were and still are valuable property, willingly passed on to relatives but taught to nonrelatives only for a stiff price. It is even said that a few crucial elements of navigation were often explained to nonrelatives in somewhat garbled form despite their having paid well for their instruction. This was especially true of the component of navigational knowledge referred to in the next chapter as "sealife." Suffice it to say here that sealife is one of those tantalizing examples of a body of esoteric knowledge which from our "rational" Western point of view we cannot believe a reasonable man would take seriously. Yet even now with the passing of belief in the supernatural, sealife is still learned and cherished with deadly earnestness and is still highly valued, with a conviction that one day it may save a navigator's life. However, it is no longer considered any more critical than the other arts of navigation. All are still intrinsically so valuable that instruction must remain somewhat confidential. You do not give away something which you could sell. However, some parts are more carefully protected than others.

Although the divisions are not rigorously maintained, distinguishable subsystems exist within the overall system of navigation. Some of these subsystems are separately named and taught as separate courses in a larger curriculum, while others are considered more in the nature of general knowledge to be taught whenever they seem to fit in. At the heart of the whole system, which will be described in detail in the next chapter, are the stars, specifically the points or directions where certain stars rise and set around the horizon. The identities and positions of these stars are so basic to travel at sea that everyone claims to know them, although it turned out that when nonnavigators were asked, their identifications invariably contained some discrepancies. The stars are taught by placing a circle of pebbles on the ground, each standing for a star which the student must learn to name. This placement in a circle is itself interesting because earlier German accounts from Puluwat describe arranging the pebbles in a square, and this is still done on some of the islands to the west. On Puluwat, however, the instructors have apparently long since adopted the circular shape of a compass card even though compasses were quite rare until recent postwar years. The points of a compass are even identified with the same names as the navigation stars.

Next come the star courses. These are the courses, with respect to the rising or setting of stars, which are sailed in order to get from one island to another. They must be learned for every pair of islands between which a navigator might conceivably find himself sailing. When it is borne in mind that there are at least twenty-six separate islands or atolls to which living Puluwat navigators have sailed, plus a number more for which a navigator is expected to know the sailing directions so he could sail there if called upon to do so (for example, Hipour's trip to Saipan), and furthermore that nominally one could sail from any one of these islands to any other, the number of possible island pairs between which star courses must be learned grows to formidable size. The directions for fifty-five commonly made journeys were recorded (one hundred and ten if return routings are included) and the more remote islands add as many more.

This is a body of knowledge which is not kept secret, but there is scarcely any need to do so. No one could possibly learn it except through the most painstaking and lengthy instruction, so no outsider could pick it up merely by occasional eavesdropping. Instead it is taught and memorized through endless reiteration and testing. The learning job is not complete until the student at his instructor's request can start with any island in the known ocean and rattle off the stars both going and returning between that island and all the others which might conceivably be reached directly from there. Although this recitation of a sequence of stars between a given island and all the other islands around it is occasionally used even by an accomplished navigator to refresh his memory, it is not a litany memorized by rote. Not only did my instructor Hipour state flatly that it was not (I suggested to him an analogy between this recital of stars and prayers chanted in church), but in addition a navigator the moment he is asked can usually give at will not only the star course but also a lot of other information about sailing between any two islands. In other words, all this information is learned so that each item is discretely available, as it were floating on the surface of the navigator's mind rather than embedded in a long mnemonic chain. This is a long task, and one which requires patient commitment by both instructor and student.

After the star courses, or frequently along with them, come the many other subjects which will occupy us in the chapter to follow. These include knowledge of currents and other special conditions affecting travel between each of the many island pairs; *etak* (eh-tack), the system used for keeping track of distance traveled; how to read several kinds of information from the waves; navigation in storms, including keeping track of position while drifting; navigation when tacking upwind; techniques for locating, even in the dark, passes through the reefs of various islands; forecasting the weather through an almanac of rising and setting stars (not the navigation stars) and the moon; sealife; star courses, and sometimes long sequences of star courses, for remote and occasionally mythological islands; and, in the past, spells of magic and divination and the taboos governing the work of the sea.

There is some variation in the teaching of these subjects. Not surprisingly the differences between teachers are generally greater the farther the subject matter is removed from practical techniques of actual navigation, that is, the more it becomes esoteric. Although there are doubtless minor individual variations in what is known and taught and what is not, most of the differences can be attributed to the existence of two schools or traditions of navigation and navigators. (There are said to be still other schools in the islands to the west, but Puluwat knows only two.) These are known by the names of their mythical founders, Warieng (Wa-ree-eng) and Fanur (Fan-oor, "under the banana plant").

Because there are so few differences between them in technical aspects of navigation the practical consequences of having two divergent schools are almost nil. Nevertheless, sectarian rivalries are often strong between them, rivalries which are still evident but were most forcefully expressed in the past during the initiation ceremonies for navigators. In those ceremonies (which being of the past will not be described in any detail here) the navigators of each school would vie with their rivals in their display of knowledge. All the pent-up secrets of navigation flooded forth before laymen as well as fellow navigators, but the volume of information was so great it could not possibly be remembered. Although there is no longer any occasion for public rivalry a real reluctance remains to pass along secret names and other esoterica if they might fall into the hands (or rather ears) of a navigator of the other school.

At his initiation the neophyte was sponsored by his instructor, reflecting honor on both. Sometimes several men were initiated at once. The change in status of the student was obvious, but the teacher also grew in stature through being the one privileged to "uncover the bowl," that is, to perform the act which symbolized the right of his student to eat in the company of navigators. Nowadays both instructor and student must settle for the diminished symbolism of the student navigator making his first voyage, usually accompanied by his instructor. These voyages were made in the past also, but then they represented only a final phase of instruction (after the initiation) of minimal significance.

Now as in the past instruction beyond the first stages of intensive learning takes place alternately on land and at sea. There are many things which can only be observed, practiced, and tested when under way on a canoe. Some of these are relatively easy for one born to the sea, but others are difficult, especially the judgments of direction and speed upon which the accuracy of navigation ultimately depends. Of those students who are unable to complete the course, as many fail in the seagoing part of the course as in the learning of factual material on land.

The instructor who labors so long and patiently with his student is almost always a relative of some sort. Although it is possible to purchase instruction, and some Puluwat navigators have gone to other islands (especially Pulap) to teach students for a good price, out of slightly more than forty instructions recorded of native Puluwat navigators only one was purchased by a man for whom there was available no master navigator sufficiently closely related. The ideal relationship is father teaching son. In many cases this is realized, sometimes literally, sometimes for an adopted son or brother's son. Many other relationships, however, are called upon, including brothers and even the son of a wife's brother. This being an essentially matrilineal society it is to be expected that a number of men would teach their sisters' sons or similar relatives. This does happen, but surprisingly infrequently. In the relationships recorded, which include not only all living navigators but also some from the past and some current apprenticeships of necessarily uncertain outcome, less than one-quarter were determined by matrilineal ties of one kind or another. The trend instead is clearly patrilineal: over two-thirds of the relationships were established in a variety of ways through a male line of descent.

It follows from this, since instructors teach their students in the school of navigation to which they themselves belong, that affiliation with the Warieng or Fanur traditions of navigation by being patrilineally determined is completely unrelated to membership in the various matrilineal clans which dominate the social structure of Puluwat. In canoe-house membership, however, many of the same factors are at work which determine the selection of navigation instructors, making this a largely patrilineal group also. In addition, there is obvious convenience in having instructor and student living and working under one roof and having rights usually to the same canoes. Thus it is more common than not to find all the men in one canoe house belonging to the same school of navigation, many of them taught by the same master navigator and free to share whatever secrets and skills their degree of accomplishment may warrant.

Having described the professional training and associations of navigators, only one task remains before taking up the analysis of the navigation system. This is to recount the circumstances of my own instruction—how I came to have Hipour as my instructor, and how the instructional process unfolded—and then to describe the nature of the intellectual as well as personal relationship which developed between us. This is necessary not only as documentation for the analysis which will follow, but also because it may offer some insights into the building of bridges between diverse cognitive traditions.

Because my primary purpose was to learn and understand a body of expert knowledge, it was evident that I would need an instructor who was not only fully qualified but would also be able to communicate effectively with me. Communication in this situation was a matter both of language and of explanatory ability. The language was Trukese; this is fairly closely related to Puluwat but not mutually comprehensible. However, all Puluwat men learn Trukese in order to be able to talk to the people with whom they have their most extensive trade relations. In a short time I regained the fluency in Trukese which I had acquired twenty years earlier, but the combination of minor dialectical differences and the fact that Trukese was a second language for both me and my Puluwat informants made it more difficult to talk with some people than with others. This variation was a function of their articulation, their fluency in Trukese, and perhaps also of the island in the atoll where they had learned the language since there are noticeable local differences within Truk—I had learned on Romonum, in the western part of the atoll.

In addition to differences in language it appeared likely that some people would be able to explain procedures and concepts to me more readily than others. This proved to be markedly true. Selection of an instructor on this basis necessarily introduced a possibility that a person so chosen would be more "Western" in his style of thinking than the average Puluwatan. This was not because explanation is a uniquely Western accomplishment, but rather because to be useful explanations in this case had to be cast in a form which would in some fashion be meaningful to me, a person of Western intellectual upbringing. The effect of such selection—if indeed there was any—could not even be guessed, especially at the outset. However, since a principal purpose of this research was to discover *differences* in logical style between Puluwat and the European tradition, selection along these dimensions was bound to be conservative in result. However, of overriding importance was the fact that if my instructor could not explain the system of navigation to me I would never be able to learn it at all and the entire enterprise would have been in vain. The precaution was well taken. As it turned out for two or three key aspects of navigation literally days of work were needed before Hipour and I were satisfied that I truly understood how those principles worked and were used.

To assure that my instructor would be fully competent and at the same time able to communicate his art I obtained a list of all the master navigators on the island and spent some time with each. Getting a list proved very simple. Within a couple of days of our arrival on Puluwat I had retained a young man in his late twenties, Teruo (Tare-oo-oh), to be my increasingly useful research assistant. At his suggestion I asked the island magistrate (actually a substitute, because the elected magistrate was at a meeting on Truk) and the traditional chiefs of the two main villages to draw up such a list. They readily agreed and after some discussion arrived at five names.

There were a few others who were excluded from the list for various reasons. One man was unavailable, being away from Puluwat for some time. Two were senior navigators too old and

Teruo, ready for sea in a borrowed hat and watch

sick to be effective instructors. As it developed, there was also an effort by the chiefs not to include more than one man who had been trained by a given instructor at one time; they had assumed incorrectly that I sought some range or variation in skills. It is not certain how many additional names might have been included were it not for this misunderstanding. However, judging later from records of recent trips only two other men appeared to be able to assume full responsibility for navigation on long journeys. These were Rapwi, the exceptionally young navigator mentioned above, and—of all people—Hipour, the man who became my instructor. When I approached each of the men on the list to ask their cooperation, one of the older men insisted upon deferring to Hipour as a person better able than he to explain navigation to me. I discovered then that he and Hipour were closely related and had learned together from the same instructor, which explained the omission of Hipour from my original list. I am not sure why this man demurred, but on one later occasion he surprised me with another unexpected reluctance, although he was otherwise very cordial. In any event I checked with the chiefs and they agreed that Hipour would probably be a better instructor.

The final list included: Angora (Aang-oh-rah), the oldest active navigator on Puluwat and teacher of Rapwi; Ikuliman, also old but considered the most skilled navigator of all; Tawaru (Tah-wah-roo), an old friend who was magistrate on Puluwat years before when I used to visit the island in an administrative role; Hipour; and one other competent but not outstanding man whose inclusion on the list I never fully understood. With each of these men I spent a day or two recording an account of a recent long trip made to some other island, starting with their first intent to make the trip and concluding with hauling out the canoe at the end of the journey. I asked a lot of questions. Thus I not only had an opportunity for many interchanges with each man but also obtained an excellent general introduction to the nature of voyaging from Puluwat. Teruo was present at all the interviews to be sure language would not be an insurmountable barrier: he had spent several years in school on Truk and his Trukese was excellent. To my surprise (I thought they would consider it childish), all of the navigators were also willing to undertake a psychological assessment procedure (described in Chapter 6) involving pairing different colors of poker chips.

Upon completion of the interviews there was little doubt that Hipour offered the best combination of skills of communication and of explanation among the five navigators. Although Ikuliman could often explain things very well and had great knowledge, he had lost most of his teeth and as a result I had difficulty in understanding him. Later, when we got to know each other better in less formal contexts, I became used to his speech. Then I did use Ikuliman quite extensively both for my instruction in canoe design and to obtain the Fanur version of navigation to contrast with the Warieng school to which Hipour belonged.

As soon as I had informed the other navigators of my decision Hipour and I began our work. My colleagues and I paid all our informants for the time they spent with us, but I paid Hipour more than twice the amount the others received. This was intended to compensate at least symbolically for the transfer of his professional knowledge in addition to the expenditure of his time. Although the total amount paid was far less than would be demanded for full training in navigation from a non-relative, it seemed to both of us about right for the special circumstances of my instruction.

As an introduction I explained to Hipour and to others my interest in understanding and recording something so obviously intelligent as the work of a Puluwat navigator, and also my desire to make known to history their detailed techniques should the day come when the art is no longer practiced. At the same time I promised to report it in such a way that no one, however fluent in English, could read the book I would soon be writing and thereby learn without additional instruction all that was needed in order to be able to navigate. (Even if my notes should contain that degree of detail, which they do not, their publication would require a volume several times the size of this.)

Most of the instruction was verbal. We sat at a table, a chart of the Central Caroline Islands between us and a typewriter in front of me. I recorded everything in English on the typewriter as we went along. Hipour cannot read or write. Although he had never previously used a chart he soon learned to "read"

Hipour the navigator, his son behind him

this one, easily distinguishing the conventional signs for islands, reefs, soundings, and the like. We made no effort to follow a traditional form of instruction; that is, I did not try to play the role of an actual neophyte learning to navigate. This would have been artificial and clumsy, especially as there were some things a Puluwatan would bring to his instruction which I could not know, such as the various things one can sense when riding on a canoe in the dark, and other things which I had no need to know, such as the specific names of each of the fishes and other beings which comprise the navigational "sealife" around each island.

Instead Hipour began by telling me of the star courses and other information necessary to sail from Puluwat to each of its surrounding islands near and far. When we had finished Puluwat we went on to the sailing directions back and forth between each of the other island pairs until we had covered every seaway he knew. When something came up which I did not know or understand we digressed to discuss it. Only a few quite discrete topics such as weather forecasting were saved for separate discussion later.

In addition to short trips with other men I went on one all-day fishing trip with Hipour in order to learn things I could not learn on land—waves, canoe handling, the flight of birds, the look of deep reefs in sunlight and shadow, and many other discriminations which have to be seen and felt as well as told. Finally, when we both felt my knowledge was complete Hipour took me on his canoe to Pulusuk and back. It was a relatively short trip of only forty miles each way, but was planned so that we would have some travel both in the daylight and at night under the stars. Thus it provided a sample of most of the circumstances of normal navigation.

In the course of this instruction, which lasted slightly over a month, we had many arguments. Neither Hipour nor I was willing to concede an issue until it had been fully resolved. Sometimes I won, as when he occasionally proposed a star course between two islands which did not seem to me appropriate to their positions on the chart. On those occasions he would talk in the evening with Apwi (Ah-pwee), his own teacher of navigation many years before. Apwi was old and crippled with the infirmities of his years (he has since died), but he could still be-rate Hipour as if he were a little boy who had forgotten his lessons. If he was wrong, in the morning Hipour would show up, amused but chagrined, to confess his error. At other times we argued over principles. These arguments I usually lost, most commonly when Hipour would patiently explain that I had failed to take into account something which was obvious to him and should often have been obvious to me had I thought it through carefully. In any event we never left a topic until I had summarized for him in my own words my understanding of the subject and he had agreed it was correct.

Hipour showed no curiosity about matters of history. Unlike many Trukese of my earlier experience he never asked any questions about the role of Japan or the United States in World War II, even though Puluwat was seriously dislocated by the building and operation of a fighter strip on Allei. As another example he had a compass, a great heavy affair obviously designed for use on a ship of some size. It had been given by a Spanish priest on Truk to a great-uncle of Hipour's who gave it to his nephew, who in turn passed it on to Hipour. It had been made by Plath in Hamburg and carried a serial number, so I offered to see if I could trace its history and let him know. Although he was polite he was completely uninterested.

In contrast he was very interested in a star chart, as were a number of other men. This interest surprised me since seeing stars on paper could add nothing to his already complete knowledge of the heavens. However, it illustrated well the flexibility and insight of Puluwatans in perceiving spatial relationships. *Bernard's Nautical Star Chart,* published in Glasgow, is a schematic diagram designed solely for the use of Western celestial navigators. It is laden with conventions and symbols. The stars are shown as five-pointed, magnitude is represented by size, the stars listed in nautical almanacs are in red while the rest are black, lines are drawn between those which are linked in the constellations of our European folklore, the projection is Mercator's with gross distortion of the polar regions, and finally east and west are reversed so the chart must be held over the head to look "right." It is doubtless fine for a Scottish mariner but one would think its many cabalistic signs would render it utterly incomprehensible to a Puluwatan. Far from it. After my first lesson in star identifications I could point to a few stars on the chart by their Puluwat names. Hipour at once understood what I was demonstrating. After puzzling over the whole chart scarcely a minute he began pointing to other stars and naming them. I got out the list of equivalents given by Goodenough (1953) and all the identifications agreed. I later tried this with some other men. The navigators in particular understood the chart with no more trouble than Hipour. Tawaru was so delighted he insisted I leave the chart with him on my departure. I did so even though I felt sure he knew more than the chart did. I was also personally delighted because this saved me many late nights of peering into the heavens to verify star identifications.

Another example of Hipour's presumably not unique spatial and angular sophistication followed upon my turning over to him, shortly before my departure, the chart we had both been using of the islands around Puluwat. This was laminated in flexible plastic for protection, and had the familiar circles which show degrees of bearing and magnetic deviation. After taking the chart along on a trip to Pikelot, Hipour brought it back to me and inquired how to transfer a line of bearing between two islands on the chart to an adjacent bearing circle. He believed that if he could do this, even though he could not read the bearing numbers he could count divisions on the circle on the chart and thus transfer readings to his compass. Unfortunately in the last days before I left the United States I had been unable to purchase the parallel rulers which are customarily used for this purpose and instead had brought along an adjustable protractor. The protractor was especially inconvenient because it moved only through a 45-degree span and had to be turned around to complete the 90-degree sector. All in all the process was so complicated and confusing that I put it aside for use only if in an emergency I had to navigate myself. No such emergency arose and I forgot it. So I got out the protractor and did my best to explain it to Hipour. To my amazement he soon said he understood, and showed me by applying the device a couple of times in ways that seemed appropriate. I was not on the island long enough thereafter to follow up and determine if he really had mastered the protractor, but he was at least enthusiastic and delighted to have it.

It is difficult to sum up my relationship with Hipour. In a colonial situation it is unhappily meaningless to talk of equality, but on a personal level we attained a mutual respect and affection which I believe he valued as fully as I. Intellectually we were able to insist upon discussing issues each within his own frame of logical premises and constructs. Hipour explained things to me in his terms and I reinterpreted them back in mine. As time went on each of us became familiar with the thinking of the other so we could borrow analogies from the other's system to develop a point, but I believe we remained throughout true to the logic particular to each of our traditions.

The consequence of this, which probably should not have surprised me but nevertheless did, was that I found there were very large domains in which we were inclined to process information by identical logics, even though we might sort it into different kinds of cognitive boxes. At the same time there were ways in which he surpassed me, and others in which I went beyond him. In some perceptual modes, such as sensing the direction of waves of the presence of reefs deep below the surface, Hipour could work with discriminations I not only could not perceive but could scarcely conceive. For my part I was able, indeed eager, to explore in my mind the implications of novel and imaginary relations between facts, relations which to Hipour (I felt) were meaningless simply because they were not real or useful.

However, in these speculations I anticipate issues better discussed after we have before us the navigational system which is the finest expression of the Puluwat intellectual tradition. While attending to this it is essential to bear constantly in mind the point just made. The system I present is the one used by Puluwat navigators, described as faithfully and accurately as I can, but the terms in which it is described are necessarily my own, that is, Western. This means not only the use of English words and English categories of thought. It means also that explanations of why and how various elements in the system are effective must be cast in a logical mold familiar to me, and to you the reader, or else they will not make sense. Most of these explanations can easily be made in ways which do violence neither to Puluwat nor to Western modes of understanding, but some are more difficult. Therefore, the account which follows is a description of a cognitive system organized to make sense to us, not an attempt through words to get inside a Puluwat navigator's head and think his thoughts in his way.

5 Navigation under the Big Bird

Two statements about Puluwat navigation will serve to locate it among methods used elsewhere in the world. First, it is entirely a dead reckoning system. Second, it depends upon features of sea and sky which are characteristic only of the locality in which it is used, that is, the chain of islands in the Western and Central Carolines from Yap to Truk and the Mortlocks, where it was historically known and in which its use survives with varying degrees of vitality today.

Navigation by dead reckoning means that one's position at any time is determined solely on the basis of distance and direction traveled since leaving the last known location. Put the other way around it means that if you lose track of how far you have come from where you were, you are lost. In contrast to this, Western celestial navigation, loran, and other techniques make it possible to establish a precise position without any knowledge of where you have been, except in the most general sense of knowing what part of the world you are in. The latter methods depend, however, on a very complex technology either of time-keeping and star-tracking or of electronics. Yet dead reckoning is inherently no more or less accurate than they are. If there are available sophisticated techniques for keeping track of direction and distance traveled it is possible by dead reckoning alone to establish a position with great precision. Inertial navigation, for example, is a system solely of dead reckoning which is widely used as a primary method of navigation on everything from submarines to missiles, and a lot of ships and aircraft in between. True, with less sophisticated technology the accuracy of dead reckoning declines. Yet it must be remembered that none of the Western techniques are even conceivable in the absence of a complex technology. Celestial navigation had to await astronomy and the engineering marvel which is a chronometer, while loran and other still more sophisticated techniques were born only in the last quarter-century of our electronic age.

The fact that the navigation methods of Puluwat and its neighboring islands are localized to the area is of significance principally to students of the Pacific. Interest in native navigation on the Pacific Ocean was at first stimulated and later stultified by an increasingly sterile argument over whether our fragmentary knowledge of ancient Polynesian navigation would support a hypothesis of the peopling of Polynesia by deliberate exploration or by accidental voyages only (Golson, 1963; Sharp, 1964). Because this dispute has become largely futile, when I say that navigation in the Caroline Islands is specialized to the locality I do so in part to declare that the description on the following pages is largely irrelevant to the Polynesian controversy.

This is not to say that Caroline Islanders use a completely unique set of principles or depend upon observations of quite different natural phenomena than other Pacific navigators. There are limits to what is available for detection by the unaided human senses in any tropical ocean. Waves, winds, clouds; stars, sun, moon; birds, fish, and the water itself comprise about all there is to be seen, felt, heard, or smelled. All of these have probably been used by every native navigator in the tropical Pacific. However, they may be used for quite different purposes in different areas. The Carolinian navigator uses waves principally to maintain a steady course, while in the Marshall Islands to the east the large number of closely spaced atolls interferes with the regular run of the swells, making them of little value for course holding. Instead the Marshallese navigators were until recently students of the patterns of interference set up in waves by the islands and could use these characteristic patterns as guides for sailing from one nearby island to the next, an entirely different principle. In the Society Islands, much farther to the east and south, we are told the navigators also used waves for steering, but probably on the same principles as the Carolinians. However, the weather systems in those southern waters are entirely different and would create wave systems different from the Carolines not only in direction and size but probably also in steadiness and therefore in reliability; thus the principle would be the same but practice would differ. Comparable local characteristics are evident in the latitude of stars, in the maximum distances to be navigated between islands, in the species and habits of seabirds, in the distribution and typical depth of reefs, and in the size and visibility of islands.

No one set of observed phenomena will suffice to guide a sailing craft under all the conditions it will encounter at sea. Many categories of information must be integrated into a system whose diverse elements supplement each other to achieve a satisfactory level of accuracy and reliability. What is to be considered satisfactory is also a relative matter, depending among other things on the difficulty of the navigational problems to be solved. Any system which guides people to their destination without incurring risks which they find unacceptable must be judged satisfactory. The fact that the Puluwat navigator does not use the wave interference patterns upon which the Marshallese depended (until they recently ceased sailing in canoes between islands), or that he ignores the zenith stars said to be known by some Polynesians, or conversely that the Marshallese were not as sophisticated in their knowledge of stars as the Carolinians and therefore could not make as long voyages, none of these should suggest that one was superior to the other. If a particular kind of knowledge is not known or not used in an area, it is probably because such knowledge is either inappropriate or unnecessary there. There can therefore be no absolute basis for comparing one system with another. There is no question as to the adequacy of the Carolinian system as it is used on

Puluwat. Since our information on virtually every other system used in the Pacific is in one respect or another incomplete, the description which follows will be confined to Puluwat.*

Successful navigation from one island to another under a system of dead reckoning falls into three phases or sets of tasks. First, one must set out in a direction such that, knowing the conditions to be expected en route, one will arrive in the vicinity of the island of destination. Second, while on the way to this island the canoe must be held steady on its course and a running estimate maintained of its current position. Finally, when the craft is near its goal there should be available techniques for locating the destination island and heading toward it. If the system is to work it is necessary that the amount of absolute error introduced during the first two phases, that is, in the initial heading and the en-route course, be less than the maximum range at which it is possible to locate and home in on the final island. In other words, when you are heading for an island you must be able to come close enough to it to find it. These three logical divisions of the navigation process—initial course plan and heading, en-route course and position-keeping, and homing on the destination—will guide our discussion of Puluwat navigation. However, underlying all of these steps is an understanding of the stars and star courses used by the Puluwat navigator. Accordingly, I will begin with a description of these, and also incidentally of the way in which the magnetic compass has been integrated into the star system in recent years.

The stars, as we all know, rise in the east and set in the west, as do the sun and the moon. Away from the equator, as in the United States and Europe, they rise above the horizon at an angle and describe a sloping arc through the sky, an effect produced by being located toward the "top" of the spinning globe. Near the equator, however, the stars appear to rise and set vertically, except those in the extreme northern and southern sky. This means that even though a star is sighted some distance

*The reader interested in comparative studies is referred to Lewis (1964), Golson (1963), and Sharp (1964) for the Polynesian navigation controversy; to Hornell (1936) for a summary of major early sources on various areas of the Pacific; to Sarfert (1911) and Damm and Sarfert (1935) for Puluwat and adjacent islands sixty years ago; and to Burrows and Spiro (1957) on Ifalik and Alkire (1970) on Woleai for relatively contemporary accounts of navigation on neighboring islands.

above the horizon it is nevertheless almost directly over the spot where it has risen or where it will set. In other words, a star anywhere near the horizon does not change appreciably in its bearing or direction as it rises or sinks. It is this quality of vertical movement in equatorial stars which has been observed and utilized by Carolinian navigators. They have selected various stars both for their prominence and because the places of their rising and setting are spaced around the horizon. In this way the sky on a clear night becomes a vast compass, the various headings picked out by familiar stars as they move up and down near the horizon. Yet the particular star which is named and stands for a given bearing is visible in a setting or rising position only part of the time. At some seasons it does not appear at all. Even when it is visible it spends part of the night so high in the sky that it is not possible to obtain a bearing by looking at it. For these reasons other stars are noted and remembered which are at the same celestial latitude—"travel the same road"—and can substitute for the named navigation star when it is unavailable.

Thirty-two directions or bearings are defined by the navigation stars, which happens also to be the number of points on a traditional mariner's compass. The thirty-two stars in the Puluwat navigation system are, however, historically much older than the advent of the Western compass in this area, and are therefore not derived from it. Although the stars are spaced around the horizon they are not exactly the same distance apart, and therefore do not quite coincide with the points of the mariner's compass.

On Puluwat the cardinal direction is east, under the rising of Altair, the "Big Bird." However, the star compass system can most readily be described to a Westerner by beginning with the North Star, Polaris, "the star which never moves." The North Star is low at the latitude of the Carolines, roughly 7 degrees north, and frequently obscured by cumulus clouds which often ring the tropical horizon even at night. Nevertheless, it is highly valued because it is always there and, being close to the horizon, can provide a good bearing when sighted. Near the North Star, and thus rising a little to the east of it, is the Little Dipper. Being so far to the north, the Little Dipper swings in a fairly tight circle about the North Star and does not stay directly over

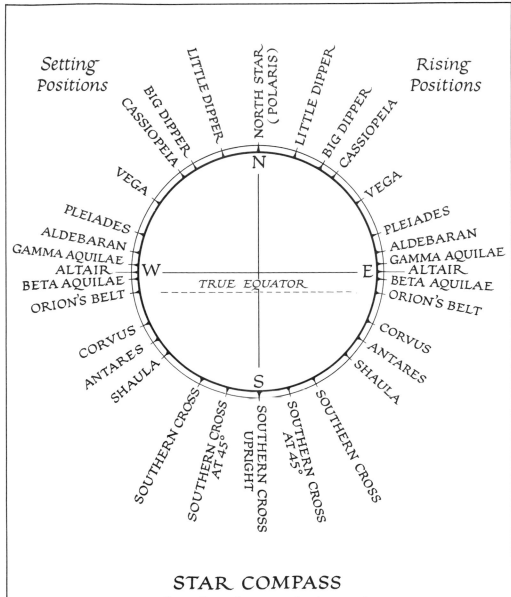

STAR COMPASS
after Goodenough (1953)

its point of rising for as long as the other stars do. It has the further disadvantage of being a constellation of several stars, although its brightest star, Kochab, catches the eye and provides the most obvious bearing. Just as the Little Dipper rises a little to the east of the North Star, so it sets to the west by an equal amount. Therefore it, like most of the other navigation stars (or constellations), defines two points or bearings on the circle of the horizon, its positions of rising and setting being equal amounts to the east or west.

Next around the circle of the sky both east and west (rising and setting) come two large constellations, the Big Dipper and then Cassiopeia. Although the Puluwat navigator does not include in these constellations precisely the same stars which we do, each still covers a great deal of the sky. If they were swung toward each other around the pole without changing their latitude to north or south they would overlap. How then with their great extent and their overlap can they provide the navigator with clearly defined bearings distinct one from the next? The answer appears to be that they do not. Goodenough (1953) in his definitive digest of the published sources on Caroline Island native astronomy, a compendium which was invaluable not only in relieving me of much work but also I suspect in saving me from some blunders, discovered numerous inconsistencies between the sources for various islands with respect to which star in each of these two constellations was used as *the* star to pinpoint the bearing. For his synoptic presentation Goodenough resolved the dilemma by more or less arbitrarily selecting the northernmost star in the Big Dipper and the southernmost in Cassiopeia (which happened to be the "alpha" star in each case). By confining his attention to these stars alone, Goodenough eliminated the overlap between the constellations and could show bearings fairly evenly spaced around the circle of the horizon. However, when I presented these two stars to Hipour and later to Ikuliman, they not only disagreed that they were the correct stars to use, but they did not agree between themselves on which stars were the actual ones used for sighting a course. I even had the feeling that they were groping with an unfamiliar question when I demanded the identification. Hipour was forced to consult his old teacher overnight before giving me an answer.

Before trying to make sense of the vagueness of these northern star bearings we must include in the discussion the southern stars. In the south the situation is little better. Due south is located by the Southern Cross in its upright position. When in this position the Southern Cross is a little too high in the sky for a really good bearing, but otherwise it is satisfactory: it is actually very close to true south and is a neatly symmetrical cross whose center is unambiguous. But the next position to one side, corresponding to the Little Dipper in the north, is the same Southern Cross leaning over at approximately 45 degrees, and next to that is the Southern Cross yet again, lying on its side as it rises and sets. The disadvantages of this arrangement are obvious. By using a single constellation to define five different star positions (two on each side of due south) it is sure that at least four of the positions will be vacant at any one time since the constellation cannot be in two places at once. Almost half the time all five are vacant when the Southern Cross is below the horizon entirely. Furthermore, except for the outside rising and setting positions of the Southern Cross, which have the Centaur at the same apparent latitude, there is no other star or constellation to provide an equivalent bearing when the Southern Cross is not available.

I was puzzled through most of my stay on Puluwat by this, which seemed to me sloppy and vague in a system otherwise so precise. However, the more I pressed for the same consistency and rigor in the northern and southern extremes of the star compass as obtains in the remainder, the more the people I asked became confused, and so did I. It was not until I took my instructional voyage to Pulusuk and back with Hipour that I realized the dilemma was created by a different set of expectations of the system on my part and on theirs. I took it for granted that a star "compass" which formed the heart of a demonstrably accurate system of navigation must itself necessarily be accurate—and therefore I assumed equally accurate—in all its parts. In actuality, however, the Puluwat navigator requires of his star "compass" only two qualities. First, it must be systematic enough that it can be explained and taught. The named star positions ranged around the horizon serve this purpose. Second, it must be sufficiently accurate to guide him to any destination he needs to reach, but gains nothing from being more accurate than is necessary. It is the latter which I was slow to recognize.

The return trip from Pulusuk to Puluwat was intentionally made largely at night. The course was nominally just west of north—toward the setting of the Little Dipper—but in order to make good this course against a westward current and a generally northeasterly wind we held a heading as close to north as possible during much of the journey. Small cumulus clouds were scattered across the sky but, except when distance made them appear to bank up at the horizon, they did not interfere with periodic star sightings until the weather turned bad near the end of the trip. The Little Dipper was up, but was rising during the early hours of the night when we were watching the stars. Thus it was on the wrong side of the North Star for our purposes. The North Star was up as always, but the clouds and some haziness made both it and the Little Dipper hard to keep in sight. The Big Dipper, however, was high and sparkling bright.

As we sailed along through the beautiful night, the wind just right and the sea not too rough but glistening with splashes of phosphorescence, I was watching the stars and asking questions. Occasionally the North Star would shine through the clouds slightly to the right of the heading of the canoe. Even when the North Star was obscured the Big Dipper was there above the clouds, at least part of it in sight all the time. The two "pointer" stars of the Dipper showed where the North Star was hidden. I soon became used to how the Dipper lay and unthinkingly shifted my attention from the North Star's projected position to just the Dipper alone in gauging when we were on course or off. Then I realized that in this northern part of the sky, where all the significant stars are more or less bunched together, it is not necessary to have a discrete point on which to set a course. Instead, to borrow an expressive image from the Mississippi River pilots of Mark Twain's day, you steer by the shape of the sky. You are sailing into a part of the heavens, not toward a dot of light. Even more must this be true on a southerly heading because the extreme southern sky much of the time holds only one bundle of significant stars, the Southern Cross. In both cases the configuration of the stars is sufficiently distinctive that one can estimate a course with considerable ease and accuracy.

Is it accurate enough? Certainly enough for the journey of only forty miles from Puluwat to Pulusuk, but how about more extended passages? Casting about for longer north-south trips with which to make comparisons I was reminded of the configuration of the Central Carolines. The islands are strung out in a long chain running east and west. This has a number of consequences for navigation and one of them is that there are no really long north-south passages to be negotiated anywhere. The longest in the customary Puluwat repertoire is between Pulap and Ulul, almost sixty miles, but even here there are reefs stretching for miles to the side of each destination, reefs which can act as a screen to catch any canoe which might stray from its course. The only really risky north-south passage is between Losap and Namoluk, south of Truk, but this is far from home and is therefore made only by the more experienced navigators. Even this is only sixty miles, less than half the one-hundred-thirty-mile east-west trip between Puluwat and little Satawal alone in the ocean. Thus the sectors wherein the star compass is least accurate are also those where the least accuracy is needed. Add to this that the patterns of the stars near each of the poles lend themselves so well to steering by the shape of the sky rather than to a point and it becomes evident why Puluwat navigators are unconcerned with, almost unaware of, the inconsistency which troubled me between the overlap and ambiguity of the polar regions and the precision of the system to east and west. They feel no intellectual need to maintain uniform standards of precision throughout the directional system and are satisfied that it meets their pragmatic requirements.

Moving south from Cassiopeia through a fairly wide arc of the sky devoid of navigation stars we come to the first of a succession of individual stars or small constellations which occupy positions fairly close together in the eastern sky at their rising and correspondingly in the western sky at their setting. There are nine closely grouped star positions, beginning with Vega on the north and ending with Antares on the south. When these nine rising positions are combined with their setting counterparts on the west, they embrace in the intervals between them sixteen or half of the thirty-two intervals into which the entire star compass is divided. The arc, however, between these same stars is only about 66 degrees on either side, adding up to little more than one-third of the whole 360-degree circle of the sky. This bunching together of star positions to east and west, as well as the precision possible with single bright stars or such compact constellations as the Pleiades, reflects the greater demands for accuracy which are placed on the navigation system as a whole by longer east-west passages.

In the middle of this arc, rising due east, is Altair, the "Big Bird." Just to the north and south of Altair, in the same constellation which we in the West also call a big bird, the Eagle, are its wings, Gamma and Beta Aquilae. Altair is where the count of stars on Puluwat begins, the greatest navigation star of all. Although it actually rises and sets 7 degrees north of the equator, because Puluwat is 7 degrees north, Altair always bears true east and west. Not only that but it has two bright companion stars, Procyon and Bellatrix, on almost exactly the same latitude but around on the other side of the heavens, so that when one is down another is up. Between the three of them they can provide a rising or setting bearing at almost any season or time of night. Altair is the star for Satawal to the west and Truk to the east, the two longest passages Puluwat navigators regularly make without intermediate stops. When navigators show off their knowledge by reciting chains of islands real and mythical reaching across the ocean they try to make these follow Altair, that is, run in lines from west to east. Sometimes they knowingly cheat a little to make it come out this way, so great is the aura which surrounds the Big Bird.

Altair is not the only navigation star which has alternate companion stars around the sky at the same latitude, that is, rising and setting at the same locations. A number of other stars have at least one substitute, and for almost any position there are other recognized stars which rise and set close enough to the right or left of the position of the navigation star when it is not itself up to provide at least an approximate bearing. Furthermore, it is not necessary that the star to be used lie straight ahead. A sight to the rear will serve as well because the navigator is concerned only with lining up the heading of the narrow hull of his canoe with the star. He can do this by looking in either direction. As a matter of fact, when on a reach with the canoe drifting somewhat sideways and the hull pointed 15 degrees or so more into the wind than its actual course there is some advantage in looking backward and gauging the actual direction of travel of the canoe as revealed by its wake. However, by the time a man is qualified as a navigator he knows where the canoe is going without looking at the wake, so the advantage is only one of confirmation.

A backsight is somewhat inconvenient for the navigator, who usually sits facing forward, because he has to swing around and look directly behind. However, this is necessary only at intervals. Whether he has a helmsman or is steering with the trim of the sheet alone it is possible for the navigator to keep a fairly steady heading just by sensing how the canoe is running over the waves, and any errors are likely to be random and therefore not cumulative. In addition, a steady wind will help keep a properly trimmed canoe on course, and there is usually a compass to look at as well as slow-moving clouds distant on the horizon. By keeping watch on all these things the navigator need not take more than an intermittent look at any stars. He can also use a star off to one side, adjusting his sitting position so that when he is on course the star he has chosen rides near a stay, or perhaps just above an end of the outrigger float. In this way he can sail almost indefinitely without attending to his acutal course star as long as the substitute is in sight—and as long as he does not shift his own position. Especially advantageous for this purpose is the North Star since if clouds do not intervene it can be kept in view all night long.

Before leaving the discussion of stars a word must be said about the magnetic compasses which are by now virtually standard equipment upon any Puluwat canoe planning a voyage to another island. At present at least compasses are not primary navigational tools. They are used principally to hold steady a course which was originally established by stars or other means, and also to keep track of the direction of drift if a canoe is caught in a large storm. They do not serve the purpose to which we put them of providing a sole or principal basis for determining courses and headings. There is no technical reason for not using them in this way. In fact the virtually complete lack of metal in the construction of a Puluwat canoe should make a magnetic compass exceptionally reliable and simple to use. However, in practical terms the correlation of the Western compass card with its thirty-two equally spaced points and the Carolinian star compass with its thirty-two *un*equally spaced star positions would present formidable problems. Granted, every Puluwatan who uses a compass is not only aware that a discrepancy exists but is able also to describe with considerable accuracy where the points of one fall relative to the other. Nevertheless, despite this known divergence, the points of the mariner's compass are referred to by the same names and in the same sequence as the navigation stars themselves. A result of this is that at some points in the circle a star bearing and a compass bearing both called by the same name are a full point (11¼ degrees) apart. Therefore, a direct substitution of the course-setting function from the stars to the compass would introduce gross errors. Even the roughly 5-degree magnetic variation eastward which prevails in this area would, if not compensated, use up all the error a navigator can allow himself on a long passage.

Taking these difficulties into account it is easy to understand why the nominally simple conversion of star courses to compass courses actually would generate all sorts of problems. The entire inventory of star courses between island pairs would have to be adjusted, usually by half points and less, differing for each bearing. Furthermore the system of star directions, now symmetrical between its eastern and western halves, would become asymmetrical by virtue of the 5-degree magnetic correction which must be applied to compass readings in this part of the world. Again the navigators are aware that the magnetic compass does not point quite true to the North Star or to the Big Bird, but it would be quite another matter for them to learn to make a correction for this declination routinely on top of all the other adjustments necessary. In sum, the practical difficulties which would loom in the work of the Puluwat navigator trying to convert to primary reliance on compass headings would probably not appear any less formidable than the prospect for us in the United States of converting from feet and inches to a metric system of measurement. Small wonder then that he sets his course by the stars and other traditional means and uses the compass only to help hold steady the course so defined.

Thus far, however, thanks to our digression into Puluwat astronomy and the star compass we have not yet fairly gotten under way on a voyage. The activities at the outset of a voyage have already been described: the work of adjusting rigging, stowing any last-minute items of gear which are still loose, a lot of tacking and changing course to get out of the lagoon, and perhaps paying out fishing lines if the canoe is to be running over reefs right away. At this time too the sailing plan for the voyage is implemented by setting an initial course. This course in effect synthesizes the total plan as far as it can be formulated in advance.

The foundation of any sailing plan is the star position which provides a bearing between the destination island and the island from which the journey begins. Satawal is due west of Puluwat so the star course is "under," as the Puluwatans express it, the setting of Altair. Pikelot, northeast of Satawal, lies under the setting of Pleiades from Puluwat. One can go on around the islands which, near or far, encircle Puluwat, calling off the course star for each. For Pulap from Puluwat the star is under the rising of Vega (although Pulap and Tamatam are so close to Puluwat one scarcely bothers with stars), for East Fayu it is under the rising of Pleiades, for the big pass into Truk from the west it is under the rising of Altair, and so on for each island to which one might conceivably sail. A similar round of star courses to other islands can be recited for each of the islands in the area, and every navigator knows them all.

For some more distant islands the star courses are known even though a direct journey is never made. The course from Puluwat to Namoluk is an example. There is not only a star for Namoluk, the rising of Antares, but also complete sailing directions. Yet no one ever sails directly to Namoluk. It would be risky, a trip of two hundred and fifty miles to a tiny atoll alone in the ocean. Instead, canoes go first to Truk and thence south to Namoluk via Losap. There are stars too for islands which no one from Puluwat has ever visited, islands such as Eauripik far to the west under the setting of Orion's Belt, or Kapinga-marangi to the southeast under the rising of Shaula in Scorpio.

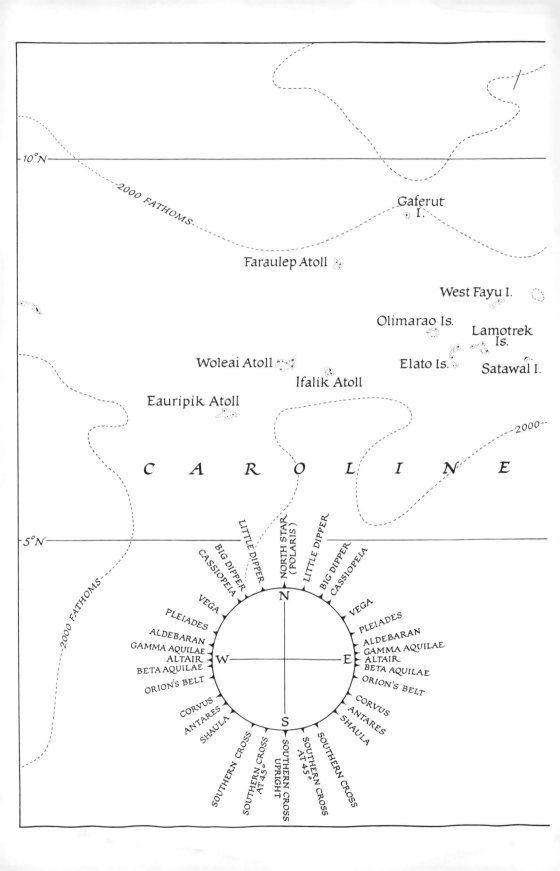

10°N

2000 FATHOMS

Gaferut I.

Faraulep Atoll

West Fayu I.

Olimarao Is.

Lamotrek Is.

Woleai Atoll

Elato Is.

Satawal I.

Ifalik Atoll

Eauripik Atoll

C A R O L I N E

2000

5°N

2000 FATHOMS

LITTLE DIPPER
NORTH STAR (POLARIS)
LITTLE DIPPER
BIG DIPPER
BIG DIPPER
CASSIOPEIA
CASSIOPEIA
VEGA
VEGA
PLEIADES
PLEIADES
ALDEBARAN
ALDEBARAN
GAMMA AQUILAE
GAMMA AQUILAE
ALTAIR
ALTAIR
BETA AQUILAE
BETA AQUILAE
ORION'S BELT
ORION'S BELT
CORVUS
CORVUS
ANTARES
ANTARES
SHAULA
SHAULA

N
W
E
S

SOUTHERN CROSS
SOUTHERN CROSS AT 45°
SOUTHERN CROSS UPRIGHT
SOUTHERN CROSS AT 45°
SOUTHERN CROSS

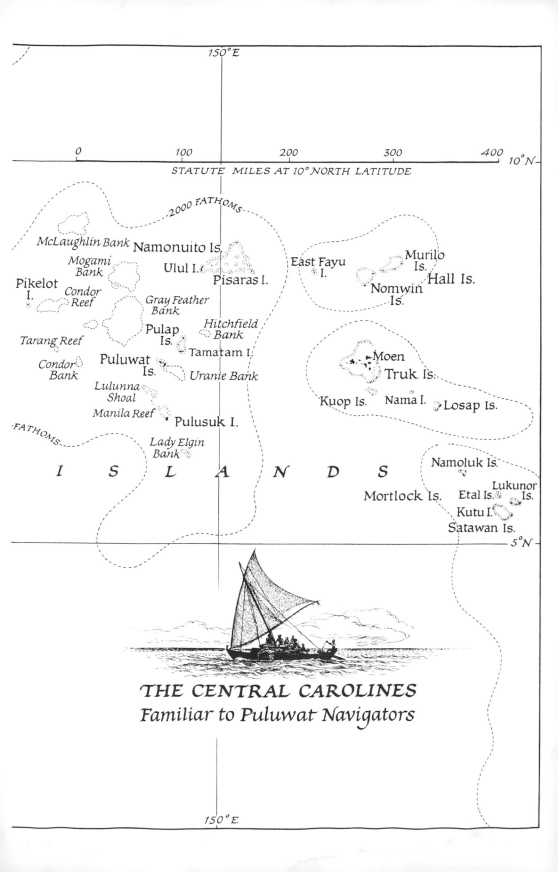

100   200   300   400   10°N

0   100   200   300   400

STATUTE MILES AT 10° NORTH LATITUDE

2000 FATHOMS

McLaughlin Bank   Namonuito Is.

Mogami   Ulul I.   East Fayu   Murilo
Bank   I.   Is.

Pikelot   Pisaras I.   Hall Is.
I.   Condor   Nomwin
    Reef   Gray Feather   Is.
            Bank
                Hitchfield
            Pulap   Bank
Tarang Reef   Is.
                Tamatam I.   Moen
Condor   Puluwat   Truk Is.
Bank   Is.   Uranie Bank

    Lulunna   Kuop Is.   Nama I.   Losap Is.
    Shoal
    Manila Reef   Pulusuk I.

FATHOMS   Namoluk Is.
        Lady Elgin
        Bank   Lukunor
I   S   L   A   N   D   S   Mortlock Is.   Etal Is.   Is.
                                Kutu I.
                            Satawan Is.

                                                    5°N

THE CENTRAL CAROLINES
Familiar to Puluwat Navigators

One can only guess how the stars were originally determined for such distant islands. There are stars too for courses between island pairs so remote that navigators are not even sure which are real and which are mythical.

The derivation of a star course such as that from Puluwat to Namoluk is, however, less speculative. Although Namoluk standing alone with no nearby reefs or islands presents too small a target to hit at such a distance, the same is not true of Puluwat as seen from the direction of Namoluk. Puluwat is flanked on both sides by a screen of reefs and islands so wide that a navigator could miss by forty miles and still find a familiar seamark or island. It is thus probable that impatient navigators in the past occasionally made the journey straight home to Puluwat rather than dallying among the foreign islands of Truk.

Knowing from these journeys that the star from Namoluk to Puluwat is the setting of Vega it follows that the star for Namoluk going in the opposite direction should be the rising of Antares. This is because the star compass, despite its uneven intervals between the star positions, is remarkably symmetrical between its northern and southern quadrants as well as its eastern and western. Therefore, for every position of a rising star there is almost exactly opposite (180 degrees away on the horizon) a setting position of another star. The star courses are for this reason often given together with their reciprocals— "from Pulusuk you steer under rising-of-Cassiopeia to Pisaras and under setting-of-Shaula back again"—so it takes no real thought to translate a known course in one direction into its equivalent return. Nevertheless, even the Namoluk-Puluwat passage has almost certainly not been made for a long time. This is attested by a difference between the star course given for it by Hipour from the Warieng school of navigators—under the setting of Vega as cited above (which is close to the true bearing)—and Ikuliman's insistence on behalf of Fanur that the proper star course is under the setting of the Pleiades. This is one of the few discrepancies between the two of them in local star courses and strongly suggests that the sailing directions between these islands have not been put to practical test by either school of navigation for many years, perhaps generations.

Although the nominal star course between any pair of islands usually reflects the true bearing between them, this true course in some cases is virtually never used, at least at the start. A deviation of one star position, sometimes even two, is often introduced to compensate for or take advantage of characteristics of the seaway between the two islands. Compensation is principally for the effect of currents. The run of prevailing currents throughout the seas ranged by Puluwat canoes is known to navigators. Compensation for these currents is an integral part of the package of instructions which comprise the sailing directions between island pairs. The initial course from Puluwat to Satawal offers a good example. Satawal lies under the setting of Altair. However, one usually starts out one star position to the south of this under Beta Aquilae to counter a strong current which sets from the southeast in this area. Yet sometimes even this is not enough.

In this part of the Pacific Ocean there is great variability in currents. To the north, the North Equatorial Current runs westward, while to the south the Equatorial Countercurrent goes in the opposite direction. The Caroline Islands not only lie along the line of transition between them, but here too a large proportion of the Countercurrent is actually generated by a reversal of the North Equatorial Current. Thus there are both vast eddies and abrupt changes in the direction of the currents which occur almost from day to day. Part of the routine for departure on a trip is therefore to gauge the direction and rate of the current before losing sight of the fixed positions of the island and its surrounding reefs. With respect to traveling from Puluwat to Satawal, then, if the current is especially strong toward the northwest, the sailing plan may call for a turn soon after departure to a markedly southerly course, under the setting of Orion's Belt. The length of time to remain on this course is a matter of judgment, based on how much initial southing the navigator believes must be made to compensate for the cumulative effect of the current throughout the whole passage. The way the above compensations are made means that the entire correction for the current to be encountered between Puluwat and Satawal is introduced during the first part of the trip. Thereafter a course change is made to a more northerly heading, usually under the setting of Altair, the true bearing. This produces a dogleg sailing plan, at first south of west and thereafter (as a result of the current) a little north of west. This is done for a very good reason, a reason related to the other major element in the formulation of sailing directions between island pairs, the sighting of seamarks en route.

The most common seamarks are reefs. There are extensive reefs throughout the Central Carolines, although they become rare to the south. In general they are ten to twenty fathoms (60 to 120 feet) below the surface at their edges, often deeper toward the center. They range from the great complex of the Gray Feather and Mogami Banks, which together extend more than a thousand square miles under the ocean, to single isolated heads of coral which cap hidden pinnacles risen from the ocean floor. Because of the clarity of the tropical water and its subtle shadings in sun and shadow, the reefs despite their depth can readily be detected from a canoe. This is true even when the wind is blowing the surface of the water into spume. In addition the current running over a reef roils the water and steepens the waves. Thus in the daytime a reef can often be detected a mile or two away by the whitecaps it creates, while at night it imparts a special uneasiness to the motion of a sailing canoe. The suspicion of a reef which this uneasiness engenders can readily be checked by a sounding with the fishline which is always on board, as Hipour's crew did on our return from Pulusuk (see Chapter 2).

Once over a reef it is possible to determine one's position. Often passing over a reef is part of the sailing plan and sighting it below verifies that the canoe is on course. At other times the canoe might be lost or uncertain of its position. Then it is necessary to sail along the edge of the reef until its bearing and some of its outline can be established. In the middle of a reef there is no way to tell one from another, but every reef has its unique outline. The skilled navigator knows them all. Therefore, even if dawn breaks and finds him in the center of a big bank he need only sail off in almost any direction to find its edge. Then by traveling along it for a way he can determine which reef he is over and his location along its perimeter.

Thus reefs not only can serve as guideposts along the seaway to an island but also can provide a screen to arrest a canoe if it has strayed from its course, or perhaps even gone past its destination. If a navigator who is not expecting to pass over a reef sights one under him he stops and casts about to find out where he is. Even more is this true if he should sight an island other than the one toward which he is heading. For this reason whenever possible a course is set so that reefs, or better still islands which can be seen from afar, lie in a direct line beyond the destination, a screen to catch the canoe if it should miss its mark. This is far safer than a course in which there is only open ocean beyond. It is this reasoning which determines the sailing directions described above from Puluwat to Satawal. The dogleg course, first to the south and then more northerly, places the canoe on a line such that if it should pass Satawal without sighting it the complex of Lamotrek and Elato would lie directly beyond, covering enough ocean so that something would almost certainly be sighted. If a more constant correction were instead applied throughout the voyage, resulting in true westerly travel all the way, and if through some error the canoe passed just out of range south of Satawal still heading west, it could go on almost indefinitely without encountering any seamarks while the crew grew weak for lack of food and water. This illustrates an essential characteristic of Puluwat navigation: sailing directions are always conservative, incorporating every precaution the seaway can offer.

It is conservatism as well as the turtles which inspires most navigators to make the passage from Puluwat to Satawal not directly, as just described, but via Pikelot. Pikelot is closer to Puluwat, one hundred miles instead of one hundred and thirty, but more important it is flanked on the east by Condor Reef. The true course to Pikelot lies between the setting of Vega and the Pleiades; sailing directions call for starting under the more westerly of these two stars, the setting of Pleiades, then about halfway turning northward toward the setting of Vega so that one will pass smartly over the southern edge of Condor Reef. As the canoe then turns to follow along the edge of the reef it is soon obvious that it runs straight east and west, the distinguishing sign of Condor Reef. When its end is reached the reef turns northward, and Pikelot lies straight ahead.

However, even more conservatively, most navigators making this passage actually depart not under the star for Pikelot at all, but rather under the setting of Cassiopeia, the star course for the southern tip of Gray Feather Bank. After a run of only thirty miles they are over its edge. Thereafter they can follow along over it or near it to the next reef, and so on all the way to Condor Reef. Even if they stray off course they know where they are: if they see reef under them on both sides they know they have veered too far to the north and should turn south, while if the water is deep and clear below they know they are too far to the south. No wonder men dare leave for Pikelot even when drunk! In addition, reefs teem with fish where canoes pass only occasionally. When over Gray Feather Bank canoe crews thus need only throw out a line to catch more than they can eat.

A slightly different strategy, but also conservative, is exemplified in the sailing directions from Puluwat to Ulul on the western tip of the Namonuito Atoll. The true course is slightly to the north of the rising of the Big Dipper. This would carry the canoe on a straight run for the eighty miles to Ulul, passing to the west of Tamatam and Pulap. Instead, however, most navigators set the starting course more to the east to pass through or even to the right of Pulap Atoll. Thus both Tamatam and Pulap, at either end of the atoll, can be kept in sight until the canoe approaches the Hitchfield Bank northeast of Pulap. Only then need the navigator strike out into the open for Ulul, now only fifty miles away. Furthermore, although the true course from Hitchfield Bank to Ulul is due north, under "the star which never moves," the course is actually set one position to the east, under the rising of the Little Dipper. This is needed to compensate for a current which often sets from the east in this area, but even when the current is weak the same heading is used to be sure that the canoe will head a little to the east of Ulul and thus pass over the Namonuito barrier reef rather than possibly passing to the west of Ulul and on into the open sea. However, another kind of caution must be exercised here. There is a danger of overcompensation. The course from Hitchfield Bank must not be planned too far to the east, especially if the current is slight or possibly westerly, because there is a shoal on the Namonuito barrier reef about a third of the way along its length, a place shallow enough to make wicked waves which could break up a canoe almost instantly. Warnings and special provisions for staying clear of this shoal if the visibility is poor abound in the sailing directions between all the island pairs in this part of the ocean.

Examples of sailing directions for other seaways could be multiplied almost endlessly. The ones given here have been limited to those originating on Puluwat only for convenience. From every island there are seaways radiating in all directions. Each has its unique set of sailing directions designed not merely to set a proper course but also to include every special precaution the arrangement of islands and reefs will permit. All of them are stored in the memory of the navigator. As his canoe moves away from the island, even though he may have given no thought to his itinerary until that moment, he already knows exactly what he should do and the course he should set.

Usually this departure is in broad daylight. Worse still, all the preparations for a trip are likely to be finished about noon, the most elusive time of day for establishing a course. At this hour there are not only no stars but even the sun is near its zenith and useless for determining direction. However, the island which the canoe is leaving usually can provide enough information for at least a preliminary heading. As the canoe sails away the navigator looks back. He has learned how the island should look from a canoe as it heads toward each of the various islands to which he might journey. For shorter trips the general configuration of the island provides sufficient orientation to set a course. However, for more precision there are usually two points visible from the sea which are directly in line with each possible island of destination and thus provide ranges to sight along. Puluwat is especially handy for this purpose because the complex of closely spaced little islands which form the atoll offer a multitude of distinguishable landmarks to be lined up one behind another. By sailing so that they remain in line the navigator who knows his backsight ranges can keep his canoe steadily on course for its destination until the island drops out of sight. To cite some examples, leaving Puluwat for Pulusuk the correct heading is defined by having the southwest tip of Puluwat Island overlap little Elangelab Island on the north edge of the atoll. This range can be modified to provide a correction to east or west if there is a current running. Thus, to counter a westerly current of average force the tip of Puluwat should just meet the eastern edge of Elangelab. If an easterly current is running, which is more common, the usual correction is achieved by having the tip of Puluwat blanket Elangelab and just touch the tip of Allei. All these ranges are defined by where

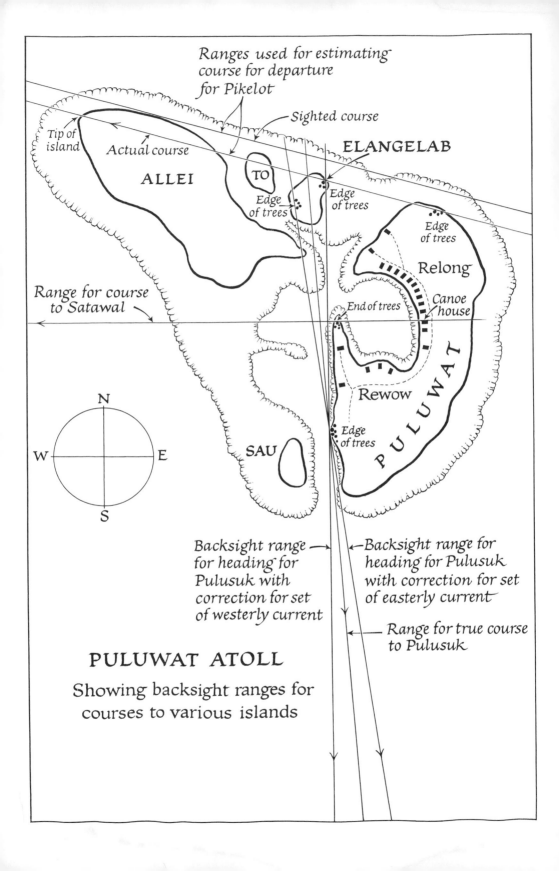

Ranges used for estimating
course for departure
for Pikelot

Sighted course

Tip of
island

Actual course

ELANGELAB

ALLEI

TO

Edge
of trees

Edge
of trees

Edge
of trees

Relong

Range for course
to Satawal

End of trees

Canoe
house

Rewow

P U L U W A T

N

W — E

S

SAU

Edge
of trees

Backsight range
for heading for
Pulusuk with
correction for set
of westerly current

Backsight range for
heading for Pulusuk
with correction for set
of easterly current

Range for true course
to Pulusuk

PULUWAT ATOLL

Showing backsight ranges for
courses to various islands

the trees rise on the shore, not by the beach where the sand meets the water.

To head for Satawal, the long spit which runs northward from the Western shore of Puluwat is lined up with some tall breadfruit trees beside one of the canoe houses on the eastern shore of the inner lagoon. The canoe houses on either side of these trees can then provide alternate range marks if changes are necessary to compensate for current. The backsight for Pikelot is a little more troublesome to obtain. However, it is no worse than those commonly encountered elsewhere in establishing headings from islands which lack the complex but tight convolutions of an atoll like Puluwat. Because there are no two simultaneously visible points which line up precisely in the direction of Pikelot it is necessary to use the northern tip of Puluwat and the western tip of Allei. The difficulty here is that the northern shoulder of Allei gets in the way of making this sight, so it is necessary to swing north of the course until the tip of Puluwat just comes in view and then drop back to an estimated alignment. This wastes time and is not very accurate, but there is nothing better. Fortunately for Puluwat navigators, Pikelot is an easy place to reach and a clumsy range is no great handicap. If it is a good day—and trips are seldom begun on bad days—the backsight operation, aside from an impressionistic glance backward, is likely to be omitted entirely when leaving for Pikelot.

A heading can also be established in some directions by passing over designated portions of reefs near the island of departure. The two arms of Manila Reef which run north and northwest of Pulusuk offer bearings when leaving there for each of the series of islands to the north from Ulul down to Puluwat as well as bearing for Gray Feather Bank and an approximate one for Pikelot. The reefs around Puluwat offer less orientation, partly at least because the principal reef, Uranie Bank, stretches off to the southeast, a direction in which no islands lie. Its northern edge, however, runs due east from Puluwat and sailing along here a canoe can line up exactly on course for the main pass into Truk. As a consequence no land-based backsight is necessary for Truk when departing from Puluwat.

Backsights and orientation courses over reefs serve two purposes. One is to establish the force and direction of any current which may be running. Once away from the fixed reference of land or reefs there is no way to estimate the current, or even to know whether one is running at all. Consequently the determination must be made early in the trip. An island with trees of average height remains in view from a canoe for about ten miles, but near the end its distinguishing features dissolve into no more than a line of dark roughness blurring the shining horizon. Reefs, as, for example, Uranie Bank, can sometimes be followed a little farther. However, for purposes of estimating current, reefs have the disadvantage that they disturb the smooth flow of the water and may thus give an erroneous impression of its speed, although the direction of flow does not change appreciably.

However accurate the initial correction for current drift may be, it will remain true only as long as the current does not change. Once clear of islands and reefs, there is no way for the navigator in the open ocean to detect changes in either direction or force of the current. This is one of many reasons for designing all voyages as conservatively as possible and taking maximum advantage of any available seamarks en route. Passing over a reef during the course of a passage between islands offers not only reassurance of one's course and position but also a chance to check the rate and direction of the current in the area at that time.

A backsight on the island or the guidance of a reef leading away from it can serve a second purpose in addition to estimating the current. This is the establishment of a course when neither sun nor stars are available at the time of departure. Such a course once set can be maintained by use of the compass and by observation of the waves until either sun or stars come into view close enough to the horizon to define a more accurate heading. In the past only the waves could be used for this purpose. Now the waves are still observed as a check and an alternative to the compass. The six to eight miles through which the backsight landmarks can be seen and utilized are barely enough to average out the compass readings, to emerge into an area of clear ocean waves free of interference from the island, and to verify that the course being held with compass and waves is a true course. Once this has been done the task of the navigator moves into its second and longest phase, that of maintaining a course and knowledge of his current position until he is close enough to his destination to home in on it. Throughout the trip both the compass and waves remain available to provide a heading whenever the sun or stars cannot be used for this purpose.

The compass is usually placed in front of the navigator on his bench which forms the inner edge of the lee platform. When not in use the compass is kept covered for protection from accident or overheating under the sun but it is easily available for consultation. As mentioned earlier, it is never used initially to set a course. Instead a compass bearing is established only after the canoe has been set on course by a backsight, by a star, or on some other basis. The proper bearing is averaged out of a series of readings as the canoe twists and swings over the waves. It is then identified with one of the thirty-two points on the compass card, points named for the star positions to which they roughly correspond. Degree readings, although also shown on most compasses on Puluwat, are never used—at least by the older navigators few of whom can read numbers or any other writing. As an additional difficulty the numbering of every tenth degree divides the circle into thirty-six segments instead of the familiar thirty-two.

Because the compass provides only a derived heading it is not essential that it be lined up exactly with the hull of the canoe. Usually the instrument is placed so that the lubber line is roughly toward the front simply because it is more readily seen there, but this is not essential provided some other reference mark is available. For the same reason a modest deflection caused by a nearby iron object would presumably not be of any consequence provided the iron were not moved en route. Many of the compasses are also large and heavy, designed for bigger craft. Their powerful magnets may therefore be less affected by stray magnetism than lighter ones would be. However, I failed to inquire whether Puluwat navigators are aware of this hazard at all. One Pulusuk canoe en route to Puluwat did go many miles off course during our stay because a piece of equipment made of iron had been laid near its compass a while after the initial course was set after leaving Pulusuk. However, technical discussion of the episode was deflected by a predictable consensus on Puluwat that no better navigation than this could be expected from any Pulusuk navigator, and from this unfortunate man in particular since he was the same who earlier in the year had been blown off course with a loss of two canoes after leaving drunk for Pikelot. Unfairly for him, in this case the offending iron object belonged to and was unthinkingly placed near the compass by an American who happened to be riding up from Pulusuk on the canoe.

It is the navigator who watches the compass. This is obviously appropriate when the canoe is on a reach and the navigator is the one who is steering by trimming the sail with the sheet he holds in his hands. However, even when the canoe is running before the wind or is on a broad reach and steering is being done with the paddle by a man aft it is still the navigator who watches the compass. The steersman is expected to observe the waves or keep an eye on a distant cloud. At intervals the navigator looks at the compass. If the heading is off he calls back to the steersman, "Come around this way, a little more, a little more . . . there!"

Thus the waves are still used even though with a compass aboard they need not be observed as assiduously or relied upon as fully as in the past. However, there are occasions at night when the sky is overcast and there is no light for the compass —no flashlight, no matches, nor coals from a fire—and at such times the waves must be used exclusively to hold the course true. The art of sensing direction by waves is thus by no means obsolete, despite its reduction to secondary status. However, as a growing number of navigators come to their maturity without ever having placed primary reliance on waves their skill is certain to decline. Hipour feels it already has even in his own case. Loss of a compass could in time prove to be a real calamity. However, this is not yet true aside from major storms.

Three wave systems are recognized and used by Puluwat navigators in maintaining a course at sea. I have observed two of them, but the third kind of wave, which is weakest, was not running at any time I was out on a canoe. Coming from due east is the Big Wave (literally the "big, big wave"), relatively steep and short and quite distinctive once you have learned to recognize it. All manner of waves cross and impinge one upon another at various angles even far from land. Two or three crests go by, then another set intrudes from elsewhere. Yet the

Big Wave has in a fashion difficult to describe more character. Perhaps the unbroken crest of the wave extends farther from side to side than do the lesser waves, or there are a few more crests which pass in review before a different set intrudes. These impressions are visual and untutored, and therefore inadequate. Puluwatans steer by the feel of waves under the canoe, not visually, so what I am able to report at first hand is several steps removed from the actual sensory inputs which guide the navigator on his way. My observations can thus testify only that the Big Wave is distinguishable, does come regularly from the east, and is therefore real, something which I found difficult to credit before I had been out on a canoe and seen it for myself.

The North Wave is the second of the major waves and actually comes in more from the northeast. Generally it runs a little east even of that, typically coming under Vega, one point east of northeast when the magnetic and star compasses are reconciled. It is a long swelling wave and would be called in English vernacular a ground swell. Other steeper waves crisscross its surface as it moves majestically past, sometimes on a calm day seeming to heave the entire surface of the ocean up on its broad crest.

The third, or South Wave, comes from a position correspondingly a little east of southeast, under Antares. It is much weaker and less regular in occurrence. I cannot describe it further because I have not seen it.

Although waves, like the compass, are used only to maintain a course which has been established by prior reference to other phenomena, the constancy of their orientation is a definite advantage. The more predictable the natural features which are used for navigation the more reliable the entire process becomes. It is therefore worthwhile to inquire into the source of the three wave systems and the basis for their regularity. Without going into technicalities, the longer the distance between one wave crest and the next the more likely it is that that wave system has traveled far from where it was generated, and that it has moved from an area of strong winds to one wherein the winds are lighter or even blowing in another direction. The North (northeast) Wave is such a wave, very long from crest to crest. Yet its great size suggests that the winds blew strongly and steadily over the ocean where it was spawned far away, building up in the moving waters vast reservoirs of energy to undulate for hundreds of miles across the sea. The Big (east) Wave, shorter between crests, must have in contrast grown under the prodding of winds closer at hand. It is not as massive as the North Wave, yet it is big enough that we should look for its origin from winds which are either quite strong or else prevail over long stretches of ocean, cumulating the energy stored in the wave by prolonged tugging at the water. About the South Wave we can only speculate by analogy from the other two.

To look for these necessary conditions we must recall the path of the great weather systems whose winds revolve clockwise about centers of high pressure as they march in succession out of Asia and across the northern Pacific. Similar systems also move eastward in the southern hemisphere but rotate in an opposite direction. Between them lies the doldrum belt, moving north and south with the seasons in an irregular but predictable line. Consider for the moment only a single mass of wind and weather swirling across the northern Pacific. We can envision near its center, at considerable distance from the doldrum belt and therefore from the Caroline Islands, steady winds of considerable force blowing out on tangents like the spurts of fire from a pinwheel. Consider more particularly only those components of the wind which at any one time are blowing toward Puluwat, generating waves on the surface of the sea as they blow. As the system moves off the Asian mainland it lies far to the north, particularly during the summer months which are the principal sailing months in the Carolines. The winds which first blow from that position toward Puluwat are northerly, generated at the front of the system as it moves eastward. However, being a thousand miles or more distant to the north they are too far away to carry either their own energy or the waves they generate over the long ocean reach to Puluwat. As the center during the next few days moves away from Asia, however, it swings south as well as east. As it moves toward and then past the Carolines to the northeast it brings its strong winds closer. Now, however, as it goes by, the strong winds from the center have, so to speak, to blow backward to reach Puluwat which it is then passing. The winds which reach Puluwat are therefore northeasterly, coming from the southeast quarter of the circle. They are the northeast trades, intermittent in the doldrum belt which blankets Puluwat during most of the voyaging seasons, but much stronger and steadier farther north. In the winter when the doldrum belt moves south the centers of weather shift their tracks southward also. Then these same trades are close enough to buffet the Carolines so strongly that sailing virtually ceases. But in the other months their greatest strength is expended at a distance, several hundred miles north and east of Puluwat and its surrounding islands. Accordingly, the waves they generate must travel far before passing under a canoe from those islands. Although these waves are sometimes accompanied and sustained—but as often are not—by the remains of the winds which gave them birth they must inevitably weaken as they travel away from the massive thrust of the originally strong central winds. Traveling and growing weaker they, like all swells which decay from lack of new energy, grow longer and more gradual but still huge. They become the North Wave.

Meanwhile the weather system moves on. Its strong central winds blow down as the trade winds of islands far to the east of Puluwat and are lost to our attention. However, the central winds are not the only ones which blow in this system. Farther out, along the edge of the galaxy of weather there are winds which also blow clockwise and at a tangent to the circle, but are lighter. As the center moves past, the southern edge of these light winds travels close; often right through the Carolines. The winds are blowing "backwards," opposite to the direction of travel of the center; that is, they blow from the east. Sometimes even in the summer the northeast winds described above, although more distant in origin, are strong enough to overcome these more local easterlies. At other times the peripheral east winds are stronger, and then on Puluwat one says the wind has swung around to the east. In any event, even if the wind is northeast at Puluwat it is as likely as not to be easterly at Truk or just beyond Truk. For our present purposes the important fact is that although they are sometimes intermittent, every time the east winds blow they store up some of their energy in waves. The waves so formed may for all we know travel thousands of miles as one circulating weather system after another nudges them along across the Pacific. There is no way to tell where they begin. However, because their most recent and continuing source of energy is relatively close at hand from the prevailing easterlies they are not as far decayed as the swells from the northeast. Thus it is that the Big Wave which these winds generate, although also a true swell in the sense that it has derived its direction and much of its energy in far places, is constantly renewed near at hand. It is therefore more youthful —steeper and shorter—just as we have found it when seen (or felt) on a Puluwat canoe.

About the origin of the South Wave I can only guess since I do not know its form. By analogy it would be reasonable to assume it is generated by the stronger winds which blow counterclockwise near the center of the weather systems of the south Pacific, in other words, by the southeast trades. This would probably be more likely during the summer months when the doldrum belt, and therefore the southern weather, moves farthest north. However, I have no information on when the South Wave is strongest. Although New Guinea and other large islands lie to the south of Puluwat, to the southeast there is a long run of open ocean north of the Solomons and the New Hebrides through which waves could build to a size large enough for their energy to carry them as swells into the Carolines.

Although this analysis accounts for the wave systems as they are known on Puluwat, it does not permit an estimate of how closely their direction holds steady. The navigators believe the orientation of the various waves is quite constant. However, because waves are used only to maintain rather than to set courses, minor or gradual changes might even go unnoticed. Certainly they should cause no concern. Difficulties would only arise if there were rapid fluctuations in the direction of the waves. This seems unlikely because the only substantial variation in their pattern would probably be seasonal rather than diurnal.

An exception to this can occur when strong westerly winds blow for several days at a time. A surprising proportion of the energy of waves is dissipated in air resistance even in still air. If there is a wind blowing steadily against the crests of oncoming waves they will decay rapidly. If the weather is clear this causes no problem for a navigator. His course can be maintained with stars and the sun. However, major changes in wind direction are often accompanied by storms, and these can obscure the sky. In the past, before compasses, this combination of losing both waves and stars left the navigator with no choice but to lower his sail and wait, sometimes for a day or two or more, for the weather to clear. Meanwhile he could drift, driven either by a strong wind or currents. Thereafter he would have to cast about to locate himself again. This need not happen any more. Even if the wave patterns break up entirely it is possible to steer indefinitely with a compass alone. For the navigator steering with the sheet by compass only is no problem at all in the daytime; he probably pays little attention to waves under these circumstances anyway. If it is dark he has to look more often at his compass if he is without the motion of regular waves to guide him, and a steersman will require more frequent correction. Yet these burdens are scarcely serious unless the crew is so improvident that it has no light at night. Even then they need drift only through the few hours of darkness.

A really large tropical storm, however, can even today create real problems for the navigator. The sky is overcast for days at a time. Rain chills and blinds the crew. Worst of all, howling winds drive across the water whipping up huge waves which orient themselves to the command of the present wind alone, all other forces being quickly overcome. The winds move counterclockwise around a center in the manner of a typhoon—which some of these storms in time become—and thus as the storm moves along the winds change direction. Yet this change in direction is so gradual it cannot be perceived on a canoe, and with the waves responding to only the local winds they no longer provide any guidance. The sail has long since been lowered, and if the storm is really severe the mast will be taken down also, despite the very heavy work of erecting it again when the wind abates. These measures cut down the rate of drift in addition to making the tortured canoe ride a little easier in the waves which fling it about. Yet a strong enough wind exerts a really solid pressure upon even the smallest exposed surface and a canoe inevitably drifts far before the storm is over.

Eventually the storm must end. If the canoe is not seriously damaged—and it is to their credit that they rarely are—it becomes imperative to find an island, or at least a reef from which position can be determined, before the crew becomes weakened by lack of food on top of the strain of their wild ordeal. In the past there was little to guide the navigator. If the center of the storm passed near him—which he would have no way of knowing—he could have started being blown in one direction and ended going just the other way. On the other hand if the storm center were more distant most of his drifting would have been in one general direction. He would have his intuition to rely upon and little else. Instead he usually made a prior assumption that he was roughly in the area where he started unless he had reason to believe otherwise. As soon as he could see the sky he would therefore set sail for the largest mass of reef or land he knew to exist in that part of the ocean. West of Puluwat this was usually the complex of reefs centered on Gray Feather Bank but extending west to West Fayu and south and east to Pulusuk. There are only a few courses through these formations which will not eventually pass over a reef or in sight of an island. To the east of Puluwat, Truk with its barrier reef forty miles across and its peaks up to a thousand feet high can be sighted many miles away. These are the wide targets toward which the navigator would usually aim his canoe and hope for an early sighting of land-based seabirds or anything at all he might recognize.

Nowadays the dangers are less severe, but by no means negligible. Again, the navigator has his compass to thank for his relief. A canoe with its sail down, it will be recalled, drifts with its outrigger upwind. This keeps it stable and slows its drift, and it also provides a ready orientation to the wind. The compass is lashed down and for once is used to establish a primary bearing. That is, the bearing of the canoe is determined solely by where the "stars" are on the compass. Although this may not be very accurate as done by a Puluwat navigator it is a lot better than guessing. What the navigator does, then, is keep track of the direction his canoe is drifting by noting the direction in which the outrigger points. He combines this with an estimate of the rate and amount of drift and thus maintains some idea of where it is. As soon as the wind drops enough to rig his sail he sets off in the direction of whatever he believes is the closest and most visible reef or island from his present estimated location. The direction of his setting off again must depend solely upon his reading of the compass unless he waits for the sky to clear, since the waves are still jumbled and therefore useless. Nevertheless this is far better than in the past when there was really almost nothing to go on.

I was unable to determine how many navigators have had an experience of this sort, or how many could actually do all the unfamiliar things necessary to keep track of position solely by drift and compass. Hipour did have such an experience and acquitted himself well, even winning an argument as to their location after two days of drifting with another younger navigator who was along on an accompanying canoe. However, Hipour was too diplomatic to reveal to me whether the other navigator (of Fanur, the other school of navigation from Hipour's Warieng) had been unable to read the compass as Hipour did. It is a new technique, but if it is not yet known by some it will be soon. Everyone is eager to learn the techniques of survival.

It remains now to describe how waves actually are used for steering. I have already mentioned that it is the motion of the canoe rather than a visual sighting which is used for orientation. Because the Big Wave has a more pronounced character and passes with greater frequency it is preferred to the North Wave. Either is more useful than the unreliable and often weak South Wave. However, the choice of a wave depends not only on which one is running strongly but also on the course to be held. In general it is easiest to steer by waves which are either at right angles or parallel to the travel of the canoe. Waves met diagonally can be confusing. Let us say a canoe is sailing fairly straight into the waves. A wave crest comes along and lifts its front, then passes amidships. The canoe begins to pitch forward as the supporting water falls away from its front end. It is possible to sense quite accurately when the wave crest passes under the center of the canoe. Meanwhile the outrigger float is also riding over the same wave. It too rises and falls. If the canoe is headed exactly perpendicular to the wave the float will pass the crest at the same instant as the hull and there will be no sideways motion at all. If, however, the canoe is turned at even a slight angle to the wave the float will pass the crest a trifle before or after the center of the hull. This will impart a discernible, even though tiny, roll to one side or the other. The direction of roll will depend on whether the hull or the float passes the crest first and is thus first to begin to drop down the other side. This roll need only be sensed for two or three waves in a row in order to define the bearing of the canoe in the wave system with considerable precision. As long thereafter as the roll remains the same going over each wave in succession it is certain that the canoe is holding its course. Correspondingly a change in the amount and timing of this little roll can be translated into a precise amount of course change.

The principle is essentially similar when steering by waves which are coming from the side of the canoe. Usually it is the float which rises first to the wave under these conditions, since wind and waves more often than not come from approximately the same direction. Either way it is possible from the relative motion of hull and outrigger float to tell the precise moment when the hull is on top of a wave crest. If it is exactly parallel to the crest it will slide over without any pitching forward or aft. However, if it is at even a slight angle to the wave the front or the back, as the case may be, will find itself out of the water and unsupported before the other end. It will drop a trifle, looking for water to buoy it up. Once again, then, there will be a characteristic movement, in this case a pitch forward or aft rather than a roll sideways, which will show not only that the canoe is not quite parallel to the waves but also in what direction and how far it is out of alignment. To steer on this heading requires only that the amount of and direction of pitch be kept constant from wave to wave. Needless to say, similar motions, slightly less clear because of pressure from the sides of the waves, occur in the troughs.

By now it probably is evident why a course diagonal to the waves is more difficult to maintain. For a canoe running at right angles to the waves there is a lot of pitch, but roll is slight and subtle differences in it are easily detected; correspondingly on a parallel heading roll is heavy but pitch changes are subtle. On a diagonal both pitch and roll are gross and it is difficult to sense small differences in direction relative to any waves. It is for this reason that the wave system to be used for steering is chosen not only for character and strength but also on the basis of the course to be steered. Even a poor wave on the beam or ahead is usually easier to follow than a good one on a diagonal.

Thus far we have reviewed the use of stars, waves, and the compass to maintain a heading or direction of travel when out of sight of land. Waves and the compass can only hold a course first defined by other means, but stars can and whenever possible do furnish the primary heading. As long as there is a navigation star in sight the navigator can set his course upon it and go forward with a light heart and a minimum of attention and effort. If he is on a reach he must compensate for the sideways drift of his canoe, expressed in a slightly upwind angle of attack, or keep watch on his steersman if running with the wind, but these come almost without thinking to a man whose life is the sea.

The sun can serve the same purpose as the stars. It too, being in the heavens, can provide a primary heading. However, the sun is more complicated to use. Like the stars it must be free of clouds, often a problem during the afternoon storms of summer. It can be used only in the morning and afternoon when it is low enough to provide a clear heading; near the zenith at midday it is useless, and there are no daytime counterparts to the substitute stars which serve at night. The sun lies in only one direction at one time, again less handy than the stars with their thirty-two positions around the horizon. Therefore an angle must be estimated between the course to be sailed and the position of the sun. This is not too difficult. Navigators know well the anatomy of their canoes. Remembering the course they want to hold and the position of the rising and setting sun (which moves conveniently almost straight up and down near the horizon), they can tell with considerable exactness over what part of the canoe the sun should ride—the end of the outrigger float, off the bow, the center of the lee platform, and so on—in order to keep the canoe headed where they wish.

Compensation for the relative movement north and south of the sun through the year is trickier. This movement results from the difference in inclination of the axis of the earth's rotation from the plane of its travel about the sun. In December the sun rises and sets far to the south and in June to the north, moving between the two during the intervening months. This is in contrast to the stars which rise and set in the same places throughout the year—aside from the planets which Puluwatans consider so unreliable as to be useless. The Puluwat navigator makes no attempt to predict the position of the sun from the date. Instead he regularly keeps track of its movement. This can be done in the open by watching any evening for the stars to appear at the place where the sun has just set. In a small atoll like Puluwat it is even simpler. The sun sets each evening over Allei. Every navigator knows where each of the navigation stars sets on Allei as seen from his own canoe house: Orion's Belt by the old dead tree; Altair over the half-sunken ship; Aldebaran between the two tall breadfruit trees; and so on. He need only glance at the setting sun. Without waiting for stars to appear he at once knows the sun's position. Next day he can set his course by equating the sun with the navigation star which sets at the sun's setting position of the evening before.

The stars, the sun, waves, and nowadays the compass, these are the tools upon which the navigator must rely to keep steady his direction as he travels from one island to the next. When expertly used—which means with skilled judgment as well as straightforward knowledge—and under reasonable conditions they can be more than sufficiently accurate. However, the navigator is conservative and conducts his voyage with all possible reserves of safety. In particular this means taking advantage of every opportunity which is available to establish a positive fix of position. Most common is passage over reefs, a matter already considered at some length. Occasionally sightings of islands are used, but it is more usual, if the island is to be passed close enough to see it, to stop overnight. This offers a chance to visit, to get fresh supplies, and to enjoy the warmth of welcome which is one of the rewards of travel in this part of the world.

When passing just out of sight of an island it can sometimes be detected by disturbances in the regular flow of waves. However, here in the Carolines where currents change so often it is not possible to predict with assurance how these disturbances will appear between one voyage and the next. As a consequence wave interferences even when they are present cannot be used as reliably as they are in the Marshalls. Nevertheless, if a navigator believes he is near an island he will watch out for irregularities in the waves and be reassured if he sees them. He may also watch for seabirds, some species of which range to predictable maximum distances from land and reliably signal that an island is near. Thus, a mark to be looked for on the course from Puluwat to East Fayu is a sighting of seabirds from Pisaras, and other seaways have similar directions.

Two major elements of the en-route navigation task remain to be described. Interestingly, although distinct in purpose they are closely linked in the logic of Puluwat navigation theory. One is estimating distance traveled, the proportion of the journey completed, through a system known as *etak* (eh-tack). The other is navigation when tacking upwind out of sight of land. They belong together because both depend upon a special logical construct or cognitive map based on the concept of a moving island. To explain this it is necessary to begin with a description of how the navigation process is conceptualized by the Puluwat navigator. In particular we must look at the way he envisions the constantly changing relation between his canoe and the islands and seas which surround it.

Like everything else in this chapter the words which follow are mine. Although Hipour and other navigators refer explicitly to a moving island when talking about etak or tacking, the larger logical context in which this concept operates is not described by them in words. This does not mean it is not real to them; it means only that they share and take for granted all the cognitive antecedents of saying that an island "moves." They find no need and therefore have had no practice in explaining this to someone like myself who starts out thinking of a voyage as a process in which everything is fixed except the voyager. The situation I suspect would be similar if an American, accomplished in interpreting the stylized symbols and distortions of a highway map, were asked to explain to our old friend the man from Mars what he really means when he points to the map and says, "We are here." I arrived, through my own style of induction, at a description of the Puluwat navigator's cognitive map, the only description I could conjure up which would account for all the different things that a number of different people said in the course of trying to explain to me what etak was all about (tacking came later). Having arrived at this construct I explained it carefully to Hipour, as was my custom whenever I felt I had mastered a particular topic. He agreed in broad outline but made one modification, one which in itself encouraged me to believe he understood what I was saying. Later in talking with other people, and in particular when it came time for me to learn about navigation when tacking, I found my perception of the system could be used without leading to any more misunderstandings. In other words it made sense out of everything which followed, both familiar and new. It is for this reason in particular that I am satisfied the cognitive map I constructed is real. That is, real in the sense that I correctly understood how the navigators organize their information. I would certainly not suggest that they believe islands actually move any more than the man with his finger on the road map believes he is really somewhere in the spot of ink on the paper.

Picture yourself on a Puluwat canoe at night. The weather is clear, the stars are out, but no land is in sight. The canoe is a familiar little world. Men sit about, talk, perhaps move around a little within their microcosm. On either side of the canoe water streams past, a line of turbulence and bubbles merging into a wake and disappearing in the darkness. Overhead there are stars, immovable, immutable. They swing in their paths across and out of the sky but invariably come up again in the same places. You may travel for days on the canoe but the stars will not go away or change their positions aside from their nightly trajectories from horizon to horizon. Hours go by, miles of water have flowed past. Yet the canoe is still underneath and the stars are still above. Back along the wake, however, the island you left falls farther and farther behind, while the one toward which you are heading is hopefully drawing closer. You can see neither of them, but you know this is happening. You know too that there are islands on either side of you, some near, some far, some ahead, some behind. The ones that are ahead will in due course fall behind. Everything passes by the little canoe—everything except the stars by night and the sun in the day.

We can call this a figure of literary style, a canoe pictured pushing through the sea with everything moving past it except the stars poised overhead. For the Puluwat navigator it is not a matter of style. It is a convenient way to organize the information he has available in order to make his navigational judgments readily and without confusion. This picture he uses of the world around him is real and complete. All the islands which he knows are in it, and all the stars, especially the navigation stars and the places of their rising and setting. Because the latter are fixed, in his picture the islands move past the star positions, under them and backward relative to the canoe as it sails along. The navigator cannot see the islands but he has learned where they are and how to keep their locations and relations in his mind. Ask him where an island is and he will point to it at once, probably with considerable accuracy.

It should be added, however, that the canoe is not at all times conceived as fixed while all else moves by. It was in this respect that Hipour had to correct my formulation. As long as the canoe is on course heading along the seaways toward its destination it is conceptually immobile. However, if it moves off course to one side, as in a storm or to chase a school of fish, the canoe is seen to move and the movement of the islands ceases —or more properly becomes temporarily irrelevant. Once the fish have been caught or the storm is over the navigator searches out his course and heads off again toward his destination. As soon as he gets under way on a proper heading the picture begins to move again, and the islands once again slide by under the stars in the unchanging heavens. It is rather like sitting on a train and looking out the window. In your little world you sit and talk while the scenery slips by. In the distance there are mountains which for long periods of time seem to pace the train. Looking at them you are distracted by nearby houses which flash backwards between you and the mountains. The mountains are the stars and the houses the islands below. The train comes to a town, slows, and a station slides into view. You cease looking out the window and get off the train and walk around. At that moment the world is not moving past and is forgotten; you are moving around by yourself in one place. Then you get back on the train and it moves out of the station. It picks up speed, the houses fly past, the mountains are again in view still pacing along with the train from their remote places on the horizon. The canoe has resumed its voyage, the constant stars are once more its guides, and the islands are again moving backwards past the canoe on either side, though unseen in the distance.

It is the passage of the islands under the stars which is used for etak, the reckoning of distance traveled on a voyage. More specifically, one island is selected for each seaway and used throughout every voyage as a reference. The identity of the etak reference island is part of the sailing directions which must be learned by the student navigator for each passage. Ideally this island is fifty miles or so to one side of the line of travel and roughly opposite the midpoint of the seaway which stretches between the islands of origin and destination. The star bearings of the reference island from both the starting and ending points of the trip are known, since on another occasion the reference island may itself become a destination. In between there are other navigation star positions under which the reference island will pass as it "moves" backward. Its passage under each of these stars marks the end of one etak and the beginning of another. Thus the number of star positions which lie between the bearing of the reference island as seen from the island of origin and its bearing as seen from the island of destination determines the number of etak, which can here be called segments, into which the voyage is conceptually divided. When the navigator envisions in his mind's eye that the reference island is passing under a particular star he notes that a certain number of segments have been completed and a certain proportion of the voyage has therefore been accomplished.

Note that the etak system does not add anything to the input of concrete information upon which the navigator bases his judgment of position and course. It is a way of organizing and synthesizing information obtained through a variety of discrete observations and nothing more. How does the navigator know where the reference island lies? A study of etak will not give us the answer. Rather we must look back to his instruction in the star courses, the little maps of islands shown by pebbles on the canoe house floor. How does the navigator know how many miles of water his canoe has pushed its way through, and therefore how far backward the reference island has "moved"? Again, the answer does not lie with an understanding of etak, but in his skill in judging the speed of his canoe under various conditions of wind, a skill sharpened by long experience, and his attention to the time which has passed as shown by the movement of sun and stars. Strictly speaking, it is not proper even to speak, as I did, of the number of miles the navigator has traveled. In our speech we find it natural to estimate (or measure) distance in arbitrary units. For a Puluwatan the estimate is

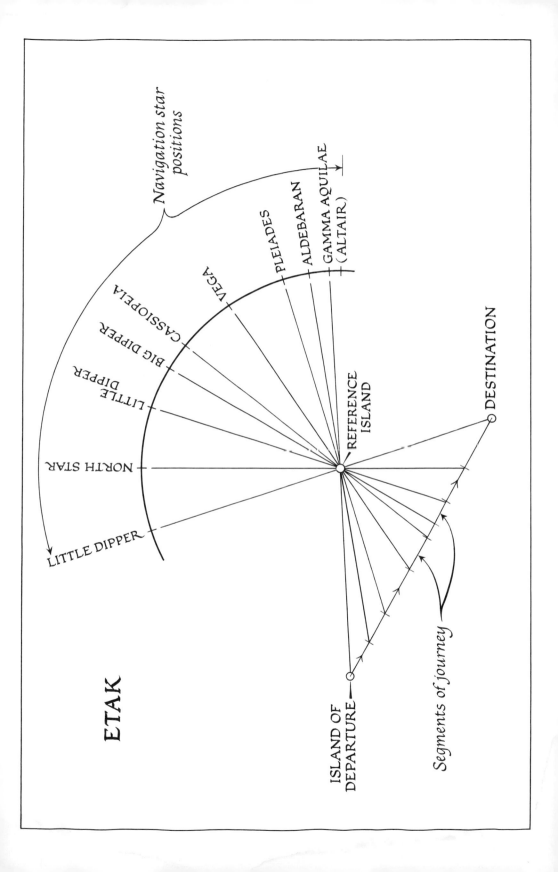

ETAK

Navigation star positions

LITTLE DIPPER
NORTH STAR
LITTLE DIPPER
BIG DIPPER
CASSIOPEIA
VEGA
PLEIADES
ALDEBARAN
GAMMA AQUILAE
(ALTAIR)

REFERENCE
ISLAND

ISLAND OF
DEPARTURE

DESTINATION

Segments of journey

relative. It is akin to a person walking across a familiar field in the dark. He is not likely to count his paces even if he knows their exact length. Instead he estimates intuitively that he is one-third or perhaps halfway across by knowing subjectively how long and how fast he has been walking.

In sum, the contribution of etak is not to generate new primary information, but to provide a framework into which the navigator's knowledge of rate, time, geography, and astronomy can be integrated to provide a conveniently expressed and comprehended statement of distance traveled. It also helps keep his attention focused on these key variables which are central to the entire navigation process. It is a useful and deliberate logical tool for bringing together raw information and converting it into the solution of an essential navigational question: "How far away is our destination?"

What has been described is the theory of etak. It has been reported in similar terms by Alkire (1970) for Woleai, although for that dialect it is spelled *hatag*. Earlier sources refer to the system throughout the islands in this area. However, considerable confusion about its purpose, and therefore its nature, arises from early informants having called the etak reference island a "refuge" island, a place to flee in storm or other trouble. Both Hipour and Ikuliman recognize a linguistic usage of this sort on Puluwat today and feel it must have some validity, but they cannot account for it. It is in the nature of the system that in order to know where the etak reference island is the navigator must also know where all the islands around him are. Therefore if he were in trouble he would flee to the most accessible or most useful of these, not necessarily the etak island. Many reference islands are actually quite useless for refuge. Some are tiny and uninhabited, others difficult to approach in bad weather, and a few are actually reefs or shoals with no dry land at all.

When one turns from the theory of etak to its practical application some complexities intrude, but they are not great. At times there is no island on either side of the seaway at a convenient distance, so an island too close or too far away must be used. If the reference island is too close it passes under many stars, dividing the journey into a lot of segments. Worse, the segments are of very unequal length. They start out rather long ("slow") and then as the canoe passes close by they become shorter ("fast") as the reference island swings under one star after another, and then at the end they are long again, a confusing effect. A distant reference island has an opposite effect, making the segments approximately equal but so few in number that they do not divide the journey into components of a useful size.

The clustering of navigation stars to east and west and their relative scarcity toward the poles creates another sort of inequality. The roughly equal triangle of West Fayu, Satawal, and Lamotrek provides an example. Between each pair the distance is a little over forty miles, and for each pair the third island of the trio is the etak reference. Therefore theoretically each of the three seaways should be divided into a roughly equal number of segments. This is, however, not so. For the east-west seaway between Satawal and Lamotrek the reference island is West Fayu. It moves during the canoe's journey under the sparse stars of the north from the setting of the Little Dipper to the rising of Cassiopeia, dividing the voyage into only four segments. In contrast, when going from Satawal northwest to West Fayu, the reference island is Lamotrek. It passes under the crowded western star positions from the setting of Gamma Aquilae to the setting of the Southern Cross to make a total of seven segments, nearly twice as many for a voyage of almost the same length.

Another kind of difficulty arises on exceptionally long passages. If a reference island is selected far enough away to make all the segments roughly equal they will also be so long that an entire day or more could sometimes be spent in completing just one. Here different solutions are sought within the two schools of navigation. As we shall see, the two schools actually differ in many of their reference island selections. In this case, even for a long voyage Fanur is inclined to adhere to the principle of only one reference island for one seaway despite the inconveniently long segments which result. Warieng, however, often selects two islands, with a shift from one to the other midway through the voyage. An example is the seaway between Puluwat and East Fayu, slightly over one hundred and fifty miles. It is commonly made with at least one intermediate stop, but non-stop passages have been made and the sailing directions are therefore careful and detailed. For Fanur, Ulul is the only reference island, dividing the voyage into ten segments. Warieng uses Ulul first then switches to Pisaras, for a total of fifteen segments. There are good arguments for doing it either way.

Less clear is the rationale for a practice which is confined to Fanur of having alternate reference islands on either side of the seaway. This is rare, and Ikuliman, my Fanur informant, knew of only one case on a commonly sailed seaway. Between Puluwat and Pulusuk a Fanur navigator can use both Truk, far to the east, and a dangerous shoal locally known as Lulunna at the end of Manila Reef very close to the seaway on the west. This case well illustrates one of the difficulties with the practice: when two reference islands are used in this way the segments are almost certain to be markedly different in length. Ikuliman was not able to offer a good explanation for using two islands, insisting only that this is the way it is taught. When I pressed him further he observed drily that Puluwat and Pulusuk are so close together that a navigator does not really need to use etak at all in order to establish his position on this seaway so in this case my question was irrelevant. With that I abandoned the argument.

A final feature of the etak system is interesting because it is completely inconsistent with the theory as described above, yet serves well the practical purpose of noting and being able to refer to segments of a journey. It consists in a special derivation and designation of the first two and last two segments of a passage. Upon leaving an island one enters upon the "etak of sighting," a segment which lasts as long as the island remains in view, usually about ten miles. When the island has at last disappeared one enters the "etak of birds" which extends out as far as the flights of those seabirds which sleep ashore each night. This is about twenty miles from land, making the first two, and therefore also the last two, segments each about ten miles long. Having four segments of the voyage absolute in length is logically incongruous (by our criteria) with the proportional derivation of the remainder of the etak divisions. In practical terms, however, the discrepancies are not severe. Around Puluwat, as Alkire (1970) independently found on Woleai, reference islands seem to be selected by preference so that they render segments roughly ten miles in length. The few examples noted above are enough to indicate that such is not always the case. There are more such examples, and some are even more divergent. However, at the practical level there are many problems more taxing than this with which the navigator must wrestle. When I tried to explore with Hipour how he resolved the discrepancy he simply replied that beyond the etak of birds he uses the reference island to establish distance. When I asked how he handled the problem of segments ending in different places under the two methods he said he did not see this as a problem. As with Ikuliman's answer to my "problem" over the dual reference islands, this ended the discussion. Although etak has for us much of the quality of a systematic organizing principle or even a logical construct, the Puluwat navigator does not let logical consistency or inconsistency, insofar as he is aware of them, interfere with practical utility. He must conform to the logic of his own system and a cardinal principle of that system is the primacy of pragmatism.

Stated theoretically navigation when tacking upwind is at least as simple as etak, possibly even simpler, but more complications intervene in its application. This is largely because the moving island construct provides the *totality* of navigational guidance when tacking, whereas etak when it is used deals with only one of several aspects of the navigator's task, distance estimation. By the same token, since the moving island is only a logical construct and thus does not contribute any factual support for the navigator's decisions, tacking over a long distance with only the moving island for guidance necessarily places the greatest demands of any routine navigational exercise upon the judgment and skill of the navigator.

The description of the theory of tacking can best begin with an oversimplified paradigm. A navigator starts from island "A" to tack directly upwind to island "B" which lies due east, that is, under Altair. (This could very nearly be a trip against an east wind from Puluwat to the west pass of Truk, except that Tamatam might get in the way.) Actually no navigator would set out on a trip this long if he knew he would have to tack into the wind all the way, but the long run allows plenty of room to work out a hypothetical example.

Tacking requires repeated changes of direction as a boat zigzags upwind toward its destination. Each time there is some loss of time and distance and the expenditure of a certain amount of work. Ideally, one might suppose a boat would make one very long tack in one direction, followed by an equally long tack the opposite way, and end at its destination. Among other things this would call for very precise navigation and no change in the wind. At the other extreme a succession of very short tacks of uniform length would keep the boat as close as possible on a direct course line and in some respects simplify the navigation problem, although at the cost of much work. The Puluwat strategy combines features of both. Initial tacks are very long but are gradually reduced each time a change is made so that near the end they become quite short. In this way near its destination the canoe courses back and forth on successively tighter tacks to assure that it will intercept the island without danger of passing by out of sight. This strategy is by no means unique; sailors all over the world use it. The only thing unique to the Carolines is the way the navigational task is set up to provide guidance for the gradually diminishing tacks.

Let us say the navigator leaves island "A" on his first tack heading in a northerly direction. (With the wind coming from the east he could equally well start in a southerly direction without affecting the outcome.) If his canoe is similar to the one whose performance was reported in Chapter 3 he will make good a course about 18 degrees east of north. The navigator naturally takes note of this heading, but his intent is only to achieve the most easterly course possible, not to head in any predetermined direction. His guidance instead comes from the "movement" of the destination island "B," which is more or less on his beam. In just the same way as an etak reference island, "B" is moving south as long as the canoe is heading north (although etak itself is disregarded during tacking). In doing so it passes under navigation stars. Being due east "B" starts under Altair. Moving south relative to the canoe it passes under Beta Aquilae, then Orion's Belt, then Corvus. The number of stars it will be allowed to slide beneath is a decision for the navigator. The more the stars the longer the tack and the fewer the changes in direction to be made. However, it is more difficult on a long tack to keep in mind the relative positions of canoe and island. It must be kept in mind that all this time the island "B" is out of sight and will remain so until near the end

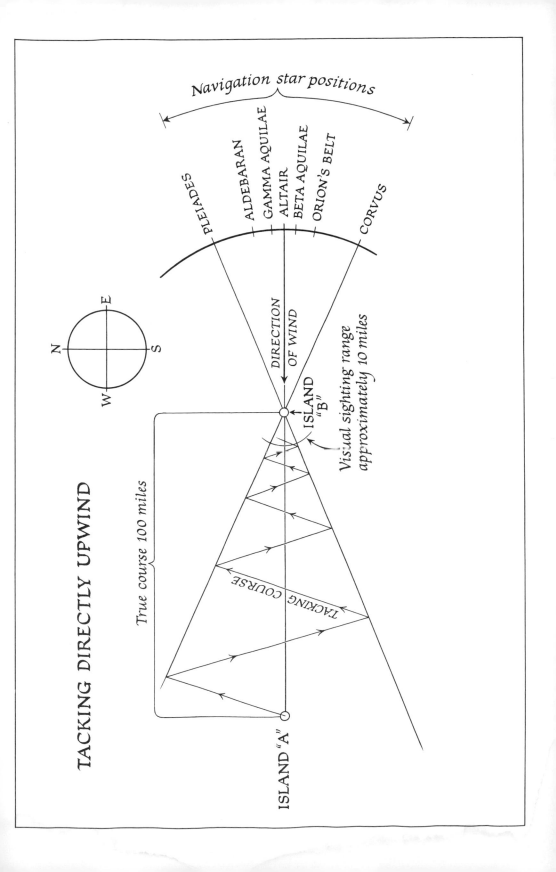

TACKING DIRECTLY UPWIND

Navigation star positions

PLEIADES
ALDEBARAN
GAMMA AQUILAE
ALTAIR
BETA AQUILAE
ORION'S BELT
CORVUS

DIRECTION
OF WIND

ISLAND "B"

Visual sighting range
approximately 10 miles

N
E
S
W

True course 100 miles

TACKING COURSE

ISLAND "A"

of the voyage. Its position must be construed solely from the navigator's knowledge of where it should be in both distance and bearing and how much progress the canoe has made on its heading through the water. The navigator therefore tries to keep the dimensions of distance and angle within whatever bounds he can readily comprehend and retain. A tack which moves the destination island three stars away, the equivalent of three segments in the etak system, is frequently the length selected. Thus, for island "B" to move from under Altair to a position under Corvus three stars away, the canoe would have to travel about forty miles to the north, requiring perhaps twelve hours of sailing.

At that point the navigator changes direction and sets a new course also hard on the wind in a southerly direction, about 18 degrees east of south. Island "B" moves back away from Corvus, then under Orion's Belt, Beta Aquilae, and Altair, and still on under Gamma Aquilae and Aldebaran to the Pleiades. Now the destination island bears from the canoe as far north of east as it did to the south at the time of the first change in direction, so the navigator again changes his tack. His run on the second tack was some seventy-five miles and his change of direction came at the end of a day and a half of sailing, perhaps more. However, as he heads northward again he can look forward to crossing the line between "A" and "B"—which is the course he is trying to make good—about forty-five miles east of "A." In other words, this third tack will complete almost half his journey. The next change in direction, when "B" has again moved south under Corvus, will come after only fifty-five miles. The tacks are getting shorter as the canoe comes closer to "B." This is because the bearing between the canoe and island "B" is the same at the end of each tack and consequently the tacking points converge on "B." Therefore the proper moment for changing direction—a bearing on the Pleiades or Corvus—comes sooner each time.

On the ninth or tenth tack island "B" should come into view about ten miles away. If it were Truk it would be sooner because the islands in its lagoon rise so high. The open ocean navigation is then over and it remains only to beat back and forth up to the pass in a way which will best suit the currents and offer a clean entry through the reef. A journey of one hundred miles has required close to three hundred and fifty miles of sailing and, because the canoe does not travel as fast hard on the wind, four or five times as long as a straight passage would take. It has also required the navigator to keep in his mind a great many things—estimates of rate, time, bearing, drift, and some complex visual images of canoe, islands, and stars. Of all these he can only see the canoe, the water, and at night the stars.

The paradigm just used is oversimplified. It is also overly difficult to sail since nothing is slower than tacking directly upwind. It is more common for tacking to be undertaken when at some angle to the wind. Under such circumstances the theoretical problem does not change, but different stars are used to conform to the different courses which must be sailed. Again using "A" and "B," let us now say the wind is blowing from the northeast instead of due east. It is thus at 45 degrees to the true course, but as even the best of Puluwat canoes can sail no better than 62 degrees or so off the wind, tacking is still required. The first tack is to the south rather than the north, but because of the more favorable wind it need be only 18 degrees off course instead of the former 62. Very gradually island "B" moves northward under the stars. It is not until it is under Cassiopeia that the island is even directly upwind from the canoe. Thereafter the canoe still goes on for three more stars, the Big Dipper, Little Dipper, and then Polaris due north. Finally it changes direction and goes on the other tack. It is, however, only a little more than thirty miles from "B" and the next tack is short. The island passes back under the two Dippers, Cassiopeia, and then on for three more stars on the other side, Vega, the Pleiades, and on to Aldebaran, where the tack ends. The canoe is now in effect tacking upwind toward island "B" from the southwest, three stars on either side of the wind. The tacks shorten rapidly and soon "B" is in sight. This time the canoe has traveled through the water on the order of one hundred and seventy miles to achieve the hundred-mile passage from "A" to "B," scarcely half that required to tack directly upwind.

Still it is not easy. It remains a long voyage and the challenge for the navigator is not relieved at all. If anything the challenge becomes more dramatic, even if objectively no more difficult. The success of the whole enterprise now rests on a single change in direction, the first, when the canoe starts tacking up

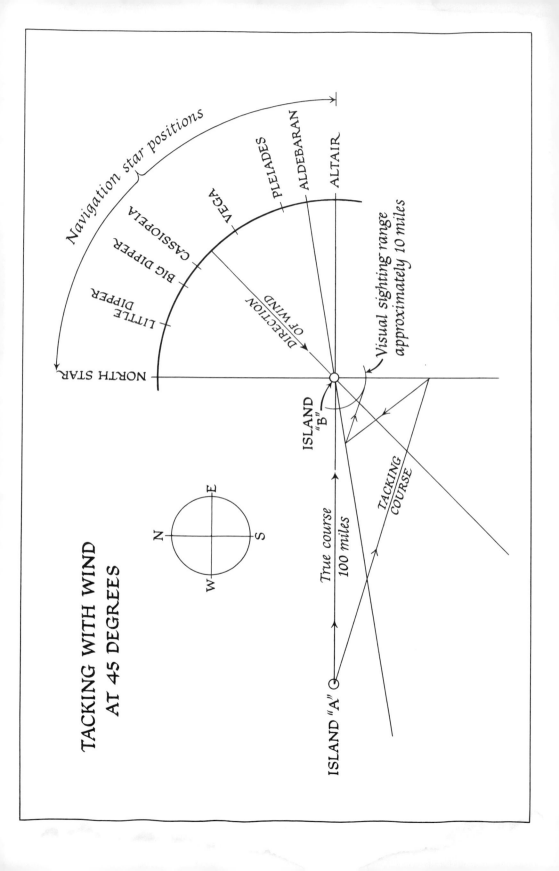

to "B." It comes after over a hundred miles of straight sailing with the canoe hard on the wind and consequently not turning in its best or its most reliable performance. The time is long and the rate not easy to judge. Mistakes are easily made. Tacking over long distances is therefore one of the most critical tests of the master navigator. Everything that really matters in the whole process goes on in his head or through his senses. All he can actually see or feel is the travel of the canoe through the water, the direction of the wind, and the direction of the stars. Everything else depends upon a cognitive map, a map which is both literally geographical and also logical.

To offset its many difficulties there is in tacking one clear advantage. The tacks back and forth, even though shortened at the end of a long voyage, cover a lot of ocean. The canoe in effect sails a search pattern. The length of its sweeps—the tacks —is added to the range from which any canoe can home on an island. As a result a fairly wide miss can still be salvaged. As a matter of fact, were it not for the safety factor introduced by the extra homing range of a tacking canoe it is likely that the potential for error would be such as to discourage all but the most accomplished navigators.

The range at which it is possible to home in on an island of destination determines the amount of error allowable in any navigation system. Navigation en route must be able to get the canoe close enough to its destination so that the navigator can find it with the techniques at his disposal. For the Puluwat navigator one technique for homing on an island which is out of sight is so heavily relied upon that it overshadows all others. This is observation of the flight of seabirds. True, there are others. Reefs can guide a navigator toward some islands. Telltale disturbances are occasionally noticeable in the waves. If freshly broken branches are found drifting they suggest that an island is near; this is especially likely after a storm, and storms are times when canoes can get lost. Gatty (1958) mentions special cloud formations in the lee of islands, and also the reflection of lagoon colors on the undersides of clouds. Neither of these appear to be used in the Carolines, perhaps because with rare exceptions the islands and their lagoons are not large enough to generate effects of this sort sufficiently strong to be detected from a distance. However, the principal reason for not using more different kinds of guides is that the seabirds locally available for observation provide such efficient homing that navigators do not need anything else.

Four principal species of seabirds are relied upon for homing on an island which is out of sight. All share the essential qualities of sleeping on land at night and flying fairly directly toward this land at dusk and away from it at dawn. In addition, none range much more than twenty or twenty-five miles away from land as they wander over the sea during the day. I determined the ranges of seabirds with Hipour by choosing pairs of adjacent islands and asking him whether the birds from one might fly out and meet the birds from the other halfway, whether there would be a gap between the ranges of birds, and so on. By selecting pairs of islands which are different distances apart and asking a variety of questions, it was possible first to establish and then to verify the range of each kind of bird as Hipour knows it. Those given are conservative, which is in keeping with the rest of the Puluwat navigation system. A navigator is not concerned with how far out he might conceivably see a given species of bird. Instead he wants to know how far out he can rely on seeing that same bird any time he needs it. Perhaps for this reason the ranges I recorded are in every instance substantially less than those given by Gatty (1958).

Noddies and white terns are the most common of the homing birds. Not only are they common, they also usually fly together, working over the ocean searching for schools of fish. Both are terns and of about the same size, but, whereas the noddy is very dark, nearly black, the white tern is luminously and almost totally white, a truly beautiful creature. At dusk they head for land, the white tern flying some distance above the water but the noddy characteristically skimming just off the surface. The aerial gymnastics which the latter requires are extraordinary. Even when the waves are relatively small a noddy heading for home will repeatedly disappear from view in the troughs of waves as he passes by, so close to the water does he fly. Nevertheless, at the end of the day both fly very straight toward land. Even a brief sighting is thus enough to tell the navigator in what direction his island lies. During the day, however, they normally give no indication of direction, ranging at apparent random over the water. One exception is the white tern if he has caught a fish too large to swallow. He holds the fish cross-wise in his bill and heads back toward land where he will pre-sumably put it down to eat it. A white tern flying with a fish sideways in his beak can be relied upon for a heading to land at any time of day he is sighted.

The sooty tern, black above and light below, also heads for land at dusk. However, sooty terns are far less common in this area than the noddy or the white tern and also may occasion-ally wander somewhat on their way home, giving a mislead-ing bearing to the navigator who has the misfortune to sight them only during an excursion. Thus the other two species of tern are more reliable as well as more commonly seen.

The booby, of a species I could not establish, is most consid-erate of all. Hipour described their habits to me in terms which were downright affectionate. He said that as the day ends and the various birds start heading for home a booby which comes upon a sailing canoe will turn and start circling over it. He acts as though he wants to land on it, but does not. At last when the sky is almost dark he finally, perhaps reluctantly, leaves the canoe and heads straight for home. By his circling he commands the attention of even the most inattentive navigator and the course he sets at last is unerringly true. What more could one ask? Not only that, but he ranges a good five miles or so farther at sea than the terns. Alas, with all these virtues boobies are common on only one island in the area, East Fayu. Elsewhere their scarcity severely limits their usefulness. There are hardly any boobies at all on Puluwat.

A number of other birds which are sighted at sea are for one reason or another of little or no value for homing. The frigate bird, ugly close at hand, is dramatic in the sky, constantly wheeling on his thin swept-back wings, a forked tail behind. He sleeps on land but is so rare and comes in to an island from so far away—up to seventy-five miles—that sightings are not only too few to be useful but may also point to land which is inaccessibly distant. He also wanders sometimes on his way home. A species of large petrel is frequently sighted but appar-ently almost never rests on land and so is useless for homing. Tropic birds nest on land but appear to fly in at any time, in-cluding late at night, so they too are not usable for locating an island. There is a large variety of plover which flies up to ten miles or so from land at night as well as by day and utters a characteristic cry, "coo-ling, coo-ling," for which he has been named. He is valueless for homing but when heard on a dark night can at least tell a crew that land is no more than ten miles away and if they wait they will sight it at dawn.

Since even the homing birds fly directly toward or away from land only at dusk and at dawn it is evident that if they are to be used actually to locate an island they can only be used at either end of the day. This means that a canoe which is really lost has to wait for the birds. Since they can initially be seen only in the daytime, the sighting to be sought is their return to the island at dusk. The flight out at dawn is helpful only if the canoe happens to have sailed within range during the night. In most recorded cases of lost canoes using birds to locate an island a bird of the proper species has first been seen during the day. If a canoe is lost everyone on board is constantly scanning the sea and sky for birds and one may thus be spied at a considerable distance. Sailing onward a little way the crew look for more birds. If they reach a point where they see birds with reasonable frequency they lower the sail and drift, waiting for dusk. Finally the birds start heading for home and the crew at last learns the bearing of the island. However, it is now almost dark and an unsafe time to approach an island of uncertain identity. Therefore, although the crew may raise the sail and travel a little way, since they do not know how far away the land lies they do not travel more than ten miles at most, for they do know the island must be at least ten miles distant or they would have seen it in the daytime. At dawn they finally sail in earnest in the direction the birds flew at dusk. Often, of course, they see the same birds flying out again for their morning fishing. Soon they find the island. This procedure may seem tedious as described, but for a canoe which is lost it is a glorious relief.

Since it is tedious, under normal conditions successful navigation should make possible a visual landfall without any recourse to birds at all, except perhaps for reassurance and minor course adjustments. This means that aside from exceptional circumstances the allowable amount of error in any passage should not exceed visual sighting distance, that is, ten miles on either side of the destination island. The total target for routine navigation is thus twenty miles wide, larger only if the island or atoll at its center is larger. However, were it not for the possibility of homing on birds it would not be safe to recognize routinely a target even twenty miles wide. It would be suicidal to work with a system of navigation in which the customarily allowable amount of error could repeatedly carry canoes to the very edge of disaster. In other words, if birds can be relied upon to provide homing guidance for a canoe which is up to twenty miles off course it is quite safe to risk the possibility of missing the island by slightly more than the ten-mile visual sighting range. If there were no birds it would probably be necessary to travel only to islands so close that the largest error one might reasonably expect would not exceed five miles either way. Then the extra five miles over which an island can be seen by eye would provide the necessary margin of safety, a margin now provided farther out by the seabirds.

The twenty- to twenty-five mile homing range of seabirds can be viewed in a somewhat different way. It has been referred to in terms of single islands. If instead one visualizes a twenty-mile radius of safety surrounding each of the islands in the Puluwat area the resultant overlapping circles, each forty miles in diameter, will be seen often to stretch across the sea in long chains or screens able to intercept a canoe crossing them at any point. One such screen extends north and south with only one short gap, from Magur at the northern end of the Namonuito Atoll over one hundred and fifty miles south to Pulusuk. The gap results from the sixty-mile span of open ocean between Ulul and Pulap. This leaves an area without homing birds perhaps twenty miles across. However, a canoe sailing west through this area would almost certainly pass soon after over Gray Feather Bank and thus locate itself, so the hiatus is even less serious than it might appear.

A far longer screen emerges if the islands of this area are viewed as they would appear from the north. This view is of some historical interest because it is the view from Saipan. Seen from the north there is a continuous screen of overlapping bird ranges extending for three hundred miles from Gaferut on the west to Pisaras on the east. If one will concede to the longer-ranging boobies of East Fayu a capability almost to close the sixty-mile gap east of Pisaras, the screen can be extended more than a hundred miles farther east to Murilo in the Halls. This screen was used deliberately on the return from Saipan in the past when that voyage of over five hundred miles was occasionally made. Going north the canoe would make a final provisioning stop at Pikelot or occasionally Gaferut. Then it took off for the grueling ordeal of at least ten, usually more, hungry, thirsty days under the sun. The navigator sailed north until he was at about the latitude of Saipan, and then if he did not sight that island he turned west. Since Saipan is in the middle of a chain of high volcanic islands, many of them (including Saipan) quite large, he was bound to hit something. However, returning to the Central Carolines some months later there were no large islands to be sighted. Instead the navigator just headed south into the long screen of islands, reefs, and birds. He always found something—or if he did not presumably never told anyone about it!

The three major operational phases of Puluwat navigation have now been reviewed: the sailing plan and initial course; maintaining en-route course and position; and locating the destination island. They have been described as I was instructed in them by Hipour and thus reflect the Warieng school. After completing my work with Hipour I went over all the sailing directions, and the secondary systems of knowledge described below, with Ikuliman, the most accomplished navigator of the Fanur school. My purpose was principally to determine how much divergence existed between the two schools in the various facets of navigation I had recorded. Not surprisingly, in areas yet to be described, which are peripheral to the central technology, many if not most of the details of systems are different, and in some cases, notably weather forecasting, even the principles differ somewhat. This is consonant, however, with the nonfunctional nature of most of this information, which shields it from the test of practice, and the jealousy with which generations of navigators have secreted their lore both from laymen and from navigators of the opposite school.

In contrast, most differences in the technical topics discussed thus far are either trifling or not such as to affect the functional integrity of the system. An example of the latter is the selection of an etak reference island. The principle is described and used identically by both schools, but the reference islands selected are different in over half the sailing directions recorded. Such a large number of discrepancies tempts the speculation that the two schools started with only the etak principle and then each selected their own reference islands within a limited number of alternatives. This can, however, remain only speculation. The point is that etak islands are a matter in which a difference in specifics does not make a difference in function.

In the all-important matter of star courses, for only one of the seaways regularly sailed by Puluwat navigators is there a real discrepancy between the two schools of navigation. Significantly, this occurs on a north-south passage, that between Satawal and West Fayu. Hipour gives the course to West Fayu as under the setting of the Little Dipper and Ikuliman under the setting of the Big Dipper. Although both have sailed this seaway themselves, it will be remembered that steering to the north or the south is more by the shape of the sky than by a specified star. In addition, the heavy easterly current which usually runs between these islands requires so much compensation that the "true" star cited above is not specified for practical use in either of their sailing directions. A few other partial discrepancies exist but can be explained even more readily than the above and need not detain us here.* It is worth noting, however, that differences do appear in star courses for some nearby seaways which, although between often-visited islands, are never actually sailed by Puluwat navigators. Examples are the seaways Ulul-Pikelot and Pulap-Satawal. Each of these four islands are regularly touched by Puluwat canoes, but only on trips to or from Puluwat, never by traveling from one island of a pair to the other.

As sailing directions are given for more and more remote islands the discrepancies become progressively greater between the two schools. This is again not surprising because these star courses between far places are used only to show off one's superior knowledge, never for real navigation. How true this may have been in the past is hard to tell. Puluwat navigators historically had a reputation as the best in the entire Caroline area. Their skills were said to link the more parochial knowledge of navigators on the islands to the east with those to the

*Findings were similar in a comparison of star courses and etak islands given to Sarfert (Damm and Sarfert, 1935: 100–103) by an earlier Puluwat navigator.

west (Hornell, 1936: 439). There is no reason why with known techniques they could not have taken trips from island to island covering in time almost unlimited distances. Some of the sailing directions in the far west from Sonsorol down to Tobi were updated and corrected in Warieng a few years ago when a navigator of that school served for a short time on a government ship which plied between them. In this regard there may be some historical significance in the fact (of which the two navigators were previously unaware) that Hipour knew from Warieng the sailing directions between far more islands in the extreme Western Carolines (in addition to those recently updated) than did Ikuliman, while the latter cited from the Fanur school sailing directions to the east well beyond Hipour's, extending from around Ponape eastward to Ebon in the Marshalls and Makin in the Gilberts.

In sum, then, in those areas where practical necessity demands accuracy the two schools converge closely. Where this is not required there are considerable differences. This would suggest at least that the divergence between the two schools goes back many generations. The even wider discrepancies found in more esoteric matters lends weight to this conclusion. Before turning to a brief description of the latter, however, it will be well to review the system of navigation as a whole, noting a few of its more striking general characteristics.

First, for a dead reckoning system of navigation it is very *accurate*. Most landfalls are made visually and the navigator expects to complete every voyage in this fashion unless a storm intervenes, relying on seabirds only for insurance against disaster. This means that the system is designed to hold the normal amount of error to within ten miles in either direction, plus the width of the destination island. Among voyages now commonly made the greatest accuracy thus demanded is on the passage from Puluwat one hundred and thirty miles to Satawal, which is less than a half mile across. An error of ten miles at the end of this journey would result from an angular deviation of less than 4½ degrees. This is through an area of ocean with quite strong cross-course currents and no en-route seamarks. (Condor Bank lies a little north of the seaway but is too small to be worth searching out just for a navigation fix.) I have to confess that once I had become familiar with the navigation system it lost some of its mystery. When in addition a number of canoes had departed on long trips and in time returned in matter-of-fact fashion, it was easy to begin taking navigation technology for granted. So at this time it was sobering to stand on the shore and watch a canoe loaded with people who had become friends grow tiny and then disappear on its way to Satawal. Like many before them, however, they found the island without difficulty, and in due time returned not even boasting of their achievement.

Second, still in the technical domain, the system is *conservative*. In both sailing directions and routine procedures the navigator capitalizes on every aid the local environment offers and never takes an unnecessary risk. Even at the cost of extra time and distance all nearby reefs or other seamarks en route and beyond are included in the sailing directions, either to be visibly sighted en route or in a position to intercept the craft if it strays. Navigators will sometimes take risks to show off their skill in handling a canoe under difficult conditions but never in their navigation.

The specificity of sailing directions for each seaway is only one of several ways in which Puluwat navigation is also highly *localized*, a characteristic noted at the beginning of this chapter. Equally localized, at least to the latitude, are the stars and the wave patterns which play central roles in the system.

If navigation is viewed as a cognitive system two additional characteristics stand out. One is that Puluwat navigation rests on a *body of theory* as well as specific techniques. This emerged most clearly in the discussion of distance estimation through etak in which theory and practice are not always congruent. However, many other aspects of navigation are also separately named and taught as distinct theoretically bounded systems. These include the navigation stars, star courses, wave systems, and navigation when tacking, along with others more esoteric in nature. Although there is no word in Puluwat for abstractions such as "system" or "theory," these subject areas are treated operationally as though they were of that order. In explaining each one of these Hipour customarily presented a functional statement of the ideal and then modified and elaborated it through working examples. Granted, this was in part a response to my requirements for learning, yet the fact that he could do this at all is significant of how the material was organized in his own mind.

The other major cognitive attribute of navigation is that the kinds of information on which the navigator must base his plans and decisions are *predetermined*. In colloquial terms, the directions are all on the package. The sailing directions, standard navigation techniques, and emergency procedures which are taught to the student navigator, combined with specified on-going observations, comprise the totality of information which he is considered to need in order not only to solve any problem he may encounter but also to make the necessary decisions regarding it. This by no means precludes skill, judgment, or careful weighing of alternatives. Superiority in just these qualities is the hallmark of the outstanding navigator. The point is that nowhere does the navigation system demand that the qualities of excellence include innovation. The navigator works at all times within the system as it has been taught to him. He expects that if he uses the system properly he will have before him in every contingency all the alternatives and all the kinds of information which could conceivably be relevant to the decisions he has to make. There is therefore no occasion to seek new techniques or strategies or to question the system as it stands. It works, and if at any time it does not work it is not the fault of the system.

More summary descriptions will suffice for the remaining aspects of the navigation complex, all of them peripheral to the central technology. One of these, alluded to earlier, is an inventory of sealife which is to be found extending outward from every known island in the direction of each of twenty-eight star-compass directions from that island. (The "wings" of the Big Bird, the stars Gamma and Beta Aquilae, are omitted.) One striking attribute of this body of knowledge is its enormous volume. The other remarkable thing about sealife inventories is that navigators seem to take them seriously. I recorded all the sealife which surrounds Puluwat as Hipour knows it, and then did the same thing with Ikuliman. (Each is familiar with the sealife for a number of other islands also but there seemed little purpose in writing it down.) Both report the same kinds of objects arranged in more or less similar ways, but the actual items they list and the sequence of items is totally different.

Each item in the list has an individual specific name by which it is known. No one knows these names except navigators. If one navigator wishes to mention to another having sighted the two porpoises' which (according to Fanur) are under the rising of Cassiopeia, he refers to them by the special sealife name which designates those two porpoises and no others. Among other things this gives navigators an opportunity to mystify the un-initiated, something which they dearly enjoy doing.

It will be sufficient to give as a sample the sealife inventories listed by Hipour for one quadrant around Puluwat, from east to south. It is given descriptively, not by the special private names. Each inventory is listed under the star toward whose rising (or setting) position it extends, starting, as does every-thing in Puluwat navigation, with the Big Bird. The presump-tion is that if you sail away from Puluwat precisely on each of these courses you will every few miles along the way encounter one after another of the things mentioned below.

Altair. A whirlpool over Uranie Bank [this really exists, and is mentioned also by Ikuliman, an exception]; a white-tailed tropic bird, alone; a frigate bird, alone; another white-tailed tropic bird, also alone [but he has a different specific name in the sealife inventory]; a large shark; a single white tern; Truk—which ends this sequence.

Orion's Belt. Two skipjack; a school of fish in the water with noddies flying and diving over them; another school of fish, mostly white terns over them; one plover [the kind which calls "coo-ling"]; two sooty terns; ends at the Kuop reefs south of Truk.

Corvus. Two sooty terns, making cries; a frigate bird, alone, flying high; two porpoises; a band of turbulence in the water with sea snails floating in it; a red-tailed tropic bird; a large porpoise, alone; ends at sea.

Antares. A large wrasse; a school of fish, noddies over them; a school of small porpoises; two dragonflies, ends on a reef which Puluwatans generally agree exists, but which does not appear on charts of the area.

Shaula. A single large barracuda; a school of fish with petrels above; two plovers; ends at sea.

Southern Cross at rising. A white-tailed tropic bird, resting on the water; about ten small plovers; this and the next sequence are short because they pass close to Pulusuk and stop.

Southern Cross at 45 degrees. A booby, alone; a school of fish with lots of noddies over it, so many because they fly out from Pulusuk; ends.

Southern Cross upright. No sealife because in this direction Manila Reef is close to Puluwat.

Similar sequences continue through the other three quadrants. Although one man could never know them all, the same kinds of sealife, each single item with its own name, surround every island in the Carolines large enough to have living things on it. Where a sequence extends from one island to another the inventory is of course the same. Thus the sealife under the setting of Altair from Truk is the same as that listed above under the rising of Altair from Puluwat, but in reverse order.

It is obvious that with rare exceptions like the whirlpool mentioned above under Altair the kinds of things included in sealife inventories would not by their nature be likely to stay long in one place, much less arrange for successors to take their places to beguile later generations of navigators.* As everyone agrees, they are sighted only rarely. Nevertheless, sealife inventories are weighty matters. Their identities and locations are never mentioned before laymen, just their names, which alone are meaningless. Sealife enters heavily into the recitations and chants of initiation ceremonies for navigators, and into the songs composed for their wives to sing while they are at sea (which used to be first sung at their initiations), but never in all of this are anything more than the names revealed, without identities.

Sealife knowledge was in the past considered so precious that, as mentioned in the last chapter, it was sometimes taught in a deliberately garbled form to people who were not related and were being trained only for pay. It was precious because sighting something from sealife could make the difference between life and death for a canoe lost at sea. Asked for examples they knew at first hand, Ikuliman reported changing course slightly once when he recognized a porpoise from sealife, and

---

*However, one is reminded of the charts prepared by early European cartographers, showing among other things the abodes of sea serpents and other vicious beings. These too were apparently in specified locations.

Hipour gave a somewhat ambiguous instance of two navigators on different canoes traveling together and sighting a single frigate bird; each gave it a different name and thus placed it under a different star. After some hesitation one decided to follow the other, who fortunately turned out to be right. Under questioning, Hipour admitted to considerably more skepticism about sealife than Ikuliman. However, when pressed further he insisted that the sealife is real and does exist as described, but because it is sighted only sporadically it is not as important as people used to think it was. One thing both agreed upon emphatically: sealife knowledge was never used, as some other esoteric things were, for magic or sorcery. In other words, it was esoteric but not supernatural. Thus I am prepared to leave the subject of sealife with the observation that if it has a deeper meaning I did not discover it. It is ambiguous, but intriguing. It must also be a dreadful subject to memorize.

Sealife inventories are worth noting for another reason. They show up repeatedly in a slightly different kind of sequence which is reported by sources both old and modern throughout the central Caroline Islands. Because a number of authors apparently have taken them seriously as a part of practical navigation, they have contributed an undeserved aura of mystery to the navigation complex. Without going into detail, of which there is much, these sequences consist of long chains of islands, reefs, and other seamarks, the star courses from one to the next, and the sealife in between. They often start or pass through distant or even mythical lands. On Puluwat there are yet wider disparities between the two schools of navigation with respect to these sequences than is true of sealife alone. About all the two schools share in common are the general characteristics outlined above and the name of the system, taken from the word for the binding on the long slender poles used to pick breadfruit. This name may be related to a tendency, especially in Warieng, to favor sequences of islands and reefs which lie more or less in a straight line, ideally a line stretching eastward under the Big Bird. It should also be added that on Puluwat at least these sequences have absolutely no practical value. They, along with other schemes for linking together islands and clusters of islands, were taught by master navigators to their students so that the latter could show off their knowledge during initiations, this possibly being the Puluwat equivalent of fraternity hazings. When these tasks of memorizing were added to sealife it is a wonder that anyone lasted through the course of study. With the end of initiations interest in the island sequences seems to be declining. It is probable that the current crop of students are not taking them very seriously.

Another class of information, technically as nonfunctional as sealife and the island sequences, differs from them in some other respects. This is the naming of seaways between pairs of islands. Most but not all seaways have secret names, known and shared among navigators but not revealed to outsiders. The names of seaways are still used, as is sealife, to bemuse the uninitiated. To this end one navigator regales another with his adventures during a past journey but never makes a reference to the name of an island or any other familiar mark, only to the seaways on which he traveled. The outsider listens in vain for some clue to where the journey took place but remains mystified to the end. The names of seaways are, however, more widely shared among navigators than is sealife. In a sense the seaway nomenclature is not really esoteric but is rather a form of specialized professional jargon, a matter of never using a common word when there is a technical one available—a form of snobbery annoying to outsiders but practiced by sailors the world around.

The common usage of seaway names among navigators is reflected in its having the highest congruence between the two schools of navigation of any category of nonfunctional knowledge. Omitting very remote island pairs I sought the names of seventy-five seaways. On forty-nine of these, essentially two-thirds, Hipour and Ikuliman were in complete agreement, either giving identical names or agreeing that there was no name. Most of the disagreements, furthermore, consisted in one giving a name and the other not—I did not reveal the list of one to the other—so only in a handful of cases did they actually offer completely different names for a single seaway. In their congruence between navigational schools seaway names stand in contrast not only to most other categories of nontechnical navigation knowledge, but even to the technical but not critical area of etak reference islands which in more than half the sailing directions differed between the two schools.

The names of seaways in days past were also of more in-
trinsic importance than the other esoterica. This was because
they were used in sorcery. Sorcery apparently died out in these
islands in the 1930's, if not before, and little has been recorded
about it. However, it was at one time rife among navigators,
principally those from different islands, and a major goal of sorcery was to bring disaster to a canoe at sea. In order to do this
one had to know and include in the spells the names of the seaways upon which the canoe would be traveling. Perhaps for
this reason one senses to this day a touch of awe associated
with the use of seaway names. Both Hipour and Ikuliman lowered their voices when pronouncing them, which incidentally made it difficult to obtain reliable phonetic transcriptions.

A final set of techniques deals with weather forecasting.
Forecasting appears here rather than in the earlier technological portion of this chapter because it has no practical effectiveness, aside from keeping track of broad seasonal changes.
As a consequence it occupies a status rather like that of sealife:
all navigators learn it, take it seriously, and declare it to be
real and effective, but in practice largely ignore it. Instead on a
short-term basis they are inclined to sail when the weather
looks favorable and remain on land when it is threatening. For
this reason I will devote only enough space to indicate its essential principles as they are taught, again differently by the two
schools of navigation, on Puluwat.

Weather forecasting utilizes both the stars and the moon,
each furnishing the basis for an essentially separate cycle or
system. The two schools agree at least on the stars which are to
be used, though Goodenough (1953) found considerable variation through the Carolines even in this regard. The stars, some
of them constellations, are fourteen in number, some but not
all coinciding with navigation stars.* Instead of being spaced

*For those interested in such matters, the stars are essentially those cited by
Goodenough from Sarfert from Puluwat of an earlier day, except that Sarfert's
tenth star is omitted and another star is introduced in thirteenth position. The
stars presently used are as follows, the first ten in a rising position and the last
four setting; (1) Antares; (2) Vega; (3) Altair; (4) Equuleus; (5) the constellation
of Pegasus; (6) a constellation including Cassiopeia, Beta, Gamma and Mu An-
dromeda, and Beta Triangulus; (7) a constellation of Hamal, Menkar, Algol, and
Mirfak; (8) the Pleiades; (9) Aldebaran; (10) a constellation of Canopus, Sirius,
and Procyon; (11) Southern Cross; (12) Spica; (13) Arcturus; and (14) the constellation of the Northern Crown. The cycle begins with Antares' appearance about
January 1, when the strong winds begin and voyaging stops.

through the sky at intervals of latitude from north to south as the navigation stars are, these are selected so as to be spaced from west to east in such fashion that they will appear at fourteen roughly equal intervals through the year, thus defining fourteen months. It should be added that their "appearance" consists for the first ten stars in being in a rising position at dawn, but the last four define the final months of the year by their "appearance" in a setting position at dusk just after the sun goes down.

The months defined by the fourteen stars are not delimited periods of time. Instead, the appearance of each of the various stars signals that a certain point has been reached in the cycle of seasons through the year, and that certain kinds of weather have become more probable at that time. Only in this very general almanac sense of forecasting do the star-months have any predictive validity.

The Puluwat word which is here translated as "month," and which has apparently always been applied to the time of appearance of the fourteen almanac stars, literally means "moon." This gave rise to an interesting bit of by-play. It had, it seems, always been assumed on Puluwat—although evidently no one paid much attention—that the somewhat irregularly spaced star months coincided approximately with the lunar months. On this basis there would be the same number of moon months as there are star months through the year, that is, fourteen. More recently the Puluwatans have learned also to work with a different system of months, the Western twelve. (Goodenough reports that some Caroline Islands have traditionally used twelve star months, but not Puluwat.) Furthermore the Puluwatans know that the lunar month has thirty days, exactly, because they have a separate name for each of the thirty days or phases of the moon. However, no one seemed ever to have placed these various discrepant systems in confrontation with each other.

One morning Hipour and I were bearing down very hard on all these matters and moving back and forth from one system to another as I tried to get clear their various relationships. Finally I felt I had it all and started my customary resumé back to him. In the course of this I was able to make clear to him that (1) the lunar month has thirty days, which he knew, (2) the American months have about thirty days, of which he was also generally aware, (3) there are twelve American months, which he knew, and (4) therefore there must be just about twelve lunar months in the year, which thus cannot be the same as the fourteen star-months. Hipour was at first incredulous, and then delighted. He could scarcely wait for our lunch break so he could go off and tell his friends. He explained it all to Angora, one of the very senior navigators, and also to a group of men who were in his canoe house, working on the lashings of his canoe whose over-haul had been delayed by our work together. Hipour reported that everyone was surprised and amused by the discovery. I was especially struck by this episode because it was the only occasion during our entire working relationship when Hipour seemed to be intrigued by a purely intellectual issue of system consistency. It is interesting to speculate whether this was re-lated to the peripheral and nonpractical nature of the systems involved. Perhaps admitting the inconsistency of systems of this sort is acceptable because it does not throw into question the validity of any working body of knowledge and therefore need induce no anxiety.

Returning to weather forecasting, the precise positions of the various stars at dawn or at dusk can, according to this system, be used to determine whether the weather will be good or bad on a given day or succession of days. For Warieng during the first ten months, when the star of one month is fairly well up in the sky at dawn and the star for the next month is just below the horizon and therefore soon to appear, the weather will be bad. As soon as the star for the next month actually appears then the weather will turn good. For Fanur the forecast runs precisely opposite: when the star for the next month is still below the ho-rizon at dawn the weather is good, and when it appears the weather turns bad. The evening forecast based on the last four stars of the year is fortunately the same for both: the weather will be bad as long as the month-star sets after the sun, that is, is visible briefly in the night sky right after sunset before it too sets. Once it sets with or before the sun, so that it is no longer visible at dusk, the weather becomes good. In addition to the contradictions between schools six of these precise-sounding determinations are made even more ambiguous by the fact that the "stars" used are actually constellations, some of which cover large sweeps of the sky and gradually "appear" over a period of many days.

All navigators know and allegedly also use a second system of short-range forecasting based on the days of the moon's monthly cycle. On some of these days one can expect good weather and on some days bad. Without going into any detail, suffice it to say that there are more days in the month when the forecasts of the two schools are contradictory than when they are congruent. No attempt is made by either school to reconcile moon forecasts with star forecasts even within their own schemes, much less between one school and the other. All of these forecasts deal only with good weather or bad. They do not differentiate between different kinds of good or bad weather, such as windy, calm, rainy, or dry.

Both Hipour and Ikuliman insisted that these short range forecasting systems are used and that, although not perfectly accurate, they do have some reliability. Each navigator follows the system of his own school of navigation. Conflicts between them are avoided even when navigators of opposite schools are traveling together in convoy by placing responsibility for all decisions in the hands of the senior navigator. Beyond that, however, there seems to be no means for reconciling star forecasting with unrelated moon forecasts, nor for determining the precise day when a large constellation can be said to have risen above the horizon. Perhaps the resolution is, as suggested before, in practice to ignore it all and look instead at the weather in the sky. However this leaves open a question, which I cannot answer, of why the star and moon forecasting systems are maintained at all.

In the several accounts I obtained of complete trips, including numerous stops on various islands, short-range forecasts were spontaneously mentioned only on occasions when a canoe was waiting for the end of bad weather on a far island. Under these conditions the navigator would forecast the number of days before the weather could be expected to clear and plan his departure accordingly. Both stars and the moon were variously referred to in this context. At that time early in my stay I did not have a basis for asking the necessary critical questions so these concrete examples went unexplored. I did not even have the sense at the time to realize that since the weather was bad on these occasions neither the stars nor the moon would have been visible for consultation!

It is perhaps appropriate that it should be on this note of mild frustration that we reach the end of the rather long technical description of the complex and sometimes tantalizing art which is navigation on Puluwat. It remains now to look at the art in a quite different way: as a process of thinking and problem-solving which makes certain psychological demands upon those who would use it.

6 Perspectives on Thinking

We have now before us a complex and organized body of knowledge, Puluwat navigation, and a somewhat less explicit and more intuitive theory of canoe design. We are ready at last to move into the psychological domain, treating navigation no longer as technology but rather as a sample of purposeful thinking in another culture. Before undertaking this, however, it will be well to restate the rationale for doing so, and particularly for making the comparisons promised earlier between the logic of Puluwat navigators and that of poor people in the United States.

Much more than just style of logic is associated with being poor, as there is more to be said about a navigator than to describe the way he thinks. The navigator is proud, assured, respected. A poor American is likely to be hungry, powerless, weak from poor health, his spirit crushed by hopelessness, in addition to whatever difficulties he may experience in solving the logical problems people ask him to solve (Gladwin, 1967). Just being "intelligent" is far from enough to assure that a poor person can escape the suffocating constraints of poverty. Yet if the child of a poor family is seen as not "intelligent," which means particularly he is not able to do well on psychological tests and with the tasks presented to him in school, he is almost certainly doomed to the lifelong misery which is the lot of the poor.

In the Western world, and throughout the world wherever change and modernization is valued, doing well in school is an almost inescapable requirement for moving upward into the ranks of privilege. Although persons who have not gone far or done well in school may regularly perform tasks which are objectively quite complex and difficult, the jobs they do are rarely accorded high prestige, and advancement is usually difficult or impossible. Furthermore, it is by now universally recognized that economically poor children generally make academically poor students. Thus any knowledge we can gain about why poor people do or do not perform well in school is relevant to the role of education as an avenue of escape from poverty.

Obviously, one important element in determining school performance is the way in which students use their minds, that is, the cognitive abilities and strategies they are able to bring to bear upon the problems presented to them in school. Many other factors are involved, especially for poor children, but there is general agreement that a child's way of going about solving intellectual problems has a major effect on his classroom achievement, and that poor children are generally less able to solve the problems presented both in class and on tests than are their more privileged fellows. Yet surprisingly little is reliably known about the nature of the logical processes which go on in the heads of children from underprivileged families, or in the minds of the undereducated and disadvantaged adults into which such children are too often transformed.

Part of the reason for this lack is doubtless that cognitive psychologists, like their colleagues in other areas of psychology, generally use as subjects for research and experimentation persons who are readily available and with whom they can communicate easily, which usually means college students or college graduates. Yet because those in our society who have been reared in poverty tend to do badly in school, they generally do not get into college. The consequence is that poor people and their style of thinking have not had a chance to play any significant role as subjects of basic research on cognition and the structure of human intellect.

This is not to ignore the large amount of research which has been done on learning deficits of poor people in the United States. The difficulty with this research, however, is that, instead of exploring the foundations of logical thinking as they are laid down in different environments, it has more commonly focused on how lower-class intellectual handicaps are manifested and distributed relative to income level, type of school, and so on (for example, Coleman, *et al.*, 1966, and Harvard Educational Review, 1969). It is perhaps historically inevitable that research on cognition in poor people should emphasize contrasts with middle-class thinking. Not only did social class differences in cognitive style first become evident through recognition of consistently poor lower-class school performance, a quantitatively defined deficit which evaluative research now seeks to specify and delimit, but in addition the research tools available for this purpose are principally measurement techniques derived from concepts of intelligence developed within educational settings. Thus, rather than trying at the outset to discover qualities of thinking in underprivileged populations, researchers seek to *quantify* divergences from the psychological baselines used by educators, baselines rooted in middle-class intellectual culture. Emphasis is therefore on measurement, with the *qualities* to be measured accepted as givens. The possibility is thereby largely foreclosed of exploring other dimensions of thinking beyond those which are traditionally recognized within educational psychology. Stodolsky and Lesser (1967: 555) succinctly state the limiting effect this has on research in lower-class cognition: "The types of achievement and intelligence tests which are most often used can have only limited value in describing the cognitive functioning of children. In almost all instances, we are concerned with scratchings on an answer sheet, not with the ways in which a student arrived at a conclusion. No matter how much we may think we know by looking at scores on such psychometric procedures, unless tests are constructed deliberately to reveal reasoning processes, these processes will not be identified." Under these circumstances it is not surprising that despite a formidable amount of research, psychology has thus far failed to create any real strategic breakthroughs in educational technology for deprived populations. Research findings point either toward broadly maladaptive personality characteristics in poor children or to contrasts between the environments of home and school so wide that they are almost unbridgeable. Programs to prevent or remedy these conditions have been forced to adopt strategies equally broad and unfocused. Lasting successes have been correspondingly rare.

In reviewing this body of research one has the sense of many people groping about, trying out their familiar tools and strategies in infinitely varied ways in the hope of stumbling upon the effective cause of a deficit which all agree exists. Failing in the search, they are forced back upon old inadequate remedies and ever more precise but not very helpful tabulations of symptoms and cases. One is reminded of some of the dramatic searches for causes of deadly diseases which at intervals have illuminated the history of public health epidemiology. The successful quest for the cause of beriberi (Williams, 1961), now known to result from vitamin deficiency, could provide a hopeful prototype for the present research. Beriberi was recognized as a distinct syndrome at a time when germ theory was revolutionizing the practice of medicine and of public health. Persistent efforts were made to isolate sources of beriberi "infection," especially on ships where mass outbreaks occurred, and to investigate the effect of the treatments then available for dealing with infections. No answer was found. Finally Western medicine turned to another area of the world, Asia. There, as we now know, eating polished versus unpolished rice can by itself make the difference between an adequate diet and thiamine deficiency, with resultant beriberi. In the Philippines a shrewd United States Army doctor, Edward B. Vedder, noting the striking differences in incidence of beriberi among troops on different diets, concluded that something left in unpolished grains of rice prevented the disease. From there to the isolation and synthesis of thiamine the road was long, but straight. Such can be the rewards of going to unfamiliar settings to seek the answer to overly familiar problems.

Thirty years ago a similar challenge confronted students of an area in psychology closely related to the focus of this book, that of personality research. Clinical studies of that time, especially in psychoanalysis, seemed to demonstrate that some aspects of personality characterized not only individuals but also subgroups in our society. Behaviors and emotions which appeared bizarre in some settings could be normal in others. The initial question raised by these seeming differences in group characteristics was whether they were real, and if so what their nature might be. Edward Sapir proposed that the first step should be to determine which aspects of personality are likely to be shaped by cultural forces and which are more idiosyncratic. To this end, he contended, one should begin with studies of people of markedly different cultures and then, enlightened by these dramatic perspectives, return to an examination of differences within one's own society. This insight inspired a research interest in culture and personality which continues to the present. Whatever their scientific merits, the resulting studies have helped clinicians discriminate between aspects of personality which are likely to be culturally determined and those which are individual or even accidental in origin. It is precisely this sort of clarification which is needed now with respect to styles of thinking and problem solving in different social groups.

There are already in existence numerous comparative studies of cognition in different cultures (Tyler, 1969). However, with but a few rare exceptions these have been concerned with the frameworks within which information is organized for use, frameworks which have been variously called cognitive maps, semantic frames, or ethnoscience. Yet the differences in cognition between middle-class and poor people in the United States seem to lie more in the way information is processed and manipulated than in the way in which it is categorized and organized. If this is true, the critical differences should be sought in styles of thinking, problem-solving, and planning. For this reason an information-processing system such as navigation seemed more appropriate than one principally devoted to classifying hierarchies of information.

It scarcely need be added that a comparison of this sort, taken between two widely different cultures, can only lead to highly speculative conclusions. To the degree that constructs derived from one culture seem to fit plausibly phenomena found in another, the comparison has at least a measure of face validity.

If the constructs in addition provoke further inquiry the effort can be judged worthwhile. It may in the end even lead to some change for the better in the human condition, in which event it must be viewed as very worthwhile. However, the goal of this book, and particularly of this chapter, is far more modest. It is only to seek and suggest new avenues of investigation in a crucial field of research, a field which seems at times to be approaching stagnation.

When we relate Puluwat navigation as a way of thinking to our own culture it is not because we think we are looking at a similar pathology, like beriberi, in both settings. Rather it is because we can look at a comparable process, like personality development, which is common to both but probably different enough in each to provide illuminating contrasts. This process is the use of one's intelligence in the solving of important problems.

Puluwat navigation is unquestionably intelligent behavior, but Puluwatans do not necessarily think of it this way. It is an obvious feat of intellect to travel far across the ocean and arrive at a tiny island through the use of nothing but one's mind and senses. We in the Western world value intelligence highly. For this reason we respect the Puluwat navigator. Puluwatans also respect their navigators, but not primarily because they are intelligent. They respect them because they can navigate, because they can guide a canoe safely from one island to another. There is, it is true, a Puluwat word one can translate as "intelligent," and in these terms navigators are considered intelligent, but etymologically it refers only to having a good memory. There are furthermore many useful ways to use one's mind in addition to remembering technical information. A Puluwatan who is asked to identify people who think well or use their minds effectively is likely to select those whose decisions are wise, who are moderate and statesmanlike in discussion, not the technicians. This does not mean that the statesman is more important than the navigator. On Puluwat nothing is more important than navigation. It means that, whereas *we* can recognize and respect navigation as a pre-eminently intelligent activity, this is not its significant quality for the Puluwatan. Because navigation is in our terms intelligent, it can provide useful perspectives on intelligence in our own culture. In thinking of navigation in this way, however, we must not slip into the assumption that Puluwatans view their navigators as highly intelligent. They do not. They view them as navigators.

In the description of navigation in the preceding chapter two qualities emerged to characterize it logically, or cognitively, in addition to its technological dimensions. It is on the one hand comprised of systems of explicit theory, and on the other hand works with a limited array of predetermined alternatives of acceptable input and output. Examined more closely, from some of our traditional perspectives on intelligence, these qualities could be seen as contradictory. First, Puluwat navigation (and canoe design) can be said to be cast in theoretical terms because it is explicitly taught and conceptualized as a set of principles governing relationships between phenomena. The phenomena are sometimes directly observed but at other times are only inferred, as in the case of star-compass bearings when the course star is not in position to be directly observed. These relationships and these inferences are unquestionably abstractions. Some, for example etak, are abstractions of a rather high order. The concept in etak of a specified but invisible island moving under often invisible navigation stars is not only an abstraction. It is also a purposefully devised logical construct by the use of which data inputs (rate and time) can be processed to yield a useful output, proportion of the journey completed. Abstract thinking is therefore a pervasive characteristic of Puluwat navigation.

The second characteristic, that all inputs of information and outputs of decision are so to speak prepackaged or predetermined, means that within the navigation system there is little room or need for innovation. Navigation requires the solution of no unprecedented problems. The navigator must be judicious and perceptive, but he is never called upon to have new ideas, to relate things together in new ways.

The contradiction, if there is one, derives from our custom in psychology in the United States of relating both these qualities, abstract thinking and innovative problem-solving to a third, superior intelligence. More particularly all three of these qualities are often attributed to middle-class intelligence, and said to be lacking in the "concrete" style of thinking of poorly educated lower-class persons. True, statements of this order are usually descriptive rather than analytic and therefore do not, for example, stipulate a causal or inevitable relationship such that innovative thinking must always be abstract, or vice versa. An association between the three is, however, so consistently noted that one is inclined to think of them as regularly occurring together. Although Puluwat navigation can "prove" nothing about cognitive styles in the United States, we may at least say with respect to one of these associations that on Puluwat abstract thinking exists as a dominant mode in the absence of any requirement for solving new problems or solving old problems in new ways.

Although it may not be contradictory in a literal sense to say that Puluwat thinking as reflected in navigation is at once intelligent, abstract, and not innovative, this appears to contrast with the conventional wisdom regarding thinking styles as related to social class in the United States. We must therefore examine the relationships more closely. The associations here are: middle class: high I.Q., abstraction, innovation; lower class: low I.Q., concreteness, little innovation. Perhaps these associations are real. It is equally possible, however, that they result from a lack of precision in our definition of the terms used. It is the latter question to which this chapter is principally directed. What are the significant dimensions of intelligence, innovation, or abstraction to which we should be addressing ourselves when we make comparisons across cultural lines, whether these are between social classes or between the United States and Puluwat?

Let us look first at the abstract-concrete continuum. Abstract thinking as it is usually conceived by psychologists in the United States deals with properties of things which are not usually obvious. Often a quality must be inferred, or its significance sought through its being shared in other things which would not otherwise be seen as related. At one extreme abstractions may consist in simple qualities such as color or size which link objects together into classes. From there they range into far more complex logical constructs embracing phenomena of several diverse orders in complex relationships. Etak with its moving island is a good example from Puluwat. So is a canoebuilder who makes statements about the unobservable flow of water around the lower part of a hull. He is dealing with abstractions about forces and movements of water which he can only infer from surface waves, sounds, and the comparative performance of different hulls. In contrast with such abstractions, concrete thinking is concerned entirely with the immediately perceived qualities of an object or situation. Once something has been observed and its distinguishing characteristics noted, this observation leads without further intellectual manipulation toward one or a very few possible responses.

Since we have already established that there is in Puluwat navigation a reliance on abstractions, we must now inquire about concrete thinking in the same context. Each observation a navigator makes of waves, stars, or birds is related directly without any logical reordering or interpretation to a conclusion about position, direction, or weather. Each such conclusion in turn permits of only one or at most two or three clearly defined alternative responses. Some of the observations are based on perceptions we (but not the Puluwatans) would consider extraordinarily acute, and some of the responses are complex, but once the initial observation has been made the steps which follow upon it are unequivocal. Is this concrete thinking? Few psychologists would argue otherwise. Not only is it concrete but direct pathways of this sort between observation and response comprise the principal operational mode of the entire navigation system. In other words, Puluwat navigation is a system which simultaneously employs fairly high orders of abstraction and yet is pervaded by concrete thinking.

If these two kinds of cognitive operations, abstract and concrete, can so intimately coexist in the working mind of a Puluwat navigator, how can these same qualities of thinking in the United States provide a basis of contrast and comparison between classes of people? In the United States the abstract-concrete, middle-class–lower-class distinctions have been elevated to particular prominence in the critically important context of remedial educational programs for poor children (Gordon and Wilkerson, 1966: 14-16). Yet it is ironic to discover that the authors who originally defined the contrast never proposed that these qualities should be used at all to discriminate between people, especially normal people. In their classic monograph on the subject Goldstein and Scheerer (1941) on the first page, before they even define the two terms, insist that abstract and concrete "attitudes" (as they call them) are mutually interdependent within each total personality. They are levels of intellectual operation differentially utilized by every person for different tasks, not necessarily differentially utilized by different people. Nor did they propose these concepts in relation to social class-determined behaviors. Their concern was better to understand the thinking of persons whose brains were damaged or who were psychotic. Although they argue effectively that both abstract and concrete thinking occur as major modalities in the cognitive processes of all persons, it is doubtful that they would have selected this particular distinction for emphasis were it not especially germane to their interests in psychopathology. However, they did. Not only that but they devised a number of tests and tasks to be used to assess these thinking styles. In time the tests were tried out on different populations from those for which they were initially designed and applied to different problems. Then, as so often happens in psychology—intelligence tests are the classic case—results of the tests came to stand for the thing they were said to measure. Thereupon all manner of distinctions became possible, including that between lower-and middle-class thinking.

Rather than test results, let us examine an example of another kind of problem-solving, an example from real life which offers significant comparisons with Puluwat navigation. There is in the United States an occupation not unlike navigation, but one which frequently engages people who are poor, have dropped out of school, and presumably cannot handle the kind of thinking usually required on intelligence tests. This is driving, specifically driving taxis or delivery trucks in a city. Not all taxi drivers or deliverymen are school dropouts or even poor, but enough are to demonstrate that this kind of driving falls within the capability of undereducated persons. Furthermore, in many (but not all) cities driving is a fairly open occupation in which a start can be made with minimum skill, education, or cash investment. Where this is true it provides an avenue leading out of poverty for many who have little more than the initiative to pursue it. To become a successful driver getting better runs, hours, and more income requires, however, the learning of new skills. It is the nature of these skills which interests us here.

What does the driver do? In some respects he responds in immediate and concrete ways to the things which happen as he moves through the traffic. He makes concrete but accurate judgments of timing and speed (his own and others'), somewhat less concrete inferences about such matters as the traction of road surfaces or the condition of the brakes on an old car next to him, and acute discriminations such as picking out the traffic light from among a welter of red and green neon signs. More than this he plans a route through the maze of city streets which will not only be as short as possible but will also take into account which streets are one-way, where the bottlenecks are, when and where rush-hour traffic will build up, and any temporary obstacles such as new construction. To do this he must have in his mind a plan of the city which is not only detailed and complete but has superimposed upon it the flux of traffic as this is governed by the time of day and day of the week. He must be able to superimpose himself on this dynamic map and project his course from start to finish upon it. Can one call this image of the city with which the driver must work anything but an abstraction? What of the inferences about other cars whose inner machinery he cannot see at all, or about what a policeman in a car is going to concern himself with next? All the specifics of what the driver does differ from the work of the navigator who in addition, with a crew aboard and no phone booth to stop at if he gets lost, bears a far more awesome responsibility. Yet in many ways both think alike: concretely, yet abstractly, and acutely. Both did a great deal of thinking while they were learning, but now both can do their work and reach their decisions with a minimum of conscious deliberation. What is so obvious in both, however, is that they are dealing constantly in complex abstractions, abstractions so essential to their tasks that they almost literally could not move without them, while at the same time responding concretely and immediately to most of the relevant observations they make.

If the driver and the navigator both do what they have to do in accordance with similar cognitive strategies, is it possible there are also significant things which neither does? More specifically, are there kinds of thinking which are not required for the routine tasks of either the navigator or the driver? In Chapter 5 it was pointed out that there were two distinctive cognitive characteristics of the navigation system on Puluwat. We have considered the explicit theoretical constructs in it and called them abstractions. The second characteristic of the system is a lack of necessity for making innovations within it. This leads to concrete thinking, but its significance goes beyond concreteness alone.

Innovation here means thinking about new things, finding new solutions to new problems. I have said the navigator does not do this because he does not have to. This is different from saying he cannot innovate. However it does mean that he has very little practice in the art. The navigation system, whatever its past origins, is now presumed to include techniques for dealing with every possible contingency. When a canoe is at sea and conditions change the navigator does not feel he must figure out a solution to the changed situation. He need only identify the new conditions, relate them to the techniques he has learned for dealing with such situations, and proceed. The experienced driver does much the same thing, for example, when he learns of an obstruction or detour along his intended route: he already has available in his mind sets of alternative routes he can use.

We say the navigator has on hand a device to lead him to the solution of every imaginable problem which could arise. Because he experiences no unfamiliar problems he need develop no new devices for solving them. Because he does not need such problem-solving devices he has little experience or skill in employing them, to say nothing of devising them in the first place. Cognitive psychology has a term for these problem-solving devices which the navigator never has occasion to develop. The word, an old one, but given a specialized meaning in computer terminology, is *heuristics*. Newell, Shaw, and Simon (1960), who were responsible for introducing the phrase into psychology, describe a heuristic as an experimental device. It is not a rule which once selected and applied guarantees a result— as do the rules of Puluwat navigation—but rather is something which should be tried to see if it works. It could not be otherwise since heuristics are used only to solve novel problems. In contrast, tried-and-true solutions are available only for old problems. Therefore, since the navigator deals only in old problems he does not usually need heuristics. Furthermore his lack of experience in developing and using heuristics is likely to make him clumsy and inept in approaching problems in this way, although it does not preclude his use of them.

The concept of heuristics is by no means new. As one example among many, the distinguished British psychologist Sir Frederic Bartlett devoted many years to experimental studies of heuristics. He pulled together his cumulated work on the subject in a book titled simply *Thinking* (1958). The title is significant in itself. Although the entire book is concerned with research on the development of intellectual devices for solving new problems, no single name is used or proposed for such devices. What we might now call heuristics are variously referred to by Bartlett as "rules" to be discovered, "gaps" in evidence to be filled, or "experimental thinking." This does not mean that Sir Frederic was diffident about coining new phrases; he clearly was not. Rather it demonstrates that for him, and for many psychologists to the present, "real" thinking, intelligent thinking, is coterminous and synonymous with what Newell, Shaw, and Simon call heuristics, which therefore need no new or special label. Thus: "More briefly thinking can be defined as: The extension of evidence in accord with that evidence so as to fill up gaps in the evidence: and this is done by moving through a succession of interconnected steps" (Bartlett, 1958: 75).

Among the many experimental problems described originally by Bartlett one has since been cited with particular frequency. It will serve here as a representative example of heuristic thinking:

> "D O N A L D
> G E R A L D
> R O B E R T

This is to be treated as an exercise in simple addition. All that is known is: (1) that D = 5; (2) that every number from 1–10 has its corresponding letter; (3) that each letter must be assigned a number different from that given for any other letter. The operation required is to find a number for each letter, stating the steps of the process and their order" (1958: 51).

Bartlett then describes a number of different heuristic sequences which were devised by participants in his experiments. Some were more successful than others, but for our purposes it is essential only to note that all subjects whose performances he recounted at once began to look for heuristics which might be helpful to them. A single example of a successful solution will suffice to make the point. I have adapted it slightly for clarity. (1958: 51-52).

1. Given $D = 5$, then $5 + 5 = T$. Therefore: $T = 0$

2. $0 + E = 0$. Therefore E must be either zero, which is impossible since T is zero, or else 9, with $N + R$ greater than 10 to cause 1 to be carried. $E = 9$

3. $L + L + 1$ (carried) $= R$. Therefore R is an odd number; but also $D (5) + G = R$, so R is 7 or 9, but E is 9. Therefore: $R = 7$

4. $D (5) + G + 1$ (carried) $= R$, and R is 7. Therefore: $G = 1$

5. $A + A = E$ and E is 9. Therefore $A = 4$, and $L + L$ is greater than 10. $A = 4$

6. $L + L + 1$ (carried) $= R$ and R is 7. Therefore: $L = 8$

7. $N + 7$ is greater than 10 and since only 2, 3, and 6 are now available, therefore: $N = 6,$

8. $B = 3,$

9. and $O = 2$

Bartlett in addition makes a number of distinctions within the thinking process which need only be mentioned. Thinking occurs within closed systems, by both interpolation and extrapolation, as in the example above, and in open systems. The latter he calls "adventurous" thinking, referring to what we now call creativity. Aside from Bartlett, many contemporary examples of thinking in closed systems are also provided in the series, analogies, and other typical subtests of standard intelligence tests. All require heuristics and all, even though they do not extend into the realms of "adventurousness" or creativity, are innovative in that they require the devising of new ways to solve problems for which no familiar tried-and-true solutions are available. With respect to the Puluwatans, then, it is precisely because they have had little or no practice in innovative problem-solving and the devising of heuristics that they and many other non-European people have difficulty with intelligence tests even when these tests are conceptually, linguistically, and perceptually appropriate to their culture.

This was well illustrated by a task I requested of a number of people on the island. It was adapted by Goodnow (1962) from Piaget and administered by her to children in Hong Kong and later to slum children in the United States. The subject doing the task is presented with stacks of colored poker chips and, after two progressive learning trials with three colors and then four is finally asked to place chips, presented this time in six stacks each of a different color, in as many unduplicated pairs of contrasting colors as possible. Most Puluwatan subjects arranged the pairs side-by-side in a row, but any arrangement was allowable. During the learning trials errors are corrected through suggestions from the examiner, and during the final trial the subject can make as many corrections as he wishes on his own. Before starting this final trial he is asked to think for a moment about the strategy he will use so that his work will be orderly, efficient, and accurate. When he declares he is through he is asked what strategy he used, if that is not already self-evident. For Puluwat the task was originally intended to provide a sample of planning behavior. Care was taken to see that each of the six colors carried a separate name despite the difference between the English and Puluwat languages in their designation of colors. From the subject's left to right the stacks as uniformly presented were red, blue, white, black, yellow, and silver. Despite the use of familiar colors, however, it proved impossible for most Puluwatans to develop any semblance of a real plan. Perhaps this was because in addition to the new kind of problem-solving required by the task the process of exploring combinations and permutations was itself unfamiliar.

Nevertheless, the Puluwatans did develop what we would have to call heuristics, albeit simple ones. This demonstrates among other things that because they usually do not think innovatively does not mean they cannot—they just cannot do it readily. In most cases the subjects only used position, the simplest and most obvious heuristic. The six stacks of different colored chips were before them, red next to blue, white next to black, and so on. It was easy to note that different colors were next to each other and so take chips off each pair of stacks and put them down together. Then there were more complicated heuristics, still based on position, such as pairing the first and third stacks from the left, the second and the fourth, and so on.

More interesting, however, some people used entirely different kinds of heuristics not based on position at all. I administered the task to, among many others, the five master navigators with whom I talked while seeking an appropriate instructor. Two of the five reported (when questioned at the end) that they had decided at the beginning there should be, when the task was finished, three of each color of chip included among the pairs. How they arrived at this heuristic I have no idea since it seems to have no parallels in the traditional culture. However, my research assistant, Teruo, also thought of the same heuristic but used the number five—which happens to be the correct number. My instructor, Hipour, to whose useful intelligence I need not further attest, was one of the two using three of each color. Not only was the number incorrect, leading to less than the total number of possible pairs, but Hipour could not carry through the task even to the partial solution the heuristic would permit. He was obviously hesitant, if not actually anxious, throughout. In other words, although when faced with the need he could devise a heuristic, he lacked the readiness to use it boldly and confidently in pursuit of a solution. I suggest this reflected lack of practice in solving problems in a new way with a heuristic of his own devising. However, this must remain speculation.

Meanwhile two men devised and used forthrightly a highly effective heuristic. Interestingly, it uses the most common "good" strategy used by Westerners for this task. Chips of each color in turn are placed in rows on the table in suitable numbers to pair with each of the remaining colors, and then one chip is taken off each pile to pair with them, thus (remembering the sequence of colors noted above, R, B, W, X, Y, S):

RB	BW	WX	XY	YS
RW	BX	WY	XS	
RX	BY	WS		
RY	BS			
RS				

The two men who used this heuristic strategy were also the only two on Puluwat, among the far larger number who had tried and failed, who had succeeded in lasting through high school on Truk.* This tells us something about the two men who went through high school and did well on the task, something about the navigators who did neither, and at least lets us infer

* Another man who also tried the task, employed from Pulusuk as an interpreter for Dr. Riesenberg, had also completed high school and did as well.

something about men in the United States who drop out of school and spend the rest of their lives driving about a city. The two Puluwat men who went through high school (and are now teachers) learned how to develop and use heuristics. One can only guess at the combinations of talent, opportunity, and incentive which kept them in school, but in any event by the time they were through they were ready to recognize a situation calling for heuristics and to devise them appropriately. Thus it appears that even on Puluwat heuristics are related to school. The navigators had little or no schooling and did not use heuristics effectively. However, there is another dimension to this. On Puluwat a navigator is still a much bigger man than a schoolteacher. His lack of heuristic skills and attendant lack of experience in innovation is no handicap.

The same is not true in the United States. Without a diploma or degree the driver will always be a driver, and that is not a very good thing to be. Yet his is a useful, essential job, and it is also one which requires forms of thinking very similar to those of the much-admired navigator. Furthermore, if one looks about at other jobs and other occupations in the United States, including middle-class occupations (aside from the academic and a few other domains), it is probable that many of these can also be handled with the same kinds of thinking, without innovation, without heuristics. How many occupations are actually innovative? Very few. They are learned and then they are performed, predictably, routinely. Yet most require a high school diploma, increasingly a bachelor's degree. To attain these degrees, moreover, one must go to school, and for that one must use heuristics. Try to solve problems in the new math—or indeed the old —without heuristics and soon you are in trouble. Try to perform on an intelligence or achievement test, such as are given increasingly in school, without heuristics and you will not make a decent score. "A rooster is to a hen as a bull is to a ——" calls for a heuristic, a search for something which will relate a rooster and a hen in a way which will tell you something about bulls and blanks. What this may be is by no means self-evident to one not used to thinking in this way.

This is not a point to be labored here, for this book is not about American schools or about employment requirements in the United States. Yet looking back upon the United States from the vantage of Puluwat, heuristics seem to loom much more important than they did before. That they are needed in school is not inherently bad. If it were not so the foundations would never be laid for the creativity and ingenuity which is an American hallmark and pride. The tragedy is that some people never learn to handle the kind of heuristics needed in school and are often thereby needlessly handicapped for life. Through lack of a diploma they are forever after held to menial jobs. Yet they are quite capable of a style of thinking which, albeit non-heuristic, is nevertheless adequate to much more complex tasks—a fact which is being demonstrated with increasing frequency in special vocational programs for dropouts, including successful training for such recondite tasks as computer programing.

Heuristics are not something readily learned in a harassed poor family. To use a heuristic means that first one must see the need for one. To see the need for a heuristic means one must perceive a problem. To see a problem means first to ask a question, literally or figuratively, and poor children do not easily ask questions. Nor are they, in contrast to middle-class children, encouraged to do so. Children's questions are a nuisance for an already overburdened mother. The lower class is in effect not a fertile breeding ground for heuristic thought as we know it. If this is true, it is a fact which has important implications for remedial education. Heuristics come before all else in school for they are the intellectual building blocks of education. Teaching this style of thinking, when needed, should therefore be an end in itself, not an adjunct to teaching mathematics or any other subject. If a child has to try to learn both mathematics and heuristic thinking at one and the same time the chances are he will learn neither.

What about abstraction? Have not the same things been said about that? They have, but if one recognizes that many people who did not get through school nevertheless use abstractions, remedial teaching of abstract thinking misses the point. More to the point, I submit, is the fact that many of the measures on which judgments of abstract thinking ability are based actually depend heavily upon heuristics for their formulation. The rooster, hen, and bull mentioned above are linked by an abstraction, in this case sex, but to discover the abstraction one needs a heuristic. What has happened is that middle-class testers, without a perspective from the other side of the cultural wall, find the heuristic in this kind of task so obvious that they assume the subject would inevitably come upon it if he were able to handle the abstraction which would result. In fact just the opposite is usually true. Why abstract thinking should be seen as more difficult than heuristic thinking is far from evident, but this seems to be the case in psychology at present. Perhaps it is simply that not enough attention has been devoted to heuristics.

A final few words need to be said about planning. As initially conceived this study was expected to discover in planning a principal basis for distinguishing the thinking processes of Puluwat navigators from Western navigators and Western thinking in general (Gladwin, 1964). It seemed likely that the plans of Western navigators were prepared in advance, whereas on Puluwat plans were made up and changed continually as the person using them went along. This does not now appear to be a valid distinction. The Puluwat navigator also has advance plans which cover the entire voyage. These are the sailing directions he has learned and they are quite as complete as those of any Western skipper. The difference is rather that the Puluwat navigator has his plans available before the voyage is even prepared. He has had them ever since he learned navigation. The Western navigator in contrast makes up a new one for each trip. Thus we come again to a matter of innovation. Yet by the time both the Western and the Puluwat navigators are ready to get under way their plans are remarkably similar. They are based on somewhat different maps, both cognitive and on paper, and the process as a whole seems superficially very different, but they cover the same things for the same reasons. Probably they could not do otherwise. However diverse the intellectual traditions of the navigator, the sea is a demanding master. No style of thinking will survive which cannot produce a usable product when survival is at stake.

Bibliography   Index

Bibliography

Alkire, William H. (1965). *Lamotrek Atoll and inter-island socioeconomic ties.* Illinois Studies in Anthopology, no. 5. Urbana and London: University of Illinois Press.

———— (1970). "Systems of measurement on Woleai Atoll, Caroline Islands," *Anthropos*, 65.

Bartlett, Frederic (1958). *Thinking, an experimental and social study.* New York: Basic Books.

Burrows, Edwin G., and Melford E. Spiro (1957). *An atoll culture: ethnography of Ifaluk in the Central Carolines.* 2nd. ed.
Behavior Science Monographs. New Haven: Human Relations Area Files.

Coleman, James S., et al. (1966). *Equality of educational opportunity.* Washington: Government Printing Office.

Damm, Hans, and E. Sarfert (1935). *Inseln um Truk.* (Ergebnisse der Südsee-Expedition 1908-10, G. Thilenius, ed., II, B, 6, ii.) Hamburg: Hamburgische Wissenschaftliche Stiftung und Notgemeinschaft der deutschen Wissenschaft.

Gatty, Harold (1958). *Nature is your guide: how to find your way on land and sea by observing nature.* New York: Dutton.

Gladwin, Thomas (1960). "Petrus Mailo, chief of Moen," in Joseph B. Casagrande, ed., *In the company of man, twenty portraits by anthropologists*. New York, Evanston, and London: Harper & Row.

———— (1964). "Culture and logical process," in Ward H. Goodenough, ed., *Explorations in cultural anthropology, essays in honor of George Peter Murdock*. New York: McGraw-Hill.

———— (1967). *Poverty, U.S.A.* Boston and Toronto: Little, Brown.

———— and Seymour B. Sarason (1953). *Truk: man in paradise*. Viking Fund Publications in Anthropology, no. 20. New York: Wenner-Gren Foundation for Anthropological Research.

Goldstein, Kurt, and Martin Scheerer (1941). *Abstract and concrete behavior, an experimental study with special tests*. Psychological Monographs, 67, no. 2, whole no. 239.

Golson, Jack, ed. (1963). *Polynesian navigation, a symposium on Andrew Sharp's theory of accidental voyages*. Memoir no. 34. Wellington, N.Z.: The Polynesian Society.

Goodenough, Ward H. (1953). *Native astronomy in the Central Carolines*. Museum Monographs. Philadelphia: The University Museum, University of Pennsylvania.

Goodnow, Jacqueline J. (1962). *A test of milieu effects with some of Piaget's tasks*. Psychological Monographs, 555.

Gordon, Edmund W., and Doxey A. Wilkerson (1966). *Compensatory education for the disadvantaged: programs and practices: preschool through college*. New York: College Entrance Examination Board.

Harvard Educational Review (1969). *Equal educational opportunity*. Cambridge, Mass.: Harvard University Press.

Hornell, James (1936). *The canoes of Polynesia, Fiji, and Micronesia*. Vol. 1 of A. C. Haddon and James Hornell, *Canoes of Oceania*. Special publication 27. Honolulu: Bernice P. Bishop Museum.

Krämer, A. (1937). *Zentralkarolinen*. (Ergebnisse der Südsee-Expedition 1908-10, G. Thilenius, ed., II, B, 10, i.) Hamburg: Hamburgische Wissenschaftliche Stiftung und Notgemeinschaft der deutschen Wissenschaft.

Lewis, David (1964). "Polynesian navigational methods," *Journal of the Polynesian Society*, 73, 364-374.

Masland, Richard L., Seymour B. Sarason, and Thomas Gladwin (1958). *Mental subnormality: biological, psychological, and cultural factors*. New York: Basic Books.

Newell, A., J. C. Shaw, and Herbert A. Simon (1960). "Report on a general problem-solving program," in, *Proceedings of International Conference on Information Processing*. Paris, Unesco.

Sarfert, E. (1911). "Zur Kenntnis der Schiffahrtskunde der Karoliner," *Korrespondenzblatt der deutschen Gessellschaft für Anthropologie, Ethnologie, und Urgeschichte*, 42.

Sharp, Andrew (1964). *Ancient voyagers in Polynesia*. Berkeley and Los Angeles: University of California Press.

Stodolsky, Susan Silverman, and Gerald S. Lesser (1967). "Learning patterns in the disadvantaged," *Harvard Educational Review*, 37, 546-593.

Tyler, Stephen A., ed. (1969). *Cognitive anthropology*. New York: Holt, Rinehart & Winston.

Williams, Robert R. (1961). *Toward the conquest of beriberi*. Cambridge, Mass.: Harvard University Press.

Index